RETHINKING T
MIDDLE EAS

CASS SERIES: ISRAELI HISTORY, POLITICS AND SOCIETY
Series Editor: Efraim Karsh
ISSN: 1368-4795

This series provides a multidisciplinary examination of all aspects of Israeli history, politics and society, and serves as a means of communication between the various communities interested in Israel: academics, policy-makers, practitioners, journalists and the informed public.

1. *Peace in the Middle East: The Challenge for Israel*, edited by Efraim Karsh.
2. *The Shaping of Israeli Identity: Myth, Memory and Trauma*, edited by Robert Wistrich and David Ohana.
3. *Between War and Peace: Dilemmas of Israeli Security*, edited by Efraim Karsh.
4. *U.S.–Israeli Relations at the Crossroads*, edited by Gabriel Sheffer.
5. *Revisiting the Yom Kippur War*, edited by P. R. Kumaraswamy.
6. *Israel: The Dynamics of Change and Continuity*, edited by David Levi-Faur, Gabriel Sheffer and David Vogel.
7. *In Search of Identity: Jewish Aspects in Israeli Culture*, edited by Dan Urian and Efraim Karsh.
8. *Israel at the Polls, 1996*, edited by Daniel J. Elazar and Shmuel Sandler.
9. *From Rabin to Netanyahu: Israel's Troubled Agenda*, edited by Efraim Karsh.
10. *Fabricating Israeli History: The 'New Historians'*, second revised edition, by Efraim Karsh.
11. *Divided Against Zion: Anti-Zionist Opposition in Britain to a Jewish State in Palestine, 1945–1948*, by Rory Miller.
12. *Peacemaking in a Divided Society: Israel After Rabin*, edited by Sasson Sofer.
13. *A Twenty-Year Retrospective of Egyptian-Israeli Relations: Peace in Spite of Everything*, by Ephraim Dowek.
14. *Global Politics: Essays in Honour of David Vital*, edited by Abraham Ben-Zvi and Aharon Klieman.
15. *Parties, Elections and Cleavages: Israel in Comparative and Theoretical Perspective*, edited by Reuven Y. Hazan and Moshe Maor.
16. *Israel at the Polls, 1999*, edited by Daniel J. Elazar and M. Ben Mollov.
17. *Public Policy in Israel*, edited by David Nachmias and Gila Menahem.
18. *Developments in Israeli Public Administration*, edited by Moshe Maor.
19. *Israeli Diplomacy and the Quest for Peace*, by Mordechai Gazit.
20. *Israeli–Romanian Relations at the End of Ceaucescu's Era*, by Yosef Govrin.
21. *John F. Kennedy and the Politics of Arms Sales to Israel*, by Abraham Ben-Zvi.
22. *Green Crescent over Nazareth: The Displacement of Christians by Muslims in the Holy Land*, by Raphael Israeli.
23. *Jerusalem Divided: The Armistice Regime, 1947–1967*, by Raphael Israeli.
24. *A Dissenting Democracy: The Case of 'Peace Now', An Israeli Peace Movement*, by Magnus Norell.

Israel: The First Hundred Years (Mini Series), edited by Efraim Karsh.
1. *Israel's Transition from Community to State*, edited by Efraim Karsh.
2. *From War to Peace?* edited by Efraim Karsh.
3. *Israeli Politics and Society Since 1948*, edited by Efraim Karsh.
4. *Israel in the International Arena*, edited by Efraim Karsh.

RETHINKING THE MIDDLE EAST

EFRAIM KARSH

FRANK CASS
LONDON • PORTLAND, OR

First published in 2003 in Great Britain by
FRANK CASS PUBLISHERS
Crown House, 47 Chase Side, Southgate
London N14 5BP

and in the United States of America by
FRANK CASS PUBLISHERS
c/o ISBS, 920 NE 58th Avenue, Suite 300
Portland, Oregon, 97213-3786 USA

Website: www.frankcass.com

British Library Cataloguing in Publication Data

Karsh, Efraim
Rethinking the Middle East. – (Cass series. Israeli
history, politics and society; no. 31)
1. Middle East – Foreign public opinion, Western 2. Middle
East – Foreign relations – 20th century 3. Middle East –
Foreign relations – Israel 4. Israel – Foreign relations –
Middle East
I. Title
956'.04
            ISBN 0-7146-5418-3 (cloth)
            ISBN 0-7146-8346-9 (paper)
            ISSN 1368-4795

Library of Congress Cataloging-in-Publication Data

Karsh, Efraim.
   Rethinking the Middle East / Efraim Karsh.
      p. cm. – (Cass series – Israeli history, politics, and society,
ISSN 1368-4795; 31)
   Includes bibliographical references (p.) and index.
   ISBN 0-7146-5418-3 (cloth) – ISBN 0-7146-8346-9 (pbk.)
   1. Middle East. 2. Arab–Israeli conflict. I. Title. II. Series.

DS44.K37 2003
956.04 – dc21
                                                        2002041580

Typeset in 11.5/13pt Erhardt by Frank Cass Publishers
Printed in Great Britain by MPG Books Ltd, Victoria Square, Bodmin, Cornwall

To the memory of my Father
Moshe Karsh
1922–2000

Contents

List of Abbreviations   ix

Preface   xi

1. Why the Middle East is so Volatile   1

2. Reactive Imperialism: Britain's Occupation of Egypt Revisited   15

3. Victim or Failed Aggressor? The Ottoman Entry into the
    First World War   30

4. Rethinking the Creation of the Modern Middle East   52

5. Cold War, Post-Cold War: Does it Make a Difference for the
    Middle East?   71

6. The Long Trail of Arab Anti-Semitism   97

7. The Collusion that Never Was: King Abdallah, the
    Jewish Agency and the Partition of Palestine   107

8. Were the Palestinian Expelled?   127

9. The Palestinians and the Right of Return   155

10. Rewriting Israel's History   169

11. Revisionists, Arabists and Pure Charlatans   186

Index   205

Abbreviations

ACC	Arab Co-operative Council
AHC	Arab Higher Committee
BBC	British Broadcasting Corporation
BMEO	British Middle East Office
CAMERA	Committee for Accuracy in Middle East Reporting in America
CIA	Central Intelligence Agency
CZA	Central Zionist Archives
FO	Foreign Office
IDF	Israeli Defence Forces
IDFA	IDF Archives
ISA	Israel State Archives
JAE	Jewish Agency Executive
JPS	*Journal of Palestine Studies*
MESA	Middle East Studies Association
MESCA	Middle East Social and Cultural History Association
OPEC	Organisation of Petroleum Exporting Countries
PA	Palestinian Authority
PLO	Palestine Liberation Organization
PRO	Public Record Office
UN	United Nations
UNRWA	United Nations Relief and Works Agency
UNSCOP	United Nations Special Committee for Palestine
UP	United Press

Preface

The 11 chapters which make up this volume – with the exception of Chapter 4, appearing here for the first time – were published over the last five years or so in the *Middle East Quarterly*, *Commentary*, *Middle Eastern Studies*, *Journal of Contemporary History*, *Review of International Studies* and *Empires of the Sand* (Harvard University Press). Permission for revising this material and incorporating it into the present book is gratefully acknowledged.

Though addressing diverse aspects of modern Middle Eastern history over a period spanning some 120 years, these essays nevertheless all point to a general view: that great power influences, however potent, constituted neither the primary force behind the region's political development, nor the main cause of its famous volatility, and that the main impetus behind Middle Eastern developments has been provided by regional factors.

This thesis runs counter to the received wisdom in modern Middle Eastern Studies. For quite some time this discipline has been dominated by what may be termed a culture of victimization. Articulated most forcefully by Edward Said (of Columbia University), it views the local populations of the Middle East, the Arabs in particular, as the hapless victims of an alien encroachment, and blames the region's endemic malaise on Western political and cultural imperialism.

As this book shows, this supine self–righteousness, with its implicit admission of political and cultural inferiority, is historically false. Even at the weakest point in their modern history, during the final stages of the demise of the Ottoman Empire and in its immediate wake, Middle Eastern actors were not passive pawns in the hands of predatory Western powers but active participants in the restructuring of their region. This reached its peak during the Cold War years, when Middle Easterners skilfully manipulated superpower anxieties and vulnerabilities to promote their local interests, and has largely persisted to the present day.

Nowhere has this 'victimization culture' been more starkly manifest than in the historiography of the Arab–Israeli conflict. Dismissing out of hand the notion of Jewish nationalism, and reluctant to acknowledge any wrongdoing on their part, Arabs have invariably viewed Israel as an artificial neo-crusading entity created by Western imperialism in order to divide and weaken the Arab and Muslim nations. Israel's ability to surmount the sustained assault by the vastly larger and more affluent Arab World has thus been seen not as an indication of its intrinsic strength but as proof of the unwavering Western, particularly American, support; the collapse and dispersion of Palestinian society – as an exclusive result of Israel's imperialist grand designs. The Jewish acceptance of the United Nations Resolution of 29 November 1947, partitioning Mandatory Palestine into two states – Jewish and Arab – is completely ignored or dismissed as a disingenuous ploy; the violent Palestinian and Arab attempt to abort this resolution is conveniently overlooked.

So successful has this misrepresentation of the historical truth been that what began as propaganda has become conventional wisdom, with aggressors portrayed as hapless victims and victims as aggressors. It is striking to see how popularity has widely come to be equated with veracity, not only in the popular press but also in 'scholarly' studies of Middle Eastern affairs, as if the most commonly held position must by definition be the correct one. Of course, fashion and popularity cannot authenticate historical facts and argument. For this reason, it is important to return to the heart of the matter and re-examine the factual basis underlying this misguided view of the past: not merely for the scholarly sake of setting the historical record straight but also with a view to a better future. For, nowhere in today's world does the past seem to have such an omnipotent hold over current events and future developments than in the Middle East. It is only when the region's nations and societies come to terms with their past, however painful, that they will be able to move towards a new stability that transcends present-day norms.

1

Why the Middle East is so Volatile[1]

Since its formation in the wake of the First World War, the contemporary Middle Eastern system based on territorial states has been under sustained assault. In past years, the foremost challenge to this system came from the doctrine of pan-Arabism [or *qawmiya*], which sought to 'eliminate the traces of Western imperialism' and unify the 'Arab nation', and the associated ideology of Greater Syria [or *Surya al-Kubra*], which stresses the territorial and historical indivisibility of most of the Fertile Crescent. Today, the leading challenge comes from Islamist notions of a single Muslim community [the *umma*]. Intellectuals and politicians, denouncing it as an artificial creation of Western imperialism at variance with Arabic yearnings for regional unity, have repeatedly urged its destruction. National leaders – from Gamal Abdel Nasser to Ayatollah Ruhollah Khomeini to Saddam Hussein – have justified their interference in the affairs of other states by claiming to pursue that unity. Yet the system of territorial states has proven extremely resilient.

That resilience raises questions. From what does it result? Does it suggest that the system of territorial states is more in line with Middle Eastern realities than the vision of a unified regional order? We review the role of pan-Arabism, pan-Syrianism, and pan-Islam, then consider how the rejection of the territorial state system has affected that most intractable conflict, the disposition of the Palestinians.

The Hashemite Attempt

Pan-Arabism gives short shrift to the notion of the territorial state, declaring it to be a temporary aberration destined to wither away before long. This doctrine also postulates the existence of 'a single nation bound by the common ties of language, religion and history ... behind the facade of a multiplicity of sovereign states'.[2] The territorial expanse of this supposed nation has varied among the exponents of the ideology, ranging from merely the Fertile Crescent to the entire territory 'from the Atlantic Ocean to the Persian Gulf'. However, the unity of the Arabic-speaking populations inhabiting these vast territories is never questioned.

This doctrine was first articulated by a number of pre-First World War intellectuals, most notably the Syrian political exiles Abd al-Rahman al-Kawakibi (1854–1902) and Najib Azuri (1873–1916), as well as by some of the secret Arab societies operating in the Ottoman Empire before its collapse. Yet it is highly doubtful whether these early beginnings would have ever amounted to anything more than intellectual musings had it not been for the huge ambitions of the Sharif of Mecca, Hussein Ibn Ali of the Hashemite family, and his two prominent sons, Abdallah and Faisal. Together, they perpetrated the 'Great Arab Revolt' against the Ottoman Empire.

When Hussein proposed to the British that he rise against his Ottoman master, he styled himself champion of 'the whole of the Arab nation without any exception'. Befitting that role, he demanded the creation of a vast new empire on the ruins of the Ottoman Empire, stretching from Asia Minor to the Indian Ocean and from Iraq to the Mediterranean.[3] When this grandiose vision failed to materialize in its full scope, the Hashemites quickly complained of being 'robbed' of the fruits of victory promised to them during the war. (They were, as it happens, generously rewarded in the form of vast territories several times the size of the British Isles.) Thus arose the standard grievance that Arab intellectuals and politicians levelled at the Western powers, Britain in particular, and thus emerged the 'pan-' doctrine of Arab nationalism with the avowed aim of redressing this alleged grievance.

Likewise, the imperial ambitions of Faisal and Abdallah placed the Greater Syria ideal on the Arab political agenda. Already during the revolt against the Ottoman Empire, Faisal began toying with the idea of winning his own Syrian empire independent from his father's prospective empire. He tried to gain endorsement by the Great Powers for this by telling the Paris Peace Conference that 'Syria claimed her unity and her independence' and that it was 'sufficiently advanced politically to manage her own internal affairs' if given adequate foreign and technical assistance.[4] When the conference planned to send a special commission of inquiry to the Middle East, Faisal quickly assembled (a highly unrepresentative) General Syrian Congress that would 'make clear the wishes of the Syrian people'.[5] In addition, by way of leaving nothing to chance, Faisal manipulated Syrian public opinion through extensive propaganda, orchestrated demonstrations and intimidation of opponents.

When all these efforts came to naught, and his position in Syria was increasingly threatened by the French, Faisal allowed the General Syrian Congress to proclaim him the constitutional monarch of Syria 'within its natural boundaries, including Palestine' and in political and economic union with Iraq. On 8 March 1920, he was crowned as King Faisal I at the Damascus City Hall, and France and Britain were asked to vacate the western (that is, Lebanese) and the southern (that is, Palestinian) parts of Syria. The seed of the Greater Syria ideal had been sown.

Faisal did not abandon the Greater Syrian dream after his expulsion from Damascus by the French in July 1920. Quite the reverse. Using his subsequent position as the first monarch of Iraq, Faisal toiled ceaselessly to bring about the unification of the Fertile Crescent under his rule. This policy was sustained, following his untimely death in September 1933, by successive Iraqi leaders. Nuri Said, Faisal's comrade-in-arms and a perpetual prime minister, did so; as did Abdallah, Faisal's older brother, who articulated his own version of the Greater Syria ideal. While Abdallah had some success, with the occupation and annexation of some 6,000 square kilometres of western Palestine to his kingdom in the late 1940s (an area to be subsequently known as the West Bank), his coveted Syrian empire remained unattainable.

Later Champions of Pan-Arabism

As Hashemite ambitions faded away, following Abdallah's assassination in 1951 and the overthrow of the Iraqi monarchy seven years later, the championship of 'pan-' movements shifted to other leaders. Cairo became the standard bearer of a wider pan-Arab ideal. Egypt's sense of pan-Arabism had already manifested itself in the 1930s but it peaked in the 1950s with the rise to power of Gamal Abdel Nasser. For a while, Nasser's hegemonic aspirations seemed to be within reach. His subversive campaign against the pro-Western states drove the Lebanese and Jordanian regimes to the verge of collapse and pushed Saudi Arabia and Iran onto the defensive. An Egyptian–Syrian union in 1958 seemed to bring the ideal of pan-Arab unity to fruition. By the early 1960s, however, Nasser's dreams were in tatters. The pro-Western regimes were weathering the Egyptian onslaught; Syria acrimoniously seceded from the bilateral union; and the Egyptian army was bogged down in an unwinnable civil war in Yemen. Nasser's inter-Arab standing took a steep plunge. Then came the 1967 Six Day War, dealing his ambitions – and the pan-Arab ideal as a whole – a mortal blow. While there would never be a shortage of contenders for Nasser's role as pan-Arabism's champion, notably Saddam Hussein, the dream of the 'Arab nation' would not regain its earlier vibrancy or appeal.

The Greater Syria scheme, pursued by Faisal and Abdallah was appropriated by successive Syrian rulers, most notably by Hafiz al-Asad. He saw Lebanon, Palestine, and Jordan as integral parts of Syria, all of them undeserving of independent self-determination. This explains Asad's denial of Israel's legitimacy and his relentless efforts to dominate the Palestinian national movement; more importantly, it accounts for Syria's *de facto* annexation of Lebanon that began in 1976 and culminated in 2000 with the Israeli withdrawal from southern Lebanon.

Why Did Pan-Arabism Fail?

Why, for all the sustained intellectual and political efforts behind it, did pan-Arabism make so little headway towards its goal of unifying the 'Arab nation'? Because there is not, and has never existed, an 'Arab nation'. Rather, its invocation has been a clever ploy to harness popular support for the quest for regional mastery by successive Middle Eastern dynasties, rulers and regimes.

If a nation is a group of people sharing such attributes as common descent, language, culture, tradition and history, then nationalism is the desire of such a group for self-determination in a specific territory that they consider to be their patrimony. The only common denominators among the widely diverse Arabic-speaking populations of the Middle East – the broad sharing of language and religion – are remnants of the early imperial Islamic epoch. However, these have generated no general sense of Arab solidarity, not to speak of any deeply rooted sentiments of shared history, destiny or attachment to an ancestral homeland, for both Islam and the Arabic language have far transcended their Arabian origins. The former has become a thriving universal religion boasting a worldwide community of believers, of which Arabs are but a small minority. The latter, like other imperial languages such as English, Spanish and French, has been widely assimilated by former subject populations, often superseding their native tongues. As T.E. Lawrence, ('Lawrence of Arabia'), the foremost early champion of the pan-Arab cause, admitted in his later days: 'Arab unity is a madman's notion – for this century or next, probably. English-speaking unity is a fair parallel.'[6]

Moreover, even under universal Islamic empires, from the Umayyad to the Ottoman, there was no unified historical development of the

Middle East's Arabic-speaking populations. There were, rather, parallel courses of development in the various kingdoms and empires competing for regional mastery. As the American-Arab scholar Hisham Sharabi aptly noted, 'the Arab world has not constituted a single political entity since the brief period of Islam's expansion and consolidation into a Muslim empire during the seventh and eighth centuries'.[7]

Arabic-speaking provinces of the Ottoman Empire had not experienced the processes of secularization and modernization that preceded the development of nationalism in western Europe in the late 1700s. When the Ottoman Empire collapsed, its Arab populations still thought only in local or imperial terms. Their intricate webs of local loyalties (to one's clan, tribe, village, town, religious sect, or localized ethnic minority) were superseded only by submission to the Ottoman sultan-caliph in his capacity as the head of Muslim community. They were wholly unfamiliar with the idea of national self-determination and so created no pressure for states.

Into this vacuum moved ambitious political leaders, proclaiming the Western rhetoric of 'Arab nationalism', but actually aiming to create new empires for themselves. The problem with this state of affairs was that the extreme diversity and fragmentation of the Arabic-speaking world had made its disparate societies better disposed to local patriotism than to a unified regional order. However, rather than allow this disposition to run its natural course and develop into modern-day state nationalism [or *wataniya*], Arab rulers systematically convinced their peoples to think that the independent existence of their respective states was a temporary aberration that would be rectified before long. The result was a dissonance that was to haunt the Middle East for most of the twentieth century, between the reality of state nationalism and the dream of an empire packaged as a unified 'Arab nation'.

A New Arab Empire?

This dissonance (speaking the language of nationalism while pursuing imperial aggrandizement) was introduced into the political discourse by the Hashemites. Though styling themselves representatives of the 'Arab nation', Hussein and his sons were no champions of national liberation but rather imperialist aspirants anxious to exploit a unique window of opportunity to substitute their own empire for that of the Ottomans. Hussein had demonstrated no nationalist sentiments prior to the war when he had generally been considered a loyal Ottoman *apparatchik*;

and neither he nor his sons changed in this respect during the revolt.
They did not regard themselves as part of a wider Arab nation, bound
together by a shared language, religion, history or culture. Rather, they
held themselves superior to those ignorant creatures whom they were
'destined' to rule and educate. David Hogarth, director of the Cairo
Arab Bureau, held several conversations with Hussein in January 1918
and reported his attitude as follows: 'Arabs as a whole have not asked
him to be their king; but seeing how ignorant and disunited they are,
how can this be expected of them until he is called?'[8] It was the 'white
man's burden', Hijaz style.

Faisal was likewise disparaging of nearly all non-Hijazi Arabic-
speaking communities. Yemenites in his view were the most docile and
easy to dominate among Arabs:

> To imprison an officer, his sheikh had only to knot a thin string
> about his neck and state his sentence, and the man would hence-
> forward follow him about with pretensions of innocence and
> appeals to be set at liberty.

Egyptians were 'weather cocks, with no political principle except dissatisfaction, and intent only on pleasure and money getting'; Sudanese –
'ignorant Negroes, armed with broad-bladed spears, and bows, and
shields'; Iraqis – 'unimaginable masses of human beings, devoid of any
national consciousness or sense of unity, imbued with religious traditions and absurdities, receptive to evil, prone to anarchy and always willing to rise against the government'.[9]

What the Hashemites demanded of the post-war peace conference,
therefore, was not self-determination for the Arabic-speaking subjects
of the defunct Ottoman Empire but the formation of a successor
empire, extending well beyond the predominantly Arabic-speaking territories and comprising such diverse ethnic and national groups as
Turks, Armenians, Kurds, Greeks, Assyrians, Chechens, Circassians
and Jews, among others, apart of course from the Arabs. As Hussein
told 'Lawrence of Arabia' in the summer of 1917: 'If advisable we will
pursue the Turks to Constantinople and Erzurum – so why talk about
Beirut, Aleppo and Hailo?[10] Abdallah put it in similar terms when
demanding from Sir Mark Sykes (in April 1917) that Britain abide by
the vast territorial promises made to Sharif Hussein: 'it was…up to the
British government to see that the Arab kingdom is such as will make
it a substitute for the Ottoman Empire'.[11] This imperial mindset
was vividly illustrated by the frequent Hashemite allusion to past
Arab and/or Islamic imperial glory, rather than to national rights, as
justification of their territorial claims.

Thus, for example, Hussein based his objection to British attempts to exclude Iraq from the prospective Arab empire on the fact that:

> ... the Iraqi *vilayets* [*sic*] are parts of the pure Arab Kingdom, and were in fact the seat of its government in the time of Ali Ibn-Abu-Talib [the son-in-law of the Prophet Muhammad], and in the time of all the khalifs [caliphs] who succeeded him.[12]

Similarly, Abdallah rejected the French occupation of Syria not on the grounds that this territory had constituted an integral part of the 'Arab homeland' but because it was inconceivable for the Umayyad capital of Damascus to become a French colony.[13]

This substitution of imperial domination for national unity was not confined to the Hashemites but is evident in the writings and preachings of successive pan-Arab ideologues and politicians. At times the justification for Arab unification has been based on the recent imperial past. The Iraqi case for the annexation of Kuwait in August 1990, for instance, was predicated on Kuwait at times having allegedly been part of the Ottoman *velayet* [province] of Basra. Baghdad presented the 1990 annexation as a rectification of a historic wrong (European disruption of the alleged unity of the Arab world in the wake of the First World War) and claimed this even would 'return the part and branch, Kuwait, to the whole root, Iraq'.[14]

More often, however, the invocation of past glory dates back to the earliest Arab and Islamic empires, or even to the distant pre-Islamic Arab past. Similarly, justifications for Greater Syria date back to the Umayyad Empire. Nuri Said defined the alleged yearning for unification among the Arab peoples as the 'aspiration to restore the great tolerant civilization of the early Caliphate'.[15] Likewise, in an attempt to prove the historic continuity of an 'Arab nation', the Palestinian intellectual and political leader Yusuf Haikal traced Arab imperial greatness to the ancient Fertile Crescent peoples such as the Hittites, Canaanites, Amourites, *et al.*, ignoring the minor problem that these diverse peoples never constituted a single people, let alone an Arab one.[16] Abu Khaldun Sati al-Husri, perhaps the foremost theoretician of pan-Arabism, lauded Nasser as 'one of the greatest [leaders] in modern Arab history, rivalled perhaps only by Muhammad Ali the Great of Egypt and Faisal I of the Arab Revolt'.[17] The trouble is, Muhammad Ali, the celebrated nineteenth-century Egyptian governor, did not speak Arabic and did not identify himself as an Arab; and Faisal, as we have seen, was not an Arab nationalist seeking to liberate the 'Arab nation' but an aspiring imperialist seeking to substitute his empire for that of the Ottomans.

Another example: at a secret meeting in September 1947 between Zionist officials and Abd al-Rahman Azzam, secretary-general of the Arab League, the latter warned the Jews of Arab efforts: 'We succeeded in expelling the Crusaders, but lost Spain and Persia, and may lose Palestine.'[18] In other words, he rejected a Jewish right to statehood not from concern for the national rights of the Palestinian Arabs but from the desire to fend off a perceived encroachment on the pan-Arab patrimony.

The Palestine Question

Which brings us to the 'Palestine Question', an issue that has constituted an integral part of inter-Arab politics since the mid-1930s, with anti-Zionism forming the main common denominator of pan-Arab solidarity and its most effective rallying cry. However the actual policies of the Arab states show they have been less motivated by concern for pan-Arabism, let alone for the protection of the Palestinians, than by their own interests. Indeed, nothing has done more to expose the hollowness of pan-Arabism than this, its most celebrated cause.

Consider, for instance, the pan-Arab invasion of the newly proclaimed State of Israel in mid-May 1948. This, on the face of it, was a shining demonstration of pan-Arab solidarity. However, the invasion had less to do with concern for the Palestinian struggle to liberate a part of the Arab homeland than with Abdallah's desire to incorporate substantial parts of Mandatory Palestine into his kingdom – and the determination of other Arab players, notably Egypt, to prevent that eventuality. Had the Jewish State lost the war, its territory would have been divided among the invading forces: not handed over to the Palestinian Arabs.

During the decades of Palestinian dispersal following the 1948 War, the Arab States manipulated the Palestinian national cause to their own ends. Neither Egypt nor Jordan allowed Palestinian self-determination in the parts of Palestine they occupied during the 1948 War (respectively, the West Bank and the Gaza Strip). Palestinian refugees were kept in squalid camps for decades as a means of whipping Israel and stirring pan-Arab sentiments. Nasser cloaked his hegemonic goals by invoking the restoration of 'the full rights of the Palestinian people'.[19] Likewise Saddam Hussein disguised his predatory designs on Kuwait by linking the crisis caused by his invasion of that country with 'the immediate and unconditional withdrawal of Israel from the occupied Arab territories in Palestine'.[20]

Self-serving interventionism under the pretence of pan-Arab solidarity had the effect of transforming the bilateral Palestinian–Israeli dispute into a multilateral Arab–Israeli conflict, thereby prolonging its duration, increasing its intensity and making its resolution far more complex and tortuous. By refusing to recognize Palestinian nationalism (or for that matter any other Arab state nationalism) and insisting on its incorporation into a wider Arab framework, Arab intellectuals, rulers and regimes disrupted the natural national development of this community. They instilled unrealistic visions, hopes and expectations in Palestinian political circles at key junctures. The consequence has been to deny Palestinians the right to determine their own fate.

The late Hafiz al-Asad was perhaps the most persistent obstacle to the Palestinians' right to self-determination. Asad pledged allegiance to any solution amenable to the Palestine Liberation Organization (PLO) – so long as it did not deviate from the Syrian line advocating the destruction of the State of Israel. When the PLO, for example, recognized Israel in 1988, Syria immediately opposed the move, and when the PLO carried this recognition a step further by signing the September 1993 Declaration of Principles with Israel, it was strongly condemned by the Syrian regime, while the Damascus-based Palestinian terrorist, Ahmad Jibril, threatened Yasser Arafat with death.

Such a patronizing attitude might have carried some weight in 1920, when Faisal advocated the inclusion of Palestine within Greater Syria; at the time, there was not yet a cohesive Palestinian nation. However, this attitude was already anachronistic by 1943, when Nuri Said, Iraq's Prime Minister, suggested that 'Syria, Lebanon, Palestine, and Transjordan shall be reunited into one state',[21] let alone in 1946 when the American academic of Lebanese origins, Philip Hitti, made his dismissive assertion that 'there is no such thing as Palestine',[22] or in 1974 when Asad referred to Palestine as being 'not only a part of the Arab homeland but a basic part of southern Syria'.[23]

There is now a Palestinian nation, just as there are now Syrian, Iraqi, Egyptian, Jordanian and other Arab nations. However strongly they may feel for each other, each of them pursues its distinct path of development within its own territorial state and in accordance with its national interests. That by the onset of the twenty-first century this reality had not been internalized by all regional leaderships, as evidenced by Asad's belief in his right to dictate to the Palestinians, is a stark reminder of the tenacity of the imperialist dream.

The Quest for the Empire of God

The other great challenge to state ideals was voiced by Ayatollah

Ruhollah Khomeini, spiritual father of the Islamic Republic of Iran that he created in 1979 on the ruins of the Pahlavi monarchy. Like pan-Arab ideologues, Khomeini viewed Western imperialism as the source of all evil. However, while the former invoked past Muslim glory as the justification for the creation of a unified pan-Arab empire, Khomeini viewed it as a precedent for the unification of the world's Muslim community, the *umma*. In his understanding, having partitioned the *umma* into artificial separate states after the First World War, the Great Powers did their best to keep Muslim communities in a permanent state of ignorance and fragmentation. 'The imperialists, the oppressive and treacherous rulers, the Jews, Christians and materialists are all attempting to distort the truth of Islam and lead the Muslims astray', he cautioned:

> We see today that the Jews (may God curse them) have meddled with the text of the Qur'an... We must protest and make the people aware that the Jews and their foreign backers are opposed to the very foundations of Islam and wish to establish Jewish domination throughout the world. Since they are a cunning and resourceful group of people, I fear that – God forbid! – they may one day achieve their goal, and that the apathy shown by some of us may allow a Jew to rule over us one day.[24]

This meant that Middle Eastern states – indeed, the entire contemporary international system – were totally illegitimate, for they perpetuated an unjust order imposed on 'oppressed' Muslims by the 'oppressive' Great Powers. Muslims were obliged to 'overthrow the oppressive governments installed by the imperialists and bring into existence an Islamic government of justice that will be in the service of the people'.[25] An Islamic world order would see the territorial state transcended by the broader entity of the *umma*.

As the only country where the 'Government of God' had been established, ran Khomeini's line of reasoning, Iran had a sacred obligation to serve as the core of the *umma* and the springboard for worldwide dissemination of Islam's holy message:

> The Iranian revolution is not exclusively that of Iran, because Islam does not belong to any particular people... We will export our revolution throughout the world because it is an Islamic revolution. The struggle will continue until the calls 'there is no god but Allah and Muhammad is the messenger of Allah' are echoed all over the world.[26]

Khomeini made good his promise. In November 1979 and February

1980, widespread riots erupted in the Shi'ite towns of the oil-rich Saudi province of Hasa, exacting many casualties. Similar disturbances occurred in Bahrain, while Kuwait became the target of a sustained terrorist and subversive campaign. Iraq suffered from a special subversive effort, whereby the Iranians sought to topple the ruling Ba'th regime, headed since July 1979 by Saddam Hussein at-Tikriti. They urged the Iraqi people to rise against their government; supported the Kurdish revolt in northern Iraq and underground Shi'ite movements; and they launched terrorist attacks against prominent Iraqi officials. When these pressures eventually led to the Iraqi invasion of Iran in September 1980, Khomeini wholeheartedly embraced 'the imposed war' as a means of consolidating his regime and furthering its influence throughout the region. The war would continue, he vowed, 'until the downfall of the regime governing Baghdad'.[27]

Eventually, the exorbitant human toll and economic dislocation of the Iran–Iraq War drove the Iranian leadership to bend its high principles and Khomeini was finally convinced to 'drink from the poisoned chalice' and authorize the cessation of hostilities. On 18 July 1988, after eight years of bitter fighting, Iran accepted United Nations Security Council Resolution 598 on a ceasefire in the Iran–Iraq War, and shortly afterwards embarked on a vigorous campaign to break its international isolation. It mended its fences with the Gulf States, re-established diplomatic ties with the major West European powers, and even alluded to a possible dialogue with the United States, the 'Great Satan'. Yet when a combination of international and regional developments offered new opportunities in the early 1990s, the mullahs' ambitions were quickly re-asserted. An expansion of the country's military arsenal was accompanied by sustained efforts to project Iranian influence in the Persian Gulf, the Middle East, and in Central Asia and Transcaucasia.

Despite these efforts, Iran's pan-Islamic doctrine has had no greater success than did pan-Arabism in denting the Middle Eastern territorial state system. Not only have most Sunnis rejected it as a distinctly Shi'ite doctrine, but even Iraq's majority Shi'ite community found it unconvincing and gave more allegiance to the Iraqi territorial state instead. And Iran's only successful revolutionary export, namely Hizbullah in Lebanon, had more to do with the struggle against Israel than with dreams of establishing a unified community of believers.

Conclusions

The Middle East's experience in the twentieth century has been marked by frustration, and much of it has resulted from the gap between delusions of grandeur and the grim realities of weakness and fragmentation. Just as the challenge to the continental order by the European 'pan-' movements, notably pan-Germanism and pan-Slavism, led to mass suffering and dislocation, so the rejection of the contemporary Middle Eastern state system by pan-Arabs and pan-Islamists has triggered many wars among Arabs and Jews, Arabs and Arabs, Arabs and Kurds, Arabs and Iranians, and others.

Over 80 years, Arab leaders have had many opportunities to undo the much-maligned international order established on the ruins of the Ottoman Empire, only to miss them all. The Iraqi and the Transjordanian branches of the Hashemite dynasty, for instance, could have promoted the unification of their respective kingdoms rather than undermined each other's regional position. So, today, could the avowedly pan-Arabist Ba'thist regimes in Syria and Iraq. However, just as Faisal and his Iraqi successors would not acquiesce in Abdallah's supremacy, so Saddam Hussein would never accept Hafiz al-Asad as *primus inter pares*. Syria did not wish to foot the bill for Nasser's high pan-Arab ideals by becoming an Egyptian-dominated province in the United Arab Republic. Nor did Kuwaitis relish their designated role under Saddam Hussein's foot.

Surprisingly enough, despite this legacy of failure, the 'pan-' dreams live on. Palestinian academic Walid Khalidi demonstrates this when he writes that:

> The Arab states' system is first and foremost a 'pan' system...
> In pan-Arab ideology, this nation is actual, not potential. The
> manifest failure even to approximate unity does not negate the
> empirical reality of the Arab nation...The Arab nation both is, and
> should be, one.[28]

This assertion could not be further from the truth. The Arab state system, as demonstrated by its extraordinary resistance to ideological assaults, is anything but 'pan-'; rather it is a regional state system of the kind that underpins the contemporary international order around the globe.

Only when the 'pan-' factor is banished from the Middle East's political scene and replaced by general acceptance of the region's diversity will its inhabitants look forward to a better future. Any attempt to impose a national or religious unity on the region's individual states is not only bound to fail but will perpetuate the violence and acrimony that have for too long plagued the Middle East. Only when the political elites reconcile themselves to the reality of state nationalism (*wataniya*) and forswear the imperial dream of a unified 'Arab nation' will regional stability will be attained.

NOTES

1. Reprinted from *Middle East Quarterly* (December 2000), by permission; all rights reserved.
2. Walid Khalidi, 'Thinking the Unthinkable: A Sovereign Palestinian State', *Foreign Affairs* (July 1978), pp. 695–6; Hisham Sharabi, *Nationalism and Revolution in the Arab World* (New York, 1966), p. 3.
3. Hussein to McMahon (Cairo), July 1915–March 1916, presented to British Parliament, Cmd. 5957, London, 1939, p. 3 (hereinafter, Hussein to McMahon). For further discussion of this issue, *see* Chapter 4 in this volume.
4. 'Memorandum by the Emir Faisal, 1 January 1919', FO 608/80.
5. Abu Khaldun Sati al-Husri, *Yawm Maisalun: Safha min Tarikh al-Arab al-Hadith* (rev. edn Beirut, 1964), p. 261.
6. *T. E. Lawrence to his Biographers Robert Graves and Liddell Hart* (London, 1963), p. 101.
7. Sharabi, *Nationalism and Revolution*, p. 7.
8. David Hogarth, 'Mission to King Hussein', *Arab Bulletin* (27 January 1918), pp. 22–3.
9. T. E. Lawrence, 'Faisal's Table Talk', report to Colonel Wilson, 8 January 1917, FO 686/6, pp. 121, 123; Abd al-Razaq al-Hasani, *Ta'rikh al-Wizarat al-Iraqiyya*, Part 3 (Sidon, 1939), pp. 189–95.
10. Lawrence, 30 July 1917, FO 686/8.
11. Mark Sykes, 'Notes on Conversations with the Emirs Abdallah and Faisal', 1 May 1917, FO 882/16, p. 233.
12. Hussein to McMahon, p. 10.
13. Munib al-Madi and Suleiman Musa, *Ta'rikh al-Urdunn fi-l-Qarn al-Ishrin* (Amman, 1959), pp. 132–6.
14. Baghdad Domestic Service, 8 August 1990; Iraqi News Agency, 28 August 1990.
15. Nuri Said, *Arab Independence and Unity: A Note on the Arab Cause with Particular Reference to Palestine, and Suggestions for a Permanent Settlement to which are attached Texts of all the Relevant Documents* (Baghdad, 1943), p. 8.
16. Yusuf Haikal, *Filastin Qabla wa-Ba'd* (Beirut, 1971), pp. 20–41.
17. Khaldun [Sati] al-Husri, review of: Anthony Nutting, *Nasser*, in *Journal of Palestinian Studies* (Winter 1972), p. 135.
18. Aharon Cohen, *Israel and the Arab World* (London, 1970), p. 381.
19. Gamal Abdel Nasser, 'Speech to National Assembly Members on 29 May 1967', in Walter Laqueur (ed.), *The Arab–Israeli Reader* (Harmondsworth, 1970), p. 228.
20. Baghdad Domestic Service, 12 August 1990.
21. Said, *Arab Independence and Unity*, p. 11.
22. Hearing before the Anglo-American Committee of Inquiry, Washington DC, State Department, 11 January 1946, Central Zionist Archive (Jerusalem), V/9960/g, p. 6.
23. Damascus Domestic Service, 8 March 1974.
24. Ayatollah Ruhollah Khomeini, *Islam and Revolution* (trans. and ed. Hamid Algar), (Berkeley, CA, 1981), pp. 127, 140.
25. Khomeini, *Islam and Revolution*, pp. 31, 48–9; James P. Piscatori, *Islam in a World of*

    Nation-States (Cambridge, 1986), p. 113.

26. Farhad Rajaee, *Islamic Values and World View: Khomeini on Man, the State and International Politics* (Lanham, 1983), pp. 82–3.

27. *Summary of World Broadcasts*, British Broadcasting Corporation (BBC), 4 April 1983.

28. Khalidi, 'Thinking the Unthinkable', pp. 695–6.

2

Reactive Imperialism:
Britain's Occupation of Egypt Revisited[1]

In analyses of the modern Middle East, it has become commonplace to view the British occupation of Egypt in the summer of 1882 as a quintessential feat of imperialism – a premeditated land grab by the largest empire on Earth in its ceaseless quest for world domination. 'The pretext for the British invasion was the claim that the government was in revolt against legitimate authority, and that order had broken down', wrote the British historian, Albert Hourani. However, 'the real reason was that instinct for power which states have in a period of expansion, reinforced by the spokesmen of European financial interests'.[2]

However intriguing, this standard interpretation is fundamentally misconceived. Far from being an act of imperial aggrandizement, the British invasion of Egypt affords a vivid illustration of the limits of Great Power control over regional dynamics. Unaware of the brewing Egyptian crisis until it exploded in their faces, policy-makers in London found themselves sliding down a slippery slope that had escaped their timely notice without a preconceived idea of how to arrest this slide. It was only after Egypt's imperial master, the Ottoman Sultan Abdul Hamid II, and his subordinate ruler of Egypt [Khedive], Tawfiq Pasha, had miserably failed to put their house in order, and after cooperation with France had proved stillborn, that the British cabinet reluctantly took the plunge. At the end of June 1882 Britain declined an Ottoman plea to take over Egypt; two months later it was sufficiently alarmed to do precisely that, only this time without the Sultan's formal approval.

I

The origins of the Egyptian embroglio can be traced back to the rule of Muhammad Ali's grandson, Ismail Pasha, between 1863 and 1879. His tireless efforts to transform Egypt into a regional empire drove the country to financial ruin and internal turmoil, implicating it in the tangled web of Great Power interests, fears and greed.[3] Ismail's dismissal by Abdul Hamid in June 1879 and his succession by his son, Tawfiq Pasha, brought no improvement, as the burden of the father's unsavoury bequest proved too heavy for his young and lacklustre son to shoulder. The treasury was empty, the people disgruntled and the military rebellious.

Even during Ismail's reign Egyptian officers had grumbled over the privileged status of their Turco-Circassian military élite. When Tawfiq appointed a Circassian General, Osman Rifqi, as the minister of war and charged him with restructuring the armed forces, all repressed anger burst out. In January 1881, a group of officers handed the Khedive a petition criticizing Rifqi's policy and demanding his dismissal. Their leaders were arrested and put on trial the following month, but as they were being court martialled their troops raided the building and secured their release. The Khedive was terrified. He fired Rifqi and appointed one of the mutineers, Colonel Mahmud Sami al-Barudi (himself a Circassian), as the minister of war.

However, the moving spirit behind the officers, and the real beneficiary of their defiant stand was Ahmad Urabi Pasha (1841–1911). The son of a village sheikh, he was taken for military service at the age of 14, rising meteorically to reach the rank of lieutenant-colonel by 1870. When his promotion ground to a halt owing to Ismail's cultivation of the Turco-Circassian élite, Urabi joined the widening club of frustrated officers. Though poorly educated and of less than brilliant military talents, he had an imposing figure and peasant authenticity that made him *primus inter pares* among his fellow officers. Now that Tawfiq's arm had been publicly twisted, Urabi was rapidly establishing himself as a popular hero, the leader of a widespread coalition comprising provincial notables and chamber deputies alongside the officers.

Intoxicated by his newly-gained prowess, and fearing a backlash by the Khedive, who seemed to be recuperating from the February debacle, Urabi brought things to a head. On 9 September 1881, shortly after Barudi had been replaced by a member of the royal family, Urabi handed the new minister of war a strong message. 'I, together with the officers and men, have ascertained that an order has been issued by your Excellency to the third Regiment of Infantry to proceed to Alexandria', he wrote.

> And inasmuch as such an order is intended to disperse the military power with a view of revenge upon us, and as we cannot deliver up ourselves to death, we hereby give notice to your Excellency that all the regiments will assemble today at 9 o'clock, Arabic time, in the Abdin Square for deciding this question...No regiment will march

in obedience to the orders given by your Excellency until ample security be given for the lives and interests of ourselves and our relatives.[4]

Urabi made good his promise. Appearing in front of the royal palace, sword in hand, at the head of a large throng of troops, he presented Tawfiq with three demands: to dismiss the cabinet, to reactivate the Chamber of Deputies and to restore the army to the authorized limit of 18,000. After some haggling through the British consul in Alexandria, Sir Charles Cookson, who stood in for Consul-General Sir Edward Malet, on leave in London, the Khedive gave in. The Cabinet was disbanded and the former Prime Minister Sharif Pasha, dismissed by Tawfiq two years earlier, formed a new Cabinet, with Barudi reinstated as the minister of war. The Chamber of Deputies, suspended since Tawfiq's accession, was to resume its activities at the end of December 1881. The officers relaxed; the threat of khedival reprisal had been removed. It was their turn to call the shots.

II

The confrontation in Cairo caused some concern in London but no undue alarm. The Liberal leader, William Ewart Gladstone, who in April 1880 had succeeded his lifelong rival, Benjamin Disraeli, as Britain's Prime Minister, was scarcely aware of the Egyptian imbroglio, having concentrated his energies on the resolution of a Boer uprising in the Transvaal and the pacification of Irish restiveness. When his foreign secretary, Lord Granville, informed him of the events in Egypt, Gladstone hoped that the episode would resolve itself without external interference. Should extraneous force be nevertheless required, the Ottoman Empire, in its capacity as Egypt's suzerain, was the obvious candidate. The moment he heard Granville's reassurance that 'there seems to be a lull in Egyptian affairs, and I do not think it impossible that it may last', the Prime Minister breathed a sigh of relief. Meanwhile Edward Malet visited Istanbul on his way back to Egypt and tried to convince the Sultan to reassert his authority over Egypt in case of further deterioration.[5]

Gladstone's hopes for a quick diffusion of the Egyptian crisis were shared by his French counterpart, Jules Ferry, who feared that France's tenuous grip over Tunis, occupied in April 1881, could be further weakened by the spread of nationalist fervour. However, in November 1881 the French premiership passed to Léon Gambetta, perhaps the most flamboyant and unpredictable of French politicians, for whom imperialism was the key to the restoration of French greatness. He viewed the occupation of Tunis as an important milestone on this path, and he rejected Ottoman intervention in Egypt lest the precedent be repeated in Tunis. If Egypt were to fall again under the sway of an imperial power, this power should be France, not Turkey or Britain.

As the scheduled reopening of the Egyptian Chamber of Deputies approached amidst rumours that the officers were seeking to topple Prime Minister Sharif, the gap between Gambetta and Gladstone gradually narrowed. The former advocated a joint action to save the Khedive, the latter a careful balancing act short of physical intervention. Gambetta insisted on keeping the Sultan out of the picture, whereas Gladstone insisted on his active involvement. The outcome of these conflicting preferences was the Anglo-French note of 8 January 1882, expressing support for Tawfiq and implying the possibility of a joint action on his behalf.

This was a high-risk bluff. Intervention was the last thing on Gladstone's mind. As a sworn anti-imperialist he was bent on reducing Britain's overseas commitments, not increasing them. Moreover, he had no intention of allowing the Egyptian irritant to stand in the way of Britain's real problem: Ireland. Restiveness there was rife, the Irish Land Act prepared by Gladstone fractured his cabinet, and the Prime Minister's thoughts could not be further removed from Egypt. His sole concern in the Egyptian crisis was the maintenance of stability, and he hoped that the joint note would settle the problem without actual intervention; at the very least, it would preempt a unilateral French action without damaging Anglo-French relations. Personally he harboured no hostility towards Urabi and his fellow nationalists. On the contrary, as a self-styled champion of small nationalities, Gladstone was sympathetic to their cause, and deemed their demand for greater control over Egypt's finances as quite reasonable. 'I am not by any means pained, but I am much surprised at this rapid development of a national sentiment and party in Egypt,' he wrote to Foreign Secretary Granville:

> The very ideas of such a sentiment and the Egyptian people seemed quite incompatible. How it has come up I do not know: most of all is the case strange if the standing army be the nest that has reared it... 'Egypt for the Egyptians' is the sentiment to which I should wish to give scope: and could it prevail, it would[,] I think[,] be the best, the only good solution of the 'Egyptian Question'.[6]

The Prime Minister was by no means the only British official to sympathize with the nascent Egyptian nationalism. So did his Egyptian envoy, Edward Malet, and even Auckland Colvin, a member of the Anglo-French Dual Control of the Egyptian debt and an arch-proponent of intervention. 'The liberal movement now going on, should, I think, in no wise be discouraged,' he wrote. 'It is essentially the growth of the popular spirit, and is directed for the good of the country, and it would be most impolitic to thwart it.'[7]

III

This, however, was not how the Anglo-French note looked in Cairo. Rather than stabilize the situation, it set in motion a chain of events that would culminate in Britain's immersion in Egyptian affairs in ways that Gladstone neither desired nor contemplated. Since his appointment as Prime Minister in September 1881, Sharif had been trying to appease the Khedive, on whom he had been imposed, the Urabist officers, who had instated him, the Chamber of Deputies, which pushed for greater powers, and the anxious Europeans. As the officers and the Chamber closed ranks in an attempt to tighten their control over the national finances at the expense of the European controllers, Sharif found himself increasingly cornered. After the Great Power note, he was painted as protector of foreign interests in Egypt. On 2 February he tendered his resignation. Barudi became Prime Minister; Urabi was promoted to a major-general and made minister of war.

From here the situation snowballed. Comfortably calling the shots from his new office, Urabi pressured Barudi to dismiss the European members of the Cabinet and to bring the Chamber under his control. To consolidate his own power base, he embarked on a wholesale promotion of officers of Egyptian origin. This drove the Turco-Circassian military élite into a rearguard action. Some left the country under protest; others allegedly conspired to assassinate Urabi and his comrades. Whether or not this threat was real, Urabi took no chances; he spent his nights in the well-protected Abdin barracks, and his mother confided to a British friend that she was keeping her son's drinking water under lock and key to prevent him from being poisoned. In a thorough purge of political opponents, some 40 officers, including the former minister of war, Osman Rifqi, were stripped of their ranks and privileges and exiled to the Sudan. When the Khedive commuted the sentences, Urabi refused to comply and pushed Barudi to convene the Chamber of Deputies, which had already adjourned for the year, to gain its support. Tawfiq condemned the move and Barudi resigned on 15 May. Though left without a Prime Minister, Urabi and the rest of the ministers refused to resign. Rumours of plots and counter-plots spread through the capital.

In their eagerness to resolve the situation without committing themselves to Egypt's occupation, Britain and France took yet another high risk. On 19 May, an Anglo-French naval squadron arrived off Alexandria in a show of support for the Khedive. Six days later the president of the Chamber was handed an ultimatum demanding the dismissal of the Cabinet, the temporary exile of Urabi and the retirement of some of his closest associates into the interior of Egypt.

As in January 1882, the Anglo-French action backfired. The Egyptian Cabinet resigned in protest and Tawfiq was all too happy to accept their move. This nevertheless brought him under harsh nationalist criticism and he backed down in fear. On 27 May Urabi was reinstated as minister of war and the Khedive retreated to Alexandria, closer to the Great Power gunboats. Westerners fled Egypt by the thousands. Impending disaster was in the air.

This came, on 11–12 June, in the form of ferocious anti-Christian riots in Alexandria, in which some 50 Europeans and 250 Egyptians were killed. In one account the riots were incited by Tawfiq in an attempt to discredit Urabi and the army; another account put the blame on Urabi, whose security forces did little to contain the raging mob. The truth, however, is that the arrival of the naval squadron off Alexandria had unleashed widespread anti-Western sentiments that had been brewing in Egypt since Ismail's days. Urabi might well have been fighting for his political survival, but his actions had generated a huge nationalistic wave; initially he might not have been anti-Western, but the Anglo-French muscle-flexing had made the temptation of an extremist stance irresistible. Urabi's open defiance and his immediate reinstatement by the Khedive were taken by Egyptians as a sign of their imminent deliverance from foreign subjugation. To them Urabi was not only a national hero who would restore 'Egypt for the Egyptians', but also *al-Wahid*, the only one in living memory who dared rise against the ruling élites and foreign powers alike.[8]

The Alexandria riots caused a general uproar in London. There was widespread indignation at the killing of European subjects and exasperation with members of the Government for allowing themselves to be humiliated by a local leader. Yet Gladstone held his ground against an increasingly militant Cabinet, and his restraint received an unexpected boost from Prime Minister Charles de Freycinet, who at the end of

January 1882 had replaced Gambetta. Losing his nerve following the Alexandria riots, de Freycinet acquiesced in the British view that the reassertion of Ottoman sovereignty over Egypt might be the least of all evils. An international conference thus convened in Constantinople on 23 June to discuss the Egyptian situation, with the participation of Britain, France, Austria-Hungary, Germany, Russia and Italy. There was however one complication: the Sultan would not join them.

IV

From his palace in Istanbul, Abdul Hamid followed with horror the events that were unfolding in Egypt. Three years earlier he had removed Ismail in the hope of stabilizing the situation and restoring Ottoman control over Egypt; now the country seemed to be moving towards yet greater catastrophe. The financial situation had not improved but had rather attracted tighter foreign control. Egyptian nationalism had not subsided, only risen to unprecedented peaks. The presence of a strong man at the helm augured the possible revival of the Egyptian imperial dream. Under the weak and indecisive Tawfiq this was a virtual impossibility; under a powerful and ambitious Urabi, the 'Ismail Syndrome' could well recur. Repeated pleas of innocence by the Urabists did little to quiet Abdul Hamid's suspicion. He urged Tawfiq to crush the mutineers and, if possible, 'to give Urabi [poisoned] coffee'. When he gradually realized that the Khedive was not up to the job and that the officers enjoyed far wider support than initially assumed, Abdul Hamid decided to remain on the sidelines in the hope that mutual exhaustion would eventually force the rival camps to request the restoration of Ottoman authority in Egypt.

When the crisis defied all attempts at resolution and shot to new heights following the Alexandria riots, the Sultan panicked. On the Friday afternoon of 23 June 1882 – a few hours after the opening of the Constantinople conference that Abdul Hamid had failed to attend for fear of being tainted as a 'Western lackey' – Reshid Bey, the Sultan's private secretary, called on the British Ambassador to Istanbul, Lord Dufferin. His master was possessed by the greatest fear and hatred for France, he said, and desired to come to an understanding with Britain about Egypt to the exclusion of France. Would Her Majesty's Government be prepared to sign a bilateral treaty whereby Britain would be given the exclusive control and administration of Egypt, with the Sultan reserving to himself only those rights of suzerainty that he possessed at the time?

Dufferin was stunned. Up to that very moment, Abdul Hamid had been violently opposed to international intervention in the Egyptian crisis. He had denounced the Anglo–French note of January 1882 and the two countries' subsequent naval show of force. Now all of a sudden Britain was being offered possession of Egypt! The shift was simply too dramatic to be true. Perhaps the Sultan was playing his habitual game of divide and rule in an attempt to drive a wedge between Britain and France? Besides, military intervention in Egypt, not to speak of its physical occupation, was still anathema to Gladstone and the majority of his ministers. Without much ado Dufferin declined the offer. 'Britain's principal aims are the maintenance of the Sultan's existing rights and of the *status quo*', he said:

> We not only accept the Sultan's sovereignty in Egypt as a fact, but regard it with benevolence. We have but two interests in Egypt – the freedom of the Suez Canal and such a satisfactory jurisdiction of Egyptian internal affairs as to preclude any power from finding an excuse to meddle with them.

In these circumstances, concluded Dufferin, 'if the Sultan were to hand over Egypt to us as a gift, with all Europe consenting, I doubt whether the British Government would accept such a burden and responsibility'. Reshid was evidently disheartened. He pleaded with Dufferin to convey the request promptly to his superiors, and to hand the official reply in person to the Sultan. This came within a day. Gladstone and Granville found the idea so absurd as to dismiss it without consulting their fellow ministers. 'We wish to see the Sultan's sovereignty maintained without any limitation excepting those which have been conceded by the Firmans,' wrote Granville to Dufferin:

> Our wish for the present is that the Sultan should by sending troops to support the authority of the Khedive, free His Highness from the risk of the continuance or renewal of the military pressure which has been exercised against him, and restore the normal *status quo*. Our desire for the future is that this state of things should continue without excluding safe improvement of internal Administration, but with entire exclusion of preponderating influence of any single power.[9]

Confronted with Britain's refusal to occupy Egypt on his behalf, the Sultan continued to equivocate. On 28 June, he conferred a high decoration on Urabi; a couple of days later the Sultan's special emissary to Egypt, Dervish Pasha, was at loggerheads with the minister of war.

When on 6 July the international conference requested that Ottoman troops be sent to Egypt, the Sultan refused, against the view of his ministers. Four days later Abdul Hamid changed his mind again: he would join the conference the following day and would propose 'a satisfactory solution of the Egyptian question'.

V

While the Constantinople Conference was progressing inconclusively, developments on the ground sucked the reluctant British Cabinet into the Egyptian marsh. Like Frankenstein's monster turning against its maker, the Anglo-French squadron assumed a life of its own, in ways unforeseen by those who had dispatched it. Once the squadron was in place, the question of how to protect it was raised in earnest. On 31 May, the commander of the British squadron, Admiral Beauchamp Seymour, reported that the Egyptians were raising earthworks in Alexandria and requested that three more ships be added to his force. At the Sultan's demand, work on these forts was suspended on 6 June, but was recommenced a few weeks later. On 1 July, Seymour reported that Urabi was allegedly planning to trap the allied fleet by sinking stone barges in the channel. Two days later he was instructed by the Admiralty to tell the military governor of Alexandria that 'an attempt to bar the channel will be considered an act of war' and that if work resumed on the fortifications, or further guns mounted, he would 'destroy the earthworks and silence the batteries'.

On 5 July the Cabinet met to approve these demands. After a heated debate members reached a compromise whereby Seymour would issue his ultimatum but would land no forces in the Canal to destroy the fortifications, as demanded by several ministers. This Seymour did the following day, only to receive the Egyptian governor's emphatic denial of both the mounting of guns and the continuation of works on the fortifications. When Seymour reported the continued mounting of guns despite the governor's reassurance, the Cabinet met again on 8 July to approve a second ultimatum to the Egyptians. By now the Sultan had declined the international request for the dispatch of Ottoman forces to Egypt, while France had decided to pull its forces from the naval squadron and was assiduously working to undercut the British position by negotiating a separate deal with Urabi. Without much fanfare Seymour was authorized to reissue the ultimatum if works on the fortifications resumed. The realization that Britain was on the verge of war in Egypt, however limited that war might be, hardly sank in. There was confidence that 'the explosion of one or two shells will send all the earthworks to glory, and there will be an end for the moment of the matter'.[10]

On 9 July, Seymour reported the resumption of works on the fortifications, and the mounting of two guns on Fort Silsileh. The following morning he informed the foreign consuls in Alexandria that he had just issued an ultimatum and would 'commence action 24 hours after, unless the forts on the isthmus and those commanding the entrance to the harbour are surrendered'.

Seymour had overstepped his authority. The Cabinet had approved the destruction of the fortifications, not their capture. It had never intended involvement to include a physical occupation that could embroil Britain in a costly adventure and entail adverse international implications. The irritated Gladstone demanded to know by what authority Seymour had issued the ultimatum. Once the Prime Minister was told that unless the fortifications were surrendered Urabi could carry on for weeks while pretending to comply with the British demand, he accepted Seymour's logic. The admiral was promptly instructed to change the wording of the ultimatum to 'temporary surrender for the purpose of disarmament'. To the Egyptian Cabinet, nevertheless, these linguistic intricacies mattered little. On 10 July, they rejected the ultimatum. The following morning Alexandria came under heavy bombardment from Seymour's forces.[11]

Contrary to British expectations, the shelling failed to topple Urabi. Instead, he called a general conscription and declared a holy war against Britain. Alexandria was put to the torch as a raging mob indulged in a spree of killing and pillaging. When the Khedive dismissed Urabi, the latter countered with a religious ruling [*fatwa*] signed by three al-Azhar sheikhs, which deposed the Khedive on grounds of betraying Islam by inviting foreigners to occupy Egypt.

This unexpected resilience put Gladstone in a quandary. What had been grudgingly approved as a brief and limited operation was rapidly developing into a massive undertaking, the consequences of which were difficult to predict. Yet he felt that there was no way back. The most powerful empire on earth could not afford to be publicly humiliated by the subject of a much weaker empire. The job had to be completed, preferably under a Great Power mandate; however, as Gladstone told the House of Commons on 22 July, 'if every chance of obtaining co-operation is exhausted, the work will be undertaken by the single power of England'.[12]

This indeed seemed to become a distinct possibility. Fearing a unilateral British intervention, de Freycinet re-donned his activist mantle and agreed to a joint Anglo–French occupation of the canal zone. However, when the proposal was put to the French Chamber of Deputies on 29 July, it was decisively defeated. Attempts to harness Italy to the protection of the canal, and to convince the Constantinople conference that Britain had no desire to occupy the canal indefinitely, all came to nought. This made the Sultan Britain's only hope. As the official suzerain of Egypt and the caliph of the largest Muslim empire, the Sultan could at the very least give the operation a much needed air of legitimacy; in the best-case scenario, his support for the suppression of Urabi could exempt Britain from the need to occupy Egypt, something which was still anathema to Gladstone. After all, if Abdul Hamid was prepared to allow Britain rule Egypt on his behalf, why should he be averse to the far-less-dangerous option of a joint Anglo–Ottoman expedition?

On 12 July, while gunfire still reverberated throughout Alexandria, Gladstone dined with the Ottoman ambassador to London, Musurus Pasha. The British action had cleared the way for the dispatch of Ottoman troops to Alexandria, he argued, and the Sultan had a great opportunity at hand; the Ottoman Empire had unwittingly stumbled across 'a supreme moment, which…it was still possible to use for good; but time was precious, and this opportunity would probably be the last'. The ambassador concurred with Gladstone's assessment and expressed his confidence that the Sultan would agree to send the requested troops, provided that he was not to act as a representative of Europe. The Prime Minister responded that to the best of his knowledge, the idea of the Sultan being a *mandataire* had not been entertained. What was of critical importance for the mission's success, however, was that there should be a unity of purpose.[13]

The ambassador's optimism was well placed, if largely premature. Even more than Gladstone, Abdul Hamid now dreaded the adverse implications of an Urabist victory. For him it was not a question of lost prestige or a mere strategic setback; it was a matter of life and death, and he knew that Britain was the only power capable of helping him stop the chain reaction caused by Urabi's nationalist surge. However, much as they needed each other, the Ottoman and British Empires could not overcome mutual prejudice and distrust. At the end of July, the Ottoman delegates to the Constantinople Conference informed their European counterparts of the Sultan's agreement to send forces to Egypt, but insisted that foreign troops evacuate the country upon the arrival of the Ottoman forces. The British Government welcomed the offer, but demanded precise details of the planned intervention: the number of troops the Sultan intended to send, the date of their likely departure, and their proposed disposition. As a guarantee that Ottoman forces would not join with Urabi against the Khedive, the British insisted that the Sultan 'should at once, and before the dispatch of his troops, issue a proclamation upholding Tawfiq Pasha and denouncing Urabi as a rebel'. Ottoman officials were quoted as saying that 'the only reason for sending Turkish troops to Egypt would be to drive the English away'. While this assertion might have been designed to neutralize domestic opposition to the impending intervention, it raised suspicions in London of the Sultan's real intentions.

Abdul Hamid's erratic negotiating style, with its constant shift of tack in accordance with the latest advice he received from his coterie, did not win him any friends in London. Particularly influential was the xenophobic Sheikh Abu al-Huda al-Sayyadi, an Arab from the province of Aleppo who arrived in Istanbul in 1878 to establish himself as Abdul Hamid's Rasputin. He worked indefatigably to prevent an agreement with 'infidel' Britain and warned the Sultan of the (alleged) backlash it would cause among Muslim communities. The Ottoman representatives to the talks, Said and Assim Pashas, thus found themselves in the unenviable position of trying to make sense of the contradictory instructions given to them. On 18 August, they finalized a draft convention with Lord Dufferin, only to have it thrown back at them the following day by the Sultan. Even the provision of donkeys and mules for the expedition became a bone of contention when the Sultan suspended the delivery of these beasts of burden, purchased in Asia Minor, and arrested their drivers; nearly a week of unremitting pressure by Dufferin was required to end this bizarre episode.

The most frustrating aspect of the talks was the Sultan's evasiveness over the condemnation of Urabi. On 3 September, after months of procrastination, Abdul Hamid gave his consent to the immediate issue of the condemnation, apparently removing the last obstacle to the signing of an Anglo-Ottoman convention. However, when Dufferin read the official proclamation in the morning papers three days later, his heart sank. In a blatant repudiation of the agreed draft, the Sultan had changed the wording in the proclamation on some material points. Enraged at 'such an inconceivable act of bad faith', Dufferin refused to sign the convention or to accept the Porte's apologies. It was only on 15 September, after another round of futile negotiations, that Abdul Hamid decided to bring matters to conclusion. He invited Dufferin to his palace, and for 11 hours haggled with the ambassador over the amendments he wished to introduce in the convention and the proclamation.

At 1.15 a.m. Dufferin's young secretary and brother-in-law, Arthur Nicolson, who waited with him for the Sultan's reply, observed 'the sinister figure of the Sultan's astrologer [Abu al-Huda] creeping across the anteroom toward his master's room'. Half an hour later Said and Assim returned to their British interlocutors. 'His Majesty was unable to approve the compromise agreed to and further discussions would be required.'

It was nearly three o'clock when the distraught Dufferin arrived at the embassy. There, to his surprise, he was handed a ciphered telegram from Granville stating that a British force under the command of Sir Garnet Wolseley had routed Urabi's army in Tal al-Kabir, some 60 miles from Cairo, and that in view of this victory 'Her Majesty's Government contemplated shortly commencing the withdrawal of the British troops from Egypt, and presumed that, the emergency having passed, the Sultan would not now consider necessary to send troops'. Three days later, on 18 September, Dufferin was instructed to inform the Sultan, 'in the most courteous terms', that Britain was dropping the negotiations of the military convention.[14] The Sultan had lost yet another golden opportunity to reassert his suzerainty over Egypt.

VI

It was a considerable historical irony that one of Britain's staunchest anti-imperialist Prime Ministers managed to accomplish what his avowedly imperialist precursor had carefully avoided: entangling his country in the largest and most enduring imperial acquisition in the Middle East. Indeed, while portraying the Egyptian venture as an undesirable burden passed on to him by Disraeli, Gladstone himself recognized the irony in the situation. On 10 August 1882, he had stated that an indefinite occupation of Egypt would be 'at variance with all the principles and views of Her Majesty's Government, and the pledges they have given to Europe, and with the views, I may say, of Europe itself'.[15] Now that Egypt had inadvertently come under British occupation, it became a hot potato that had to be disposed of before scorching the Prime Minister's palms. As early as 14 September, a day after Urabi's crushing defeat, Gladstone outlined his ideas for an Egyptian settlement. British forces were to be withdrawn as soon as possible and Egypt set on the road to self-rule. Egyptian military and police forces were to be reorganized, self-governing institutions developed, and privileges enjoyed by the Europeans, such as exemption from taxation, terminated. The Sultan's suzerainty over Egypt would be retained, albeit on a more restricted basis: he would still receive tribute, but he would not nominate the Egyptian ruler or command the service of Egyptian troops. The conduct of the Suez Canal company was to be reviewed, and the possible neutralization of the canal discussed.

Dufferin was instructed to inform the Sultan that 'Her Majesty's Government contemplated shortly commencing the withdrawal of the British troops from Egypt'. In a circular to the Great Powers on 3 January 1883, Granville promised that Britain would withdraw from Egypt 'as soon as the state of the country, and the organization of proper means for the maintenance of the Khedive's authority, will admit of it'. This promise was to be repeated 66 times between 1882 and 1922, when Egypt became an independent state.[16] What had begun as a brief and decisive military action in 1882 had turned into a long occupation that was to have a profound impact on the making of the modern Middle East.

NOTES

1. Reprinted by permission from A. Klieman and A. Ben-Zvi (eds), *Global Politics: Essays in Honour of David Vital* (London, Frank Cass, 2001).
2. Albert Hourani, *A History of the Arab Peoples* (London, 1991), p. 283. For variants of this received wisdom, *see*, for example, Ronald Robinson and John Gallagher, with Alice Denny, *Africa and the Victorians: The Official Mind of Imperialism* (2nd edn), (London, 1981), p. 159; Juan R.I. Cole, *Colonialism and Revolution in the Middle East: Social and Cultural Origins of Egypt's Urabi Movement* (Princeton, NJ, 1993).
3. For further discussion of this point *see* Efraim Karsh and Inari Karsh, *Empires of the Sand: The Struggle for Mastery in the Middle East, 1789–1923* (Cambridge, MA, 1999), Chapter 4.
4. Public Record Office (PRO), Letter by Urabi to the Egyptian Minister of War, 9 September 1882, CAB 37/6, No. 24, enclosure 6. On the reasons for Urabi's show of force see also Malet to Granville, 23 September 1881, CAB, 37/6, No. 24; Ahmad Urabi, *Kashf al-Sitar an Sirr al-Israr* (Cairo, n.d.), p. 236.
5. Gladstone to Granville, 12, 13, 16 September 1881, PRO 30-29/124. *See also* Granville to Gladstone, 14 September 1881, Add. MS. 44173, fol. 151, British Library; Malet to Granville, 21 September 1881, FO 78/3324, No. 246.
6. Gladstone to Granville, 4, 12 January 1882, PRO, 30-29/160; 22 January 1882, PRO, 30-29/125.
7. Memorandum by Colvin, 12 December 1991, CAB 37/7, No. 4.
8. Abd al-Rahman al-Rafi'i, *al-Thawrah al-Urabiyyah wa-l-Ihtilal al-Inglizi* (2nd edn), (Cairo, 1937).
9. *See* Dufferin to Granville, 24 June 1882, FO 78/3397, No. 168; Granville to Dufferin, 25 June 1882, FO 78/3395, No. 302; Dudley W.R. Bahlman (ed.), *The Diary of Sir Edward Walter Hamilton, 1880–1885*, Vol. 1 (Oxford, 1972), pp. 208, 212, 297 (hereinafter *Hamilton Diary*).
10. Northbrook to Seymour, 3 July 1882, ADM 116/33; Seymour to Admiralty, 8 July 1882, ADM, 116/34; Admiralty to Seymour, 8 July 1882, ADM, 116/34; Lyons to Granville,

5, 6 July 1882, FO 27/2574; Granville's draft to Cabinet, 8 July 1882, FO 27/2753, PRO 30-29/143.

11. Gladstone to Granville, 9 July 1882, PRO, 30-29/126; Granville to Gladstone, 9 July 1882, Add. MS. 44174, fo. 160.

12. John Morley, *The Life of William Ewart Gladstone*, Vol. 3 (London, 1903), p. 82.

13. Gladstone to Granville, 13 July 1882, PRO 30-29/126; *Hamilton Diary*, p. 306.

14. Granville's dispatch to Dufferin, CAB 37/9, p. 15.

15. *Hamilton Diary*, p. 340.

16. A.J.P. Taylor, *The Struggle for Mastery in Europe, 1848–1918* (New York, 1971), p. 90.

3

Victim or Failed Aggressor? The Ottoman Entry into the First World War[1]

I

Since actions are commonly judged by their outcome, rather than the original intention, it has become customary to equate failure with victimhood. Such has been the case with the Ottoman Empire's entry into the First World War on the side of the Central Powers – by far the most important single decision in the annals of the modern Middle East.

Nearly a century after this catastrophic blunder, which led to the destruction of the then longest reigning empire and the creation of the contemporary regional order on its ruins, culpability is still apportioned to the European Powers. According to the conventional wisdom, it was primarily the 'forceful and clever German diplomacy' that 'persuaded and manoeuvred' the Ottoman leadership 'into taking such a perilous gamble'. An alternative explanation shifts the blame from Germany to the Habsburg Empire:

> By 1914 Germany had lost interest in the Ottomans who approached the Entente for an alliance. The Ottoman–German alliance of 2 August 1914 was principally the outcome of Austrian pressure, it being the object of Austria to control Ottoman ambitions in the Balkans by tying the Porte into the Triple Alliance.

Yet another popular theory portrays the Ottoman entry into the war as a desperate bid by an isolated and spurned empire for its place under the sun. 'The Unionists who seized power in January 1913…felt betrayed by what they considered was Europe's anti-Turkish bias during the Balkan Wars', runs this version, 'and therefore they had no faith in Great Power declarations regarding the Empire's independence and integrity'; hence, when their attempts to secure formal alliances with the Entente on the eve of the Great War were turned down, they had no choice but to throw in their lot with Germany. A corollary of this account is that 'although the Entente tried to keep the Ottomans out of the war they had not tried very hard' and that 'with more generous Entente offers to feed on', the pro-Entente faction within the Ottoman leadership 'might well have prevailed'.[2]

These arguments could not be further from the truth. Far from being a last-ditch attempt to ensure its survival, the Ottoman Empire's plunge into the whirlpool reflected a straightforward imperialist policy aimed at territorial aggrandizement and the reassertion of past glory. In practical terms this meant the destruction of Russian power, as overtly stated in the Ottoman proclamation of war; the liberation of Egypt and Cyprus from British occupation; and, last but not least, the taming of its former Balkan subjects and the recovery of lost Ottoman territories in Europe, first and foremost Macedonia and Thrace. Military planning envisaged the extension of the Ottoman frontier all the way to the Volga River; likewise, as late as autumn 1916, more than two years after the outbreak of the Great War, Ottoman officers in the Levant were still talking openly of an intended march on India via Iran and Afghanistan.[3]

II

Contrary to conventional wisdom, the Ottoman leadership had no reason for anti-European grievances following the Balkan Wars of 1912–13. Quite the reverse. Rather than 'betray' the Ottoman Empire during this conflict, it was the European powers that saved it from assured destruction at the hands of its former subjects. Had these powers been interested in falling upon the carcass and dismembering the Ottoman Empire, they could have easily done so at this point – not to mention several earlier occasions. Instead they tried to forestall a general Balkan conflagration, and – when war nevertheless broke out – played a key role in ending it and preventing a total Ottoman collapse. Even Russia, Turkey's longstanding nemesis, not only made no attempt to exploit the war for its own territorial aggrandizement but played the key role in halting the Bulgarians at the gates of Istanbul.[4]

These powers did not cold-shoulder the Ottoman Empire in the wake of the wars, let alone abandon their longstanding interest in its continued existence. Instead, in the summer of 1913 Britain and France agreed:

> ...that a partition into spheres of influence was not possible, for this would first of all lead to an intervention, on the part of other powers those of the Triple Entente, which must then lead to a partition of Turkey, which would bring about a crisis this time without any hope of preventing a war.

Hence, it was 'necessary to support Turkey to a certain degree, and by means, about which an agreement of all the Powers would have to be reached'. A few months later the British, Russian and German Emperors all agreed 'on the necessity of preserving the Turkish Realm in its present form'.[5]

Finally, a closer scrutiny of the alleged Ottoman overtures prior to the First World War – to Russia in May 1914, and to France two months later – would quickly dispel any notion of rejection. In the former case it was Turkey, rather than Russia, that aborted its own timid overture; in the latter case there is no hard evidence that a concrete alliance proposal was ever made.[6]

All this means that by the outbreak of the First World War the Ottoman Empire was scarcely the rejected and isolated international player it is commonly taken to be. Rather, it was in the enviable position of being courted by the two warring camps – one wishing its participation in the war (the Central Powers), the other desiring its neutrality (the Triple Entente). The fact that an alliance with the Entente had never been given serious consideration by the triumvirate, which had effectively run the Ottoman Empire since January 1913 – the Minister of the Interior, Talaat Pasha, the Minister of War, Enver Pasha, and the Minister of the Marine, Djemal Pasha – was not for want of options. Apart from their admiration for Germany and their conviction in its ultimate victory, the Entente had less to offer by way of satisfying this group's imperialist ambitions: even the allure of Egypt, since 1882 under British effective control, was secondary to the latter's designs on Russia and the Balkans.

Hence, within days of the assassination of the Austro-Hungarian heir apparent, Archduke Franz Ferdinand, in Sarajevo on 28 June 1914, Enver reportedly made his first secret overture to Berlin for an alliance; soon afterwards he informed the governor of Basra that the Ottoman Empire was ready to help Germany in return for assistance received during the Balkan Wars, and that German arms were on their way to Basra – to be followed by 32 secret German emissaries, including officers, to preach *jihad* both within and beyond the boundaries of the Ottoman Empire. A few weeks later the governor was ordered to 'arrange [Basra] for speedy mobilization', and the *vali* of Nejd, Abd al-Aziz Ibn Saud, was informed of the dispatch of officers 'so that they may put your troops in order quickly'.[7]

At the same time, Enver gathered his associates around him: Talaat, the most powerful man in Turkey beside Enver; the Grand Vizier and Foreign Minister, Said Halim Pasha, who was under Enver's spell; and the President of the Senate, Halil Bey. In secret deliberations, held at the Grand Vizier's villa on the Bosphorus, the four decided to make simultaneous overtures to the German and Austro-Hungarian ambassadors for a military alliance, while keeping the rest of the Ottoman Cabinet in the dark.

On 20 July, Enver, Talaat, and Said Halim met the Austro-Hungarian ambassador to Istanbul, Johann Margrave von Pallavicini. They warned him that the Triple Entente, primarily Russia, was hard at work in trying to engineer an Ottoman-Graeco-Romanian alliance, and that only a bold Austrian move could pre-empt such a development.

> This was Austria's last chance to restore its prestige as a Great Power in the eyes of both Turkey and the Balkan peoples. Not only Bulgaria, but also Romania and Turkey would unflinchingly ally with the Central Powers were Austria to teach Serbia a proper lesson.

Pallavicini was duly impressed.[8]

Two days later, on 22 July, Enver approached the German Ambassador, Baron Hans von Wangenheim. He told him that, 'the majority of the committee, headed by the Grand Vizier, Talaat, Halil, and himself, did not wish to become Russian vassals and were convinced that the Central Powers were militarily stronger than the Entente and would triumph in the event of a world war'. This in turn meant that 'the present Turkish Government was eager to associate itself with the Central Powers and would decide, with a heavy heart, in favour of a pact with the Triple Entente only if spurned by Germany'.

Wangenheim sought to deflect Enver's enthusiasm. He was not convinced of the necessity of an alliance for the Ottoman Empire. Was the Porte aware that the proposed alliance could jeopardize the Ottoman economic recovery? Did they consider the far-reaching political implications of such a move and its attendant military risks? As the weakest link in the Central Powers the Ottoman Empire would be exposed to Russian retribution; not even an Ottoman–Bulgarian bloc would remove such a threat or be of real value to the Central Powers unless it included Romania as well; but such a possibility was not in the offing.[9]

Wangenheim's scepticism about Turkey's value as an ally was shared by his superiors in Berlin – the Foreign Minister, Gottlieb von Jagow, and the Prime Minister, Theobald von Bethmann-Hollweg – as well as by influential members of the military, among whom the Ottoman Army was known as the *Sorgenkind* [the problem child].[10] Yet they were confronted with a formidable coalition advocating the virtue of an Ottoman alliance, notably the Marine Minister, Grand-Admiral Alfred von Tirpitz, the Under-Secretary of State for Foreign Affairs, Arthur Zimmerman, and the head of the German mission in the Ottoman Army, Lieutenant-General Otto Liman von Sanders. Above all, Kaiser Wilhelm himself was keen to see the Ottoman Empire joining his bandwagon. 'A refusal or a snub would result in Turkey's going over to Russo-Gallia, and our influence would be gone for ever', he angrily responded to Wangenheim's lukewarm reception of the Ottoman overtures. 'Wangenheim must express himself to the Turks, on the issue of an alignment with the Triple Alliance, with unmistakably plain compliance, receive their desires and report them! Under no circumstances whatsoever can we afford to turn them away.'[11]

Wangenheim was thus peremptorily ordered to accept the Ottoman offer of an alliance, and he dutifully complied. Secret negotiations were resumed in Istanbul, and on 28 July the Grand Vizier made a formal alliance proposal to Wilhelmstrasse. This envisaged an offensive and defensive alliance against Russia that would pave the way for the Ottoman Empire's incorporation into the Central Powers. The treaty was to be activated in the event of both a Russian attack on either Turkey, or Germany, or Austria-Hungary, and an attack by Germany or the Central Powers on Russia. Germany would leave its military mission in the Ottoman army for the duration of the war. In return, the Ottoman Empire would place its supreme military command and the actual command of one-fourth of its army under the German mission.[12]

The Kaiser's acceptance came within hours. The Habsburg Empire had just declared war on Serbia and Wilhelm was anxious to draw the Ottoman Empire into what increasingly appeared as an inevitable war with Russia. 'His Majesty has agreed to the proposal of the Grand Vizier', Bethmann-Hollweg cabled Wangenheim on 28 July, with the modification that if the Austro-Hungarian–Serbian conflict failed to develop into a German–Russian war the alliance would no longer apply.[13]

This qualification, however, was wholly unacceptable to the Ottomans. They insisted on an alliance that would 'protect Turkey from all the possible consequences attending its association with Germany' and would ideally last for a seven-year period; but, as a means of last resort, they would be prepared to settle for a treaty that would run 'only' until the end of 1918.[14] Yet again the Germans complied, and on 2 August 1914, 16.00 Istanbul time, Wangenheim and Said Halim affixed their signatures to the secret alliance treaty.[15]

Since Germany was already in a state of war with Russia by 2 August, it expected its new ally to abide by its treaty obligations and declare war on the latter. On 4 August, Foreign Minister Jagow informed Wangenheim that Britain would possibly declare war on Germany within the day and emphasized that 'a Turkish declaration of war on Russia this very day if possible appears to be of the greatest importance'. Helmut von Moltke, the Chief of the Prussian General Staff, who had previously dismissed the Ottoman military as insignificant, went a step further: he demanded not only immediate Ottoman action against Russia, as stipulated by the treaty alliance, but also against the other members of the Entente (something that was not required by the agreement), notably the initiation of insurrections in Egypt and India.[16]

This was not to be. To Berlin's deep dismay, on 3 August the Ottoman Empire mobilized its forces and proclaimed an armed neutrality.

III

The proclamation was phoney. The underlying principle of neutrality is the complete and unqualified impartiality on the part of the non-belligerent, and its abstention from any action favouring one of the combatants. This precludes *ipso facto* participation in bilateral and multilateral alliances, let alone those entailing military obligations. Through its treaty with Germany, the Ottoman Empire had effectively transformed itself into a belligerent in a continental conflict, though this fact was not fully recognized for some time because of the agreement's secretive nature.

For Enver, however, the proclamation provided the necessary breathing space to prepare the Ottoman entry into the war: to complete the reorganization and rearming of the military; to dispel remaining apprehensions within the Cabinet, whose members were largely unaware of the secret Ottoman–German alliance; to sway public opinion in the direction of the Central Powers, and to convince Turks, still in the throes of the Balkan Wars, that another war would be in their interest; to ensure the most favourable regional constellation in the Balkans; and to buttress the fledgling Ottoman economy. Above all, the feigned neutrality allowed Enver simultaneously to extract the utmost material and political benefits from a Germany eager to see the immediate implementation of the secret agreement, and from the Entente, anxious to keep the Ottoman Empire out of the war.

An early boost to Enver's machinations was provided from an unexpected source: the requisitioning, on 3 August, of the two Ottoman warships ordered from Britain – the *Sultan Osman* and the *Reshadieh*. And,

while this decision had nothing to do with anti-Ottoman sentiments –
Winston Churchill, the First Lord of the Admiralty, was among the
most pro-Ottoman members of the British Cabinet, yet he would not
take the risk of allowing such powerful vessels to leave home territory on
the eve of an all-European war – the requisitioning fell into Enver's lap
like a ripe plum. To the Ottomans, the vessels were a source of great
national pride. They embodied the burning ambition to regain the
Aegean Islands from Greece, and the Government had turned their
purchase into a national mission: children were urged to donate pocket
money, women to sell their hair to raise funds for the ships. Now that
the news broke that the ships would not be coming, a virulent anti-
British propaganda campaign was launched, largely inflating German
victories in the war. The Kaiser was portrayed not only as the greatest
friend of the Ottomans, but also as the pious protector of Islam – 'Hadji
Wilhelm'. As Halil Bey, the president of the Senate and Enver's close
associate, put it: 'France and Russia will have to give way before the
German army... England will not be able to get at the German fleet'.
Were the Entente to win the day, he warned, 'Turkey would be...at the
mercy of Russia, and England would not be able, even if it wished, to
prevent its present ally, Russia, from consummating its traditional policy of the destruction of Turkey'. In contrast, 'if Germany and Austria
were victorious, there would be a better chance of Turkey being supported and allowed to exist and develop itself'.[17]

This position was rapidly becoming the received view within the
Cabinet. Contrary to the conventional wisdom, there was no real
pro-Entente faction inside the government: The vast majority of
Ottoman leaders were pro-German from the outset, not only the four
who engineered the secret alliance – Enver, Talaat, Said Halim and
Halil. Djavid Bey, the minister of finance and the staunchest pro-British
Cabinet member, and Djemal Pasha (wrongly considered pro-French),
were instantaneously won over to the secret alliance on 1 August and
sworn to confidentiality, as Enver informed them of the imminent
British requisitioning of the ships (of which he had learned from a cable
from the Ottoman ambassador to London, Tewfiq Pasha); so were the
Grand Mufti and the ministers of justice and education, Ibrahim Bey
and Shukri Bey.

This pro-German disposition notwithstanding, the Cabinet was still
divided on certain critical issues. While most ministers wished to join
Germany in war against Russia, they had no desire to fight Britain and
France. Some saw the German option in more defensive terms than others; some advocated a longer waiting period than others. No one had any

intention of being drawn into the war on Germany's terms, not least Enver himself.[18] Having harnessed Germany's commitment to Ottoman defence, he skilfully exploited Germany's eagerness to bring Turkey into the war to extract substantial material and political gains from it.

Already before the conclusion of the secret agreement the Ottoman negotiators had devised a list of six far-reaching demands: requiring Germany to support the abolition of the capitulations (the longstanding economic, legal and political concessions enjoyed by Europeans in the Ottoman Empire); to facilitate the conclusion of agreements with Bulgaria and Romania; to forego a peace agreement so long as Ottoman territory remained under enemy occupation; to guarantee the restoration of the Aegean Islands to Turkey if Greece were to join the Entente; to secure the rectification of the eastern Ottoman frontiers so as to establish a link with the Muslim peoples of Russia; and, finally, to see that the Ottoman Empire was adequately compensated at the end of the war.

These far-reaching demands were eventually left out of the negotiations so as to facilitate the conclusion of the Ottoman–German treaty. Once the agreement was in their pocket, however, the Ottoman negotiators immediately tried to improve on its conditions by presenting them to Wangenheim on 3 August. Of the six demands the ambassador accepted one – to avoid making peace before the withdrawal of all enemy forces from Ottoman territory. However, three days later he relented and accepted all the demands *en bloc*, including the most imperialist of them all, namely, that the Ottoman Empire share the war spoils at Russia's expense. The reason for this concession was quite simple. The German Mediterranean squadron, commanded by Admiral Wilhelm Souchon, was steaming towards Istanbul, chased by a superior British task force, and Berlin was anxious to have it enter the safe haven of the Dardanelles.

IV

The squadron, particularly the formidable cruiser *Goeben* and its smaller sister *Breslau*, had been requested by Wangenheim and von Sanders on 1 August, following a secret conference with Enver, who for his part instructed the Ottoman military authorities to keep the Straits – closed to warships by virtue of the 1841 London Convention – open for the arrival of the German vessels. Yet once these vessels came under British threat, the Ottomans tried to make the most of the German plight. On 4 August, the Grand Vizier told Wangenheim that since granting asylum to the two cruisers would expose the Ottoman Empire to grave risks, the ships would have to stay outside the straits for the time being. Two days later Said Halim was more 'conciliatory'. The Ottoman Government had just decided to allow the ships into their territorial waters, he said; but they expected a German *quid pro quo* in the form of acceptance of the six demands. The ambassador saw no choice but to comply: the British were breathing down Souchon's neck and any delay in opening the straits could condemn the German squadron to annihilation. Four days later, in the evening hours of 10 August the *Goeben* and the *Breslau* arrived outside Istanbul. Enver's joy was overflowing: 'To us a son is born!'

The ships, however, had not yet exhausted their usefulness for the Ottomans. As a neutral and a signatory to the XIII Hague Convention of 1907 concerning the Rights and Duties of Neutral Powers in Maritime War, the Ottoman Empire was obliged either to return the German ships to international waters within 24 hours, or to intern them along with their crews for the duration of the war. To get around this obligation, on 9 August the Grand Vizier offered Wangenheim a bogus purchase of the two cruisers: the Ottomans would take possession of the ships and would pretend to have paid for them. This would put a shiny legal gloss on the ships' continued presence in Ottoman waters in full military preparedness.

The angry German rejection of this proposal did not dissuade the Ottomans. On the same day the ships arrived in Istanbul, Wangenheim was summoned to the Sublime Porte. Oblivious of his own role in introducing the squadron into the straits, and of the exorbitant price exacted for this concession, the grand vizier reprimanded the ambassador in front of the entire cabinet for the 'premature arrival' of the vessels, which allegedly put the Ottoman Empire at great peril. Thereupon he reiterated the proposal for a fictitious purchase of the ships. When the idea was declined yet again by the ambassador, the Porte dropped its bombshell: a unilateral public declaration of Ottoman purchase of the two German warships for the alleged price of 80 million marks. On 16 August Djemal Pasha received the *Goeben* and the *Breslau*, renamed *Yavuz Sultan Selim* and *Medilli*, into the Ottoman fleet.

The Germans gasped with disbelief – but complied. The Ottoman Empire was too precious an ally to alienate over this issue. Besides, despite their formal incorporation into the Ottoman Navy the cruisers remained with their German crews. Not least, coming on the heels of the British requisition of the two dreadnoughts, the bogus purchase of the German ships was immensely popular with the Ottoman public and rocketed German prestige to new heights. The Germans could hope that their effective control of the ships, their closer association with the Ottoman Navy – on 24 September Souchon was officially made commander of this force – and their burgeoning public popularity would expedite the Ottoman entry into the war.

These hopes proved to be vindicated, but not before the further exploitation of German vulnerabilities by Enver. The mobilization had placed an unbearable strain on the crumbling Ottoman economy, and on 30 September the Porte appealed to Germany for a loan of five million Turkish pounds (T£) in gold, only to be thoroughly disappointed. Germany was willing to lend Turkey the requested sum, Under-Secretary Zimmerman told the Ottoman ambassador to Berlin, Mukhtar Pasha, but only after the latter had entered the war; until then, Turkey would have to content itself with an advance payment of T£250,000.

This was not what Enver had expected, and on 9 October he called on Wangenheim. The pro-war faction in the cabinet was about to prevail, he argued, and the army was fully prepared. The only obstacle to the Ottoman entry into the war was financial: it could not assume such a demanding undertaking without full certainty regarding Germany's financial commitment. Two days later Enver paid yet another visit to the ambassador, this time with Talaat, Djemal and Halil. The four reaffirmed their commitment to war and promised to allow Souchon to attack Russian targets the moment the German government deposited T£2 million in Istanbul.

These meetings did the trick. On 12 October a shipment of T£1 million in gold left Germany on its way to Istanbul, to be followed five days later by a second shipment of T£900,000. This was manna from heaven to Enver. With the German credit he could resolve the upkeep of the army at a stroke and have an army ready to go into action. The doubting voices within the Cabinet would be silenced once and for all. As the shipments arrived in Istanbul on record time, Enver made his move. On 21 October 1914 he prepared the Ottoman war plan, which was immediately submitted to the German imperial headquarters. The opening blow was to be delivered at the Russian fleet by Admiral Souchon, who, in turn, would blame Russia for the incident. The Ottoman Army would then initiate 'defensive operations' in Transcaucasia (to be expanded later to an offensive against Russia's southern flank), while an expeditionary force would advance against Egypt. The German chief of the general staff, General Erich von Falkenhayn, immediately gave his seal of approval.

The die was cast. On 25 October Enver ordered Souchon to 'attack the Russian fleet at a time that you find suitable'. Four days later, in the pre-dawn hours of 29 October, Ottoman torpedo boats attacked Russian warships in Odessa, while the *Goeben* and the *Breslau* attacked Sebastopol.

V

Though not wholly unexpected, the attack took the Entente Powers by surprise. Even when they got wind of the existence of an Ottoman–German agreement of sorts, within a week of its signature, the Entente powers continued to bask in their self-delusion: not only did they fail to explore the real essence of this alliance, let alone exploit it as a *casus belli*, but they acted as if it did not exist and Ottoman neutrality could be indefinitely secured for the right price. They wished for this neutrality, and were willing to believe what their heart desired, despite the growing evidence to the contrary; and none more so than their three ambassadors to the Porte: Mikhail Nikolaevich de Giers of Russia, Sir Louis Mallet of Britain and Maurice Bompard of France.

The Ottomans did not fail to exploit this self-delusion. On 3 August, a day after personally signing the secret alliance treaty with Germany, Grand Vizier Halim assured Ambassador Giers and the British chargé d'affaires, Henry Beaumont (Mallet was on vacation in England), of Turkey's strict neutrality. He presented the mobilization as primarily motivated by the fear of a surprise Bulgarian attack: actually, with German help, Turkey and Bulgaria were hectically negotiating a secret alliance treaty, which was signed two days later, on 6 August, by Talaat and the Bulgarian Prime Minister, Vasil Radoslavow. As for the presence of German military advisers in the Ottoman Army, Halim was dismissive: 'Retention of the German military mission meant nothing and had no political significance. He regarded them as Turkish employees who were doing good work, and, as they had offered to remain, it would have been ungracious to refuse.' This was yet another lie: it was the Ottoman Empire, rather than Germany, which insisted that the mission remain on its soil in the event of war.

Similar reassurances were passed on by the Ottoman ambassador in London to the Foreign Secretary, Sir Edward Grey, and by Enver himself to Ambassador Giers. The Entente need not fear Germany's influence in Istanbul, the minister of war claimed: 'Turkey only follows its own interests'.[19]

This was not the final frontier of Enver's deception. On 5 August he approached the Russian military attaché in Istanbul with a staggering proposal: the Ottoman Empire was prepared to enter into a military alliance with Russia, including the commitment of Ottoman forces to the Russian war effort, in return for the restoration of the Aegean Islands and Western Thrace to Ottoman control.

The proposal was clearly bogus. Apart from providing a handy cover-up for the concentration of Ottoman forces in Thrace, in accordance with Enver's agreement with Liman von Sanders, it was made with the full knowledge of the German embassy in Istanbul and with the close co-operation of the Bulgarians, who were a day from an alliance with Turkey against the pro-Entente Balkan states. Indeed, on the same day that Enver saw the Russian military attaché, the Bulgarian ambassador to Istanbul played his own game of deception on Giers. 'The moment has come for Bulgaria to return to the Russian orbit of influence and join with the other Balkan states', he claimed, 'but it would wish to have guarantees that it would not be attacked by Turkey.' As late as mid-August Enver was laying his conditions for such an alliance, including the cession of Western Thrace and the Aegean Islands to Turkey, as well as Russian commitment to fight any Balkan state which would take on Turkey, not least Bulgaria. On 20 August Djemal made a similar pitch to Mallet, demanding *inter alia* the Entente's support for the abolition of the capitulations and for Ottoman territorial gains at the expense of Greece and Bulgaria – including the Aegean Islands and Western Thrace.[20]

VI

Coming at a time when the Ottoman Empire had successfully black-mailed Germany into accepting its territorial designs on Russia; had secretly aligned itself with Bulgaria against other Balkan states; had incorporated the *Goeben* and the *Breslau*, with their German crews, into the Ottoman fleet; and had removed the British naval mission from the Ottoman Navy, these proposals were nothing short of an elaborate smokescreen. Yet the Entente, though vaguely aware of the existence of Ottoman–German and Ottoman–Bulgarian understandings of sorts, would not read the writing on the wall. Rather, they stubbornly sub-scribed to the misperception of Turkey as the hapless victim that could still be extricated from German claws.

On 15 August, the Russian Foreign Minister, Sergei Sazonov, con-veyed his ideas to London and Paris. Were the Ottoman Empire to abide by its declared neutrality and commence military demobilization as proof of its sincerity, the Entente would guarantee its integrity and ensure that the peace treaty give it possession of all German concessions in Asia Minor. The following day, having heard of Enver's latest conditions for an alliance, Sazonov agreed to raise the reward still higher and to restore Lemnos Island, just opposite the straits, to Ottoman control. The British and the French ambassadors to St Petersburg were asked to canvass their governments for a tripartite declaration that would guarantee Ottoman integrity and its 'economic emancipation from Germany', provided the latter 'engaged to adopt [a] strictly neutral attitude during the war'.[21]

This is indeed what happened. Both Britain and France were amenable to the preservation of the Ottoman Empire, and were even willing to consider certain concessions to it in the Aegean Islands, though not in a way 'that meant injury to Greece'. Already on 7 August, Foreign Secretary Grey disowned any intention of 'injuring Turkey', emphatically denying Ottoman allegations of a British plan to alter the status of Egypt. When a week later Churchill sent a personal letter to Enver to warn him off the folly of throwing Turkey's lot with Germany, Grey inserted an unequivocal reassurance: 'If Turkey remains loyal to her neutrality, a solemn agreement to respect the integrity of the Turkish Empire must be a condition of any terms of peace that affect the near East.'[22] Now that Sazonov had suggested a tripartite declaration to the same effect, Grey gave his immediate consent. 'As soon as French and Russian Ambassadors are similarly instructed,' he wrote to Beaumont on 16 August, 'you are authorised to declare to the Turkish Government that if Turkey will observe scrupulous neutrality during the war, England, France, and Russia will uphold her independence and integrity against any enemies that may wish to utilise the general European complication in order to attack her.' Two days later, he reassured the Ottoman ambassador to London, Tewfiq Pasha, that his empire's territorial integrity 'would be preserved in any conditions of peace which affected the Near East, provided she preserved a real neutrality during the war'. On the same day, 18 August, the tripartite guarantee of Ottoman territorial integrity, in return for Ottoman neutrality, was given to Said Halim by Ambassadors Mallet, Giers, and Bompard. Five days later, at the request of the Grand Vizier and Djavid Bey, the Triple Entente put down this guarantee in writing.[23]

VIII

The significance of this proposal could not be overstated. The Entente Powers effectively offered the Ottoman Empire a defence pact; and at no price at all. True, they were unwilling to accommodate Ottoman expansionist ambitions, but then they asked nothing of it beyond staying out of the war; and they were prepared to reward this neutrality with the ultimate prize: imperial survival.

Since the Ottoman leadership had no real interest in an alliance with the Entente, having already made their deal with Germany, it made no effort to seize the rope thrown to it. Instead, it continued the policy of speaking peace while laying the ground for war. This was an increasingly difficult task, as the expanding magnitude of Ottoman war preparations did not evade the Entente's eyes. Yet the Ottomans unflinchingly denied all accusations of misconduct.

The most vivid demonstration of such duplicity was afforded, perhaps, by the question of the *Goeben* and the *Breslau*. The incorporation of the two German-manned warships – which retained their position in the German imperial fleet – into the Ottoman Navy made a mockery of the idea of neutrality and gave the Entente a clear *casus belli*, had they actually wished to attack Turkey. Yet the Ottomans never strayed from the lie that the ships had been properly purchased and that their German crews would be leaving any minute; and the Allies were prepared to give them the benefit of the doubt.

With Britain the Ottomans even found a handy guilt button which they never tired of pressing: the requisitioning of the two dreadnoughts by the Admiralty on 3 August. The purchase of the *Goeben* and the *Breslau* was a result of Britain's detention of the *Sultan Osman*, the Grand Vizier told Beaumont on the day of the bogus sale. Turkey needed the cruisers as a bargaining chip in the negotiations over the Aegean Islands, and their purchase was in no way directed against Russia. A week later, on 18 August, Mallet heard the same story from Enver. Public hostility to Britain would be 'effected immediately', the minister of war promised, if the British Government declared that the requisitioned ships would eventually be returned and that an indemnity for their seizure would be paid.[24]

These complaints were completely untrue. The Bank of England had already refunded the Ottoman down-payment on the ships (worth some £648,000) on 7 August, and the British Government had promised due compensation for the loss of the ships upon their requisition; but these facts were concealed from the Ottoman public by their own leaders, who continued their false criticism of Britain's refusal to compensate Turkey for the ships. Meanwhile the Germans not only showed no sign of removing their crews from Turkey but instead poured in fresh reinforcements, together with consignments of weapons and ammunition. On 23

August, Mallet reported the arrival of 28 German officers in Turkey; three days later another 90 German sailors passed through Sofia on their way to Istanbul, to be followed on 28 August by a 500-strong German contingent; most of these troops were deployed in fortifications along the Dardanelles. Reports from Cairo told of subversive Ottoman activities in India, Yemen, Libya and Egypt, and of military deployments in an apparent intention to attack Egypt in the event of war.[25]

IX

By September, there were nagging doubts in the Allied chancelleries regarding Turkey's ability to stay its course. Military circles in Russia viewed the Ottoman mobilization as geared to war, and demanded adequate preparations to meet this threat. Several British ministers, notably Winston Churchill and the chancellor of the exchequer, David Lloyd George, maintained that the Ottoman Empire was about to join the Central Powers and that the Entente should work towards establishing a Balkan league which would not only contain Turkey, but would also move against Austro-Hungary. On 2 September, the British Cabinet decided to extend financial aid to both Romania and Serbia, and 'to sink Turkish ships if they issue from the Dardanelles'. The following day it was decided that the two Indian divisions, then on their way to Europe, would be held for a few days in Egypt 'as a warning to the Turks to keep quiet'.

These moves, nevertheless, signalled no general shift of strategy. The overriding concern of the British Prime Minister, Herbert Asquith, Foreign Secretary Grey, and Secretary of War, Lord Horatio Herbert Kitchener, remained unchanged: to keep the Ottoman Empire out of the war. Even the advocates of a harsher line were motivated primarily out of the conviction that 'a kind word and a gun' would carry more weight with the Porte than 'just a kind word'. The Russians were even less keen to see a slide to war, as repeatedly emphasized by Sazonov to his allies and the Ottomans: early in September he poured cold water on a British enquiry as to whether Russia would join in an attack on Turkey. As for the French, having just checked the German advance on Paris, they were as keen as ever to keep Turkey out of the war.

These hopes were reinforced by the optimistic messages of the Entente's ambassadors to Istanbul. They did not shy away from warning the Ottomans, at times in the most uncompromising language, of the folly of their joining the war. Nor were they blind to the gathering storm over the Ottoman horizon. Yet, on the whole, the three ambassadors

judged the situation as anything but hopeless and urged their governments to 'go on as long as possible without provoking a rupture'. When,
at the end of August, the *Goeben* seemed poised to enter the Black Sea,
the ambassadors' advice was to withhold action against Turkey 'as time
is on our side'. Early in September, they were still willing to give a
listening ear to the reassurances of Halim, Djemal and Djavid that
'nothing will induce them to side actively with either belligerent and
that they will not go to war with anyone'. Even Enver's pledge that he
was 'determined not to go to war' was not dismissed out of hand. There
was a feeling that the situation was improving and that 'a current has set
in' against any Ottoman adventure.[26]

This deference was all the more extraordinary given that by this time
the Ottoman Empire had taken several critical steps that moved it closer
than ever to war: on 20 September, at long last, the German cruisers
entered the Black Sea; and four days later Rear Admiral Wilhelm
Souchon, commander of the German Mediterranean squadron, was
appointed commander of the Ottoman Navy. On 27 September, the
Ottomans closed the straits to international shipping in violation of the
1841 treaty regulating navigation in this waterway. Russia lost its only
ice-free link with the West, and could only be supplied through the
lengthy and precarious northern route to Archangel.

Still the Allies continued their indulgence. Giers viewed the entry of
the German ships into the Black Sea with stoic indifference, as if it was
not his own country that stood to be attacked by these ships: he
expressed confidence that no incident would ensue and proposed to
ignore the whole thing. Mallet was more wary, but only slightly so. On
16 September, he had received the strongest assurances from both Said
Halim and Talaat that there was no intention of sending the *Goeben* into
the Black Sea, and three days later he heard the same tune from Halil
Bey. Yet when the hollowness of these pledges was exposed within days,
Mallet refused to call a spade a spade, believing that this episode
reflected the Cabinet's lack of control over 'the minister of war and the
Germans'. Grey was willing to go along with this:

> We do not want to precipitate a conflict with Turkey and are not
> contemplating a hostile act by our fleet against her. But the Turkish
> Government must not suppose that because we have not taken any
> hostile action against Turkey we regard her present attitude as con-
> sistent with obligations of neutrality...Constantinople is in fact
> under German control. We have ample ground, if we desired, for
> protesting against the present state of things as violation of neu-
> trality; in the hope that the peace party will get the upper hand we

have not hitherto taken action, but the Grand Vizier should realise
that his party must succeed soon in controlling the situation and
bringing it within the limits of neutrality.[27]

The Ottomans were unimpressed. On 27 September they closed the
straits and put the blame for this act on Britain. Earlier that day a British
squadron, lying outside the Dardanelles since the arrival of the two
German cruisers in early August, had stopped and turned back an
Ottoman destroyer venturing out of the straits. This, the Grand Vizier
told the three ambassadors, gave rise to fears of an imminent British
attack and caused the abrupt closure of the straits. He reassured Mallet
'that [the] Turkish Government would never make war upon Great
Britain', and claimed that 'if His Majesty's Government will move the
fleet a little further from the entrance to the Dardanelles, the Straits will
be reopened'.

Grey was prepared to give this claim the benefit of the doubt. 'It is
the Germans who keep the Straits closed, to the great detriment of
Turkey', he cabled Mallet. 'If you concur, you may point out to the
Turks that the British fleet will move away as soon as the German officers and crews leave and the Turkish navy ceases to be under German
control. We should then have no fear of hostile action on the part of the
Turks.'[28]

This stance was still based on the general misperception, shared by
the three ambassadors and their respective governments since the outbreak of the Great War, that the Ottoman Empire was a hapless captive
of German machinations, and was therefore to be offered a helping hand
out of its undesired entanglement. Even at this advanced stage of the
crisis, despite the abundant evidence to the contrary, the Entente Powers
could not bring themselves to acknowledge the imperialist aspirations of
the leading group in Istanbul. They were increasingly aware that the
'Turks are possibly less blind to their interests than is generally supposed', and that they were possibly exploiting the situation to extract
the maximum gains from Germany, but misinterpreted these facts as
reinforcing Ottoman reluctance 'to go all lengths with Germany'.

As late as mid-October 1914 Mallet estimated that it was the Germans
who were behind the increasingly threatening Ottoman military posture
vis-à-vis Egypt, and that 'probably [the] Government as a whole have little control over these activities, but do not disapprove of them'. Enver was
still mistaken for a 'willing tool of [the] Germans', Talaat – for a strong
opponent of war.[29] The truth was, of course, precisely the opposite. By
that time Enver and Talaat had already crossed the point of no return in
their imperialist odyssey, having promised Germany to initiate hostilities

the moment a large consignment of German gold arrived in Istanbul to shore up the fledgling Ottoman economy from the effects of war.

The Entente got wind of this shipment on 16 October, as part of it crossed Bulgaria *en route* to Istanbul, and a week later they were already aware of its real magnitude. The Russians were the first to grasp the detrimental implications of this German enterprise. On 20 October, Sazonov told Britain that he expected an Ottoman declaration of war within a few days; Giers assessed that unless Turkey planned a last-minute betrayal of Germany, the possibility of which he could not completely exclude, it would wage war on Russia on receipt of the first half of the T£4 million-worth of German gold.[30]

Mallet was far more sanguine. 'Danger of attack on [the] Russian Black Sea fleet is not perhaps so great as my Russian colleague seems to think', he cabled London on 23 October. In his view, Germany had tired of enticing Turkey into an attack on Russia and had subsequently turned its attention to Egypt and to the incitement of Ottoman religious fanaticism against Britain. However, even in this arena Germany's success was far from assured:

> I do not expect that they will make regular war but we shall have raids and attempts on the part of Turks and Germans to create trouble in underhand and perhaps equally dangerous ways. Pamphlet which consul at Beirut reports as likely to be smuggled into Egypt may be one which I have seen here of a religious character and in nature of incitement to Holy War...If Egyptian campaign prove a failure, Turks will tire of it.

Grey concurred. Without much ado he instructed Mallet to disabuse the Porte of the delusion that a military move against Egypt would in some way be different from an act of war against Russia: violation of the Egyptian frontier would threaten the international Suez Canal which Britain was 'bound to preserve' and would place Turkey 'in a state of war with three allied powers'. Should this happen 'it will not be we but Turkey that will have aggressively disturbed the *status quo*'.[31]

They were looking in the wrong direction. On 29 October, as the *Goeben* and Ottoman gunboats attacked Russia's Black Sea ports, the unwitting Mallet was protesting to the Grand Vizier over the Bedouin incursion into Egypt. Even at this late stage Halim feigned innocence, claiming to have instructed the minister of war on no account to allow the movement of any forces across the frontier: 'If it were true, he would give immediate orders to recall all Bedouins, but he did not believe accuracy of the information'.[32] When Mallet questioned his ability to do so, the

Grand Vizier responded angrily. The ambassador was absolutely mistaken, he said. 'If it came to that, [the] military party would not act without full assent of the Government'. 'In that case', answered Mallet, 'time had come to put them to the test, and…unless expedition were immediately recalled, I could not answer for the consequences. As it was, I might at any moment receive instructions to ask for my passports.'[33]

X

This was precisely what Mallet was about to do, but not for the reason he mentioned to the Grand Vizier. The Ottoman attack on Russia, which the Entente (with the partial exception of St Petersburg) had so miserably failed to predict, despite the numerous signs, ended at a stroke months of self-delusion and wishful thinking. War in the Middle East was at the gate; or was it?

The Entente *still* hoped not. Though the incident was a blatant act of aggression that could have constituted a perfectly legitimate *casus belli* against the Ottoman Empire, the Entente kept cool. Repudiating the absurd Ottoman apology, which blamed Russia for the attack and offered to settle the manner amicably, Sazonov gave the Porte a last chance to avert war: the immediate dismissal of all German military officers in the Ottoman Army and Navy. London and Paris followed suit. The hopeful Mallet pleaded with his superiors to exercise the utmost restraint, for there was still a chance for the anti-German faction within the Ottoman Government to prevail. But he was instructed by Grey to warn the Porte that unless Turkey promised, within 12 hours, to divest itself 'of all responsibility for these unprovoked acts of hostility by dismissing the German military and naval missions, and fulfilling their often repeated promises about the German crews of the *Goeben* and the *Breslau*', he would have to leave Istanbul with the staff of the embassy.[34]

The Allies were asking for the impossible. The Porte had not attacked Russia with a view to averting war but rather in the hope of triggering it. For months Enver and his powerful group had been patiently bracing the Ottoman Empire for what they saw as a historic chance to reach to new imperial vistas, and they were not going to let this golden opportunity slip from their fingers. On 31 October, Giers left Istanbul, to be followed a day later by Mallet and Bompard. On 3 November, on Churchill's instructions, British warships, assisted by two French ships bombarded the outer forts of the Dardanelles. A day later Russia declared war on the Ottoman Empire. Britain and France followed suit. The Allies had been drawn into a war not of their own choice.

NOTES

1. Reprinted from Efraim and Inari Karsh, *Empires of the Sand: The Struggle for Mastery in the Middle East, 1789-1923* (Boston, MA, 1999), by permission of Harvard University Press; all rights reserved.
2. Elie Kedourie, *Politics in the Middle East* (Oxford, 1992), p. 93; Malcolm Yapp, *The Making of the Modern Middle East 1792–1923* (London, 1987), p. 266; Feroz Ahmad, 'The Late Ottoman Empire', in Marian Kent (ed.), *The Great Powers and the End of the Ottoman Empire* (London, 1996), pp. 15–16. *See also* David Fromkin, *A Peace to End All Peace: The Fall of the Ottoman Empire and the Creation of the Modern Middle East* (New York, 1989), pp. 48–50; Y.T. Kurat, 'How Turkey Drifted into World War I', in K. Bourne and D.C. Watt (eds), *Studies in International Diplomacy* (London, 1967), p. 297; Ahmed Emin, *Turkey in the World War* (New Haven, CT, 1930); Feroz Ahmed, *The Young Turks: The Committee of Union and Progress in Turkish Politics, 1908–1914* (Oxford, 1969); Joseph Heller, *British Policy towards the Ottoman Empire, 1908–1914* (London, 1983); Harry N. Howard, *The Partition of Turkey: A Diplomatic History, 1913–1923* (New York, 1966); Frank G. Weber, *Eagles on the Crescent: Germany, Austria, and the Diplomacy of the Turkish Alliance, 1914–1918* (Ithaca, NY, 1970); Howard M. Sachar, *The Emergence of the Middle East 1914–1924* (London, 1970), p. 32; John DeNovo, *American Interests and Policies in the Middle East, 1900–1939* (Minneapolis, IL, 1963), p. 90.

    Interestingly enough, even Ulrich Trumpener, who meticulously documents the extent of Ottoman eagerness for an offensive alignment with Germany, reserves judgement as to the motivation behind the Ottoman behaviour. See Trumpener, *Germany and the Ottoman Empire, 1914–1918* (Princeton, NJ, 1968), especially pp. 14–61; 'Turkey's Entry into World War I: An Assessment of Responsibilities', *Journal of Modern History* (1962), pp. 369–80; 'German Military Aid to Turkey in 1914: An Historical Re-Evaluation', *Journal of Modern History* (1960), pp. 145–9.
3. Yusuf Hikmet Bayur, *Türk Inkilabi Tarihi*, Vol. 3 (Ankara, 1953), p. 198. Further addenda to 'Report of an inhabitant of Athlit', circulated on 2 November 1916 under No. 7977, FO 371/2783/225831, 10 November 1916.
4. *See* for example, Sazonov to Buchanan in Buchanan to Grey, 2 November 1912, in E.L. Woodward and Rohan Butler (eds), *D[ocuments] on B[ritish] F[oreign] P[olicy] 1919–1939*, First Series, Vol. IX/2, No. 98, p. 79; Buchanan to Grey, 8 November 1912, FO 371/1505/47589. Interestingly enough, Sazonov also rebuffed a British 'trial balloon' to consider the possible neutralization of Constantinople. *See* Grey to Buchanan, 5 November 1912, FO 371/1505/47008; and Sazonov's response in Buchanan to Grey, 6 November 1912, FO 371/1505/47210; Bertie to Grey, 27 October and Grey to Bertie, 28 October, both in FO 371/1503/45534.

    For the French mediation attempts *see* Ministère des affaires étangères, République française, *Documents diplomatiques. Les affaires balkaniques, 1912-1914*, Vol. 4 (Paris, 1922; [hereinafter *Documents Diplomatiques Français*], pp. 310–59. *See* in particular: Poincaré to the French Ambassadors of London and St Petersburg, 30 October 1912, No. 279; Poincaré to the French Ambassadors of Berlin, Vienna and Rome, 30 October 1912, No. 284; Vol. IV, pp. 291, 295; Communication from M. Paul Cambon, 30 October 1912, DBFP, Vol. IX/2, No. 80, p. 68. For Austro-Hungary's interests in the crisis *see* Bearbeitet von Ludwig Bittner and Hans Uebersberger (eds), *Österreich-Ungarns Aussenpolitik von der Bosnischen Krise 1908 bis zum Kriegsausbruch, 1914.*

Diplomatische Aktenstücke de Öterriechische-Ungarischen Ministeriums des Ässern, Vol. 4 (Vienna, 1930), pp. 769–76.

5. The Russian Ambassador in London to Sazonov, 14–27 June 1913, No. 572, *Entente Diplomacy and the World*, No. 780; the Russian Ambassador at Berlin to Sazonov, 8–21 November 1913, *ibid.*, No. 781, p. 676.

6. For an elaborate discussion of this issue see Karsh and Karsh, *Empires of the Sand*, pp. 119–22.

7. Intercepted cypher telegrams from Enver Pasha, 10, 15, 26 and 27 July 1914. Sent by the political resident in the Persian Gulf (Major S.G. Knox) to the foreign secretary to the Government of India in the foreign and political department, Simla, on 26 September and 1 October 1914, FO 371/2144/64214.

8. Wangenheim to Foreign Office, 21 July 1914, in Karl Kautsky (ed.), *Die Deutschen Dokumente zum Kriegsausbruch*, Vol. 1, No. 99 (Charlottenburg, 1919), p. 123. On Pallavicini's warning against alliance with Greece see Wangenheim to Foreign Office, 23 July 1914, *ibid.*, Vol. 1, No. 149, pp. 162–3.

9. Wangenheim to Foreign Office, 22 July 1914, *ibid.*, Vol. 1, No. 117, pp. 134–6.

10. *See*, for example, Jagow to the ambassadors in Vienna and Istanbul, 14 July 1914, *ibid.*, Vol. 1, No. 45.

11. The Kaiser's comments on Wangenheim's report of 23 July 1914, *ibid.*, No. 149, pp. 162–3.

12. Jagow to Wangenheim, 24 July 1914, *Die Deutschen Dokumente*, Vol. 1, No. 144, p. 158; Count Wedel (minister in the Imperial Suite) to Foreign Office, 24 July 1914, *ibid.*, No. 141, p. 158; Wangenheim to Foreign Office, 28 July 1914, *ibid.*, Vol. 2, No. 285, p. 7; Admiral Alfred P. Tirpitz, *My Memoirs*, Vol. 2 (London, 1919), pp. 80–3.

13. Bethmann-Hollweg to Wangenheim, 28 July 1914, *Die Deutschen Dokumente*, No. 320.

14. Wangenheim to Foreign Office, 30 July 1914, *ibid.*, No. 411.

15. The broad contours of the Ottoman–German military collaboration in the event of war were delineated at a meeting in the German Embassy on 1 August 1914, with the participation of Enver, von Sanders and Wangenheim. For the text of the Ottoman–German treaty *see* Wangenheim to Foreign Office, 2 August 1914, *Die Deutschen Dokumente*, Vol. 3, No. 733; J.C. Hurewitz (ed.), *The Middle East and North Africa in World Politics*, Vol. 2, 2nd rev. edn (New Haven, CT, 1975–79), pp. 1–2.

16. Von Moltke to the Foreign Office, 2 August 1914, *Die Deutschen Dokumente*, Vol. 3, No. 662; Jagow to Wangenheim, 4 August 1914, *ibid.*, Vol. 4, No. 836; von Moltke to the Foreign Office, 5 August 1914, *ibid.*, No. 876.

17. Halil Bey to A. Block, 9 August 1914, as cited in Beaumont to Grey, 13 August 1914, FO 371/2138/42436.

18. On the divisions within the Ottoman government *see*, for example, Bayur, *Türk*, Vol. 3, pp. 71–2; Kurat, 'How Turkey Drifted', pp. 299–300.

19. Giers, 3 August 1914, No. 5; Giers, 4 and 5 August 1914, Nos 7 and 8; Tewfik Pasha, 6 August 1914, in Benckendorff to the Russian Foreign Office, No. 9, in Ministère des Affaires Étrangères, *Recueil de Documents Diplomatiques, Négociations ayant précédé la guerre avec la Turquie 19 juillet (1 août)–19 octobre (1 novembre) 1914* (Petrograd, 1915); Beaumont to Grey, 3 August 1914, Tewfik Pasha to Edward Grey, 4 August 1914, *DBFP*, Vol. 11, Nos 598 and 605; Beaumont to Grey, 4 August 1914, 'Correspondence Respecting Events Leading to the Rupture of Relations with Turkey', Presented to Both Houses of Parliament by Command of His Majesty, November 1914, Cmd 7628, No. 3, p. 1 (hereinafter 'Cmd 7628').

20. See Sazonov to Izvolsky and Benckendorff (ambassadors in Paris and London), 16 August 1914, Sazonov to Giers, 16 August 1914, *ibid.*, Vol. 2/6, Nos 1924 and 1939; Mallet to Grey, 20 August 1914, 'Cmd 7628', No. 24, p. 8.

21. Buchanan to Grey, 16 August 1914, FO 371/2138/39792; Sazonov to Giers, 16 August 1914, *Die Internazionalen Beziehungen*, Vol. 2/6, No. 1924.

22. Grey to Erskine, 20 August 1914, FO 371/2138/42268; Grey to Beaumont, 7 August 1914, 'Cmd 7628', No. 5, p. 2; Churchill to Enver, 15 August 1914, brought in Martin Gilbert, *Winston S. Churchill*, Vol. 3, Pt 1 (London, 1972), p. 38.

23. Grey to Beaumont, 16 August 1914, 'Cmd 7628', no. 17, p. 5; Grey to Mallet, 18 August 1914, *ibid.*, No. 21, p. 7; Mallet to Grey, 21 August 1914, *ibid.*, No. 27, p. 9; Sazonov to Giers, 23 August 1914, *Recueil des Documents Diplomatiques*, No. 34.

24. Beaumont to Grey, 11 August 1914, 'Cmd 7628', No 9, p. 3; Mallet to Grey, 18 August 1914, *ibid.*, No. 20, p. 6; Mallet to Grey, 18 August 1914, Gilbert, *Churchill*, Vol. 3, pp. 40–1.

25. Mallet to Grey, 26 August 1914, No. 39, p. 13; 27 August, No. 40, p. 14; Cheetham to Grey, 28 August 1914, No. 44, p. 14: all in 'Cmd 7628'; Mallet to Grey, 28 August 1914, FO 371/2138/44220; Gilbert, *Churchill*, Vol. 3, p. 198.

26. Mallet to Grey, 23, 27, 31 August, 2 September 1914, FO 371/2138; Mallet to Grey, 19, 20, 21 and 24 September 1914, 'Cmd 7628', Nos. 82–4, 90, pp. 27–8, 30.

27. Mallet to Grey, 16 and 19 September 1914, FO 371/2138; Mallet to Grey, 20 September 1914, 'Cmd 7628', No. 83, p. 27; Grey to Mallet, 23 September 1914, FO 371/2138/52335; Grey to Mallet, 11 October 1914 FO 371/2139/58206.

28. Mallet to Grey, 27 September 1914, 'Cmd 7628', Nos. 97 and 98, pp. 32–3; Grey to Mallet, 4 October 1914, *ibid.*, No. 107, p. 36.

29. Mallet to Grey, 15 and 16 October 1914, *ibid.*, Nos 129 and 134, pp. 48–50; Mallet to Grey, 16 October 1914, FO 371/2139/66678; acting Consul-General Heathcote-Smith (Smyrna) to Mallet, 12 October 1914, FO 371/2139/66678 (enclosure No. 1).

30. H. Bax-Ironside to Grey, 16 September 1914, 'Cmd 7638', No. 131, p. 49; Mallet to Grey, 23 October 1914, *ibid.*, No. 162, p. 68; Mallet to Grey, 22 October 1914, *ibid.*, No. 157, p. 66; Buchanan to Grey, 20 October 1914, FO 371/2139/61563.

31. Mallet to Grey, 23 October 1914, Grey to Mallet, 24 October 1914, FO 371/2139/62834.

32. Mallet to Grey, 27 October 1914, FO 371/2139/64020; Mallet to Grey, 29 October 1914, FO 371/2144/77717; Grey to Mallet, 28 October 1914, 'Cmd 7628', No. 174, p. 71; Mallet to Grey, 29 October 1914, *ibid.*, No. 176, p. 71.

33. Mallet to Grey, 29 October 1914, *ibid.*, No. 176, p. 71.

34. Sazonov to Benckendorff, 1 November 1914, FO 371/2145/66389; Grey to Mallet, 30 October 1914, 'Cmd 7628', No. 179, p. 72; Gilbert, *Churchill*, Vol. 3, p. 216.

4

Rethinking the Creation
of the
Modern Middle East

It is a commonplace among historians to blame the West for the Middle East's endemic malaise. According to this conventional wisdom, which is adhered to across the political spectrum, the record goes something like this: the European Powers, long having set their sights on the territories of the declining Ottoman Empire, exploited the latter's entry into the First World War to carve out artificial states from this defunct entity. In so doing, they paid attention only to their imperial interests and completely disregarded local yearnings for political unity. London and Paris successfully duped the naive Arab nationalist movement into a revolt against its Ottoman suzerain, then cheated it of its fruits, thereby sowing the seeds of the region's future turmoil. In short, the Middle East suffered unduly as an offshoot of global power politics during the long nineteenth century (1789–1923).

This, roughly, is the argument of such leading Western scholars as Arnold Toynbee, Bernard Lewis, Albert Hourani, George Lenczowski, Roger Owen, André Raymond and David Fromkin.[1] It is also a favourite argument of Arab nationalists, including George Antonius, Amin Said, Suleiman Musa, Abu Khaldun Sati al-Husri, Zaki Hazem Nuseibeh, Zeine N. Zeine and Edward Said.[2]

However, there is another view, one that holds that the Middle East's experience in the nineteenth century was the culmination of long-existing indigenous trends, passions and patterns of behaviour. This viewpoint leads to some radically different interpretations of the Middle Eastern experience and has many implications for the present day.

Imperialist Partners

Contrary to the conventional wisdom, European–Ottoman relations in the era preceding the collapse of the Ottoman Empire, or the Eastern Question as it is commonly known, was not an extended period 'during which European powers slowly picked the Ottoman Empire to pieces',[3] but it was a time when they shored up the ailing Muslim Empire. In the 1830s, these powers saved the Ottoman Empire from assured destruction by its ambitious subject – Egypt's governor, Muhammad Ali. Similarly, Britain and France, later joined by Sardinia, bailed out the Ottomans from their ill-conceived sacred war [*jihad*] against Russia, triggering in the process what came to be known as the Crimean War of 1854–55. When in the 1870s the Ottomans were confronted with a general revolt in their Balkan provinces, which culminated in a fully-fledged Turco–Russian war, it was yet again the Great Powers that redressed the Ottoman setbacks and kept the almost moribund Muslim Empire alive. The same scenario repeated itself as late as 1913, when Istanbul was about to be overrun by a coalition of Balkan states; only, this time, Russia played the lead role in salvaging the Ottoman existence.

This pattern of an outside power saving the Ottomans resulted not from luck but from Ottoman political acumen. The Ottomans did whatever it took to survive: be it skilfully pitting its enemies against one another, or using European support to arrest domestic disintegration and external decline; and notwithstanding its internal weakness and inferiority to its European counterparts, the Ottoman Empire managed to stay in this intricate game of Great Power politics for a surprisingly long period of time, and even to outlive (if only by a slim margin) its two formidable imperial rivals, the Habsburgs and the Romanovs.

Another source of Ottoman success derived from European imperial solidarity. Those were the high days of imperialism. The Ottoman Empire was an empire among empires; and, apart from their strategic, economic, and political interest in Ottoman survival, the European Powers were loathe to knock a fellow empire out of existence so as to avoid rocking the Continental imperial order. This solidarity had its limits, of course, and the Europeans repeatedly encroached on Ottoman territories – notably the French occupation of Algeria (1830) and Tunisia (1881) and the Italian conquest of Libya (1911–12). However, these were nibbles at the fringes of empire that had little effect on the Ottoman edifice. The only substantial Great Power infringement on Ottoman territorial integrity – the British occupation of Egypt in 1882 – was born of chance, not design; as such, it was a demonstration of Great Power immersion in an unwished-for regional crisis that it had done little to create and over which it exercised less control.[4]

Despite extensive external support, the Ottoman Empire steadily contracted, mostly due to internal fragmentation and decay, not external threats. However adept they were in manipulating European interests to their advantage, the Ottomans could not perform miracles. No foreign physician could cure the 'Sick Man of Europe' unless he helped himself. This he could not do because, like his other imperialist colleagues, he never developed an adequate response to the ultimate foe of empires in modern times: the rise of nationalism. Nationalism wrested Greece from Ottoman domination as early as the 1820s and thereafter relentlessly squeezed the Ottomans out of their European provinces, resulting in the independent states of Romania, Bulgaria, Serbia, Montenegro and Albania.

Also, it was the desire to redress these setbacks that largely accounted for the Ottoman decision to enter the First World War, by far the single most important decision in the history of the modern Middle East. It was anything but inevitable. The Ottoman Empire was not forced to take part in the war by a last-ditch bid to survive, nor cowered into it by an over-bearing German ally, or even by a hostile Great Britain. Rather, it was in the highly enviable position of being courted by both warring camps: the Central Powers wished for its participation and the Entente Powers hoped it would stay out. That the Ottoman leaders chose to ignore repeated British, French and Russian pleas for neutrality indicated a determination to go to war. Why? The Young Turk leadership made clear that it sought to reverse centuries of imperial decline and revive their country's glory, as their proclamation of war evidenced:

> Our participation in the world war represents the vindication of our national ideal. The ideal of our nation and people leads us toward the destruction of our Muscovite enemy to obtain a natural frontier to our empire, which should include and unite all branches of our race.

This terrible miscalculation led in the short run to the destruction of Turkey-in-Asia by the British Army during the First World War. In the long run, it led to the century of flux and instability that has caused so much misery to so many.[5]

The 'Great Arab Revolt'

The imperial ambitions of the Hashemites exerted a decisive impact on the modern history of the Middle East. The standard account of the revolt they led in 1916–18 holds that the British manipulated them into leading the Arabs to turn against their Ottoman overlords. In fact, the Hashemites and their imperial ambitions manoeuvred the largest empire on earth to extend itself well beyond their original plans for the post-war era.

The key turn took place in the second half of 1915. As late as June of that year, British policy-makers still accepted the continued existence of Turkey-in-Asia.[6] However, just four months later, the British High Commissioner in Egypt, Sir Arthur Henry McMahon, accepted Sharif Hussein of Mecca's vision of a successor empire (presumably headed by himself) and agreed to his main territorial demands, albeit in a tentative and highly equivocal fashion.

This achievement of the Hashemites was all the more remarkable given the almost complete lack of nationalist fervour among the Ottoman Empire's Arabic–speaking subjects. The 'Arab national awakening' that supposedly originated in the late nineteenth century and culminated in the 'Great Arab Revolt', simply did not exist. One historian has credibly estimated that a mere 350 activists staffed all the secret Arab societies operating in the Ottoman Empire at the outbreak of the First World War.[7] Even if one accepts that the leaders of these societies 'were mostly notables with substantial followings of their own',[8] they were but a drop in the ocean. Completely unaware of this handful of activists, the vast majority of the 8–10 million Ottoman Arabic-speaking subjects remained loyal to their imperial master to the bitter end.

This means that Hussein represented little more than himself, notwithstanding his pretensions to represent 'the whole of the Arab Nation without any exception'.[9] The minimal backing he received from some Bedouin tribes had nothing to do with a yearning for independence and everything to do with the glitter of British gold and the promise of booty. Hussein could not even count on the support of his own Hijaz constituency: in December 1916, six months after he began a rebellion against the Ottoman authorities, a British report found the residents of his home town, Mecca, 'almost pro-Turks'.[10] It would not be until the winter of 1917 that the pendulum would start swinging in Sharif Hussein's direction.

On a wider level, the thought of the Sharif of Mecca wresting the caliphate from the Ottoman Sultan, with whom their loyalty had rested for centuries, was anathema to most Arabs and Muslims. So entrenched was this overarching loyalty to the Sultan that in Egypt, despite three decades of British occupation, the very occurrence of the revolt was generally questioned; instead, the revolt was seen as an Ottoman–Sharifian conspiracy aimed at deceiving the British through an apparent display of loyalty into generous financial contributions to Hussein.[11] Even outside the Ottoman Empire, for example in French-occupied

North Africa, Muslim opinion was no less hostile; some condemned the revolt as an unlawful rising by an audacious subject against his lawful Muslim suzerain, others dismissed it as 'one of the habitual Arab revolts'. In the Persian Gulf principalities, the revolt was received with indifference. Even the sheikhs of Kuwait and Muhammarah, who sent hearty congratulations to the Sharif, did so only in deference to British wishes. The powerful pro-British Arabian potentates, Abd al–Aziz Ibn Saud and Muhammad al–Idrisi, also deferred to their patron and expressed sympathy with the revolt; but they lent it no material support and were bitterly resentful of Hussein's championship of the Arab cause lest this suggest their coming under his control.[12]

Nor did the revolt win popular support in the Levant, let alone whip up nationalist sentiments there. In Syria and Palestine the urban political leadership remained loyal to the Sultan and frowned on the desert uprising. It would not be before the summer of 1917, after the capture of Aqaba by sharifian forces and the British advance from Egypt into Palestine had driven home the reality of allied successes to the Levant, that mutterings of discontent began to surface; but these resulted from the serious material shortages caused by the Ottoman setbacks, not identification with the Sharif. Even in August 1918, just weeks before the end of hostilities in the Middle East, a British report stated that:

> The Muslim population of Judea took little or no interest in the Arab national movement. Even now the Effendi [middle] class, and particularly the educated Muslim–Levantine population of Jaffa, evince a feeling somewhat akin to hostility towards the Arab movement very similar to the feeling so prevalent in Cairo and Alexandria.[13]

In Mesopotamia, indifference ran even deeper and wider. There was no anticipation of national liberation – not even in the British-occupied areas. The Sharif's religious credentials were of little consequence to the mainly Shi'ite population which abhorred his desire to incorporate their lands into his future empire: many individuals served in the Ottoman Army and numerous tribal chiefs collaborated with the central authorities. The British even had great difficulties in persuading Mesopotamian prisoners of war, detained in India, to join the Sharif's revolt: most of them remained loyal to their Ottoman sultan-caliph; others were concerned for their families' safety; still others were simply indifferent to the developments in the Hijaz.

Also, those Mesopotamian prisoners of war who joined the Sharif's army did not feel any empathy towards the non-Arabian participants in the revolt, who were shipped to Arabia by the British. Relations with Syrian officers were especially acrimonious, as both groups vied for greater power and influence in the sharifian armies. Indeed, disharmony among the revolt's constituent elements was a reflection of the wider attitude of the Arabic-speaking communities towards the sharifian venture: 'The Syrian, from the height of his education and "refinement" looks down on the Bedouin in his "dirt and sand" as being beyond real consideration, while the Bedouin in turn despises the effeminacy of the Syrian.' Egyptians were particularly loathed by the Arabians. On several occasions Hussein and his sons expressed their preference for Sudanese over Egyptian troops, and the Egyptian forces sent to the Hijaz were given rough and humiliating treatment by the Bedouins: they were denied basic foodstuffs; were occasionally fired at; and their military preparations were often obstructed (a popular Bedouin pastime, for example, was to empty sandbags filled by the Egyptians and to steal the sacks). 'Most of the Egyptians are left to the mercy of the Arabs who are doubtful allies and putting up the rottenest fighting and making us responsible for the result', Lieutenant-Colonel Pierce Joyce, who served with the Sharif's forces throughout much of the war, noted in his plea for greater British control of the revolt.[14]

All this means that the Hashemites were not seen as champions of national liberation but as imperialist aspirants eager to exploit a unique opportunity to substitute their own empire for that of the Ottomans. As David Hogarth, director of the Arab Bureau in Cairo, put it in January 1918 following extensive talks with Hussein: 'It is obvious that the King regards Arab Unity as synonymous with his own Kingship.'[15] In fact, Hussein's territorial ambitions extended well beyond the Arabic-speaking territories. As he told 'Lawrence of Arabia' in the summer of 1917: 'If advisable we will pursue the Turks to Constantinople and Erzurum – so why talk about Beiruth, Aleppo and Hailo?'[16]

Perfidious Albion or Perfidious Arabia?

Though generously rewarded by the Entente Powers for their desert revolt – in the form of vast territories – the Hashemites were never satisfied with their gains. Furthermore, their complaint of being 'robbed' of the fruits of victory promised to them during the war was soon nationalized to become the standard grievance levelled at the Western Powers, Britain in particular. This gave rise to a theory of pan-Arabism premised on imperialist perfidy that has ever since dominated the Middle Eastern political discourse.[17]

'The Sykes–Picot Agreement is a shocking document', charged George Antonius in his celebrated book, *The Arab Awakening*, a study that has had wide and lasting influence among intellectual and academic circles in both the Arab World and the West:

> It is not only the product of greed at its worst, that is to say, of greed allied to suspicion and so leading to stupidity: it also stands out as a startling piece of double-dealing …The agreement had been negotiated and concluded without the knowledge of the Sharif Hussein, and it contained provisions which were in direct conflict with the terms of Sir Henry McMahon's compact with him. Worse still, the fact of its conclusion was dishonestly concealed from him because it was realized that, were he to have been apprised of it, he would have unhesitatingly denounced his alliance with Great Britain. He only heard of the existence of the Agreement some 18 months later.[18]

This claim has three main parts: that the British were duplicitous; that Sharif Hussein knew nothing of the Sykes–Picot agreement until a year and a half later; and that this agreement contradicted the deal Hussein had previously reached with London. Let us look at each of these charges.

The British were duplicitous

There was nothing deceitful about the Anglo-French talks. The two participants were war allies engaged in a mortal struggle and it was only natural for them to co-ordinate strategies, especially as this was officially required by the Declaration of London of 4 September 1914, in which the Entente Powers committed to co-ordinate their peace terms. If anything, France could lodge a grievance against Britain for breaching the terms of their wartime alliance by making unauthorized promises to a minor third party, one that had not even decided to throw in its lot with the Entente. It was precisely to staunch this grievance that the British initiated talks with the French: not to renege on their tentative understanding with Hussein but to give it the widest possible international recognition.

From the outset of the Sykes–Picot talks, the British tried to convince their sceptical ally of the merits of both an Arab revolt and the establishment of an independent Arab State, or rather an Empire. They succeeded: the Sykes–Picot Agreement contained a commitment 'to recognize and protect an independent Arab State or a Confederation of

Arab States – under the suzerainty of an Arab chief' occupying the territory from Aleppo to Rawandaz and from the Egyptian–Ottoman border to Kuwait.[19] This commitment represented a clear victory for Britain's championing of Arab independence and unity over French opposition. In other words, the Sykes–Picot Agreement constituted the first-ever Great Power recognition of an Arab right to self-determination, well before President Woodrow Wilson turned this principle into a driving force of international politics. As such, Sykes–Picot was an agent of unification rather than the divisive instrument it is commonly thought to be.

Sharif Hussein knew nothing of Sykes–Picot

Hussein was not kept in the dark regarding the other provisions of the Sykes–Picot Agreement, let alone its very existence. By October 1916, a Lebanese notable revealed details of the agreement to Syrian circles in Cairo.[20] Sykes and Picot themselves met a group of Syrian nationalists in April 1917 to inform them of the agreement's main provisions (though without divulging its precise geographical delimitation);[21] and Sykes then set out to the Hijaz to brief Hussein in person. On 2 May, he met Faisal and explained to him the gist of the agreement, to which Faisal reportedly agreed 'after much argument and seemed satisfied'. Three days later Sykes explained to Sharif Hussein 'the principle of the agreement as regards an Arab Confederation or State'.

Sykes reported to Cairo that his interviews with the two men went well. Later that same month, on 19–20 May, he held two further meetings with Hussein, this time with Picot present. After much bargaining, Hussein agreed to declare that 'he would be content if the French Government pursued the same policy towards Arab aspirations on Moslem Syrian Littoral as [the] British did in Baghdad' and that he would be 'ready to co-operate with France in Syria to the fullest extent and England in Mesopotamia'.[22]

Sykes claimed Hussein was given a thorough explanation of 'the outline and detail of the [Sykes–Picot] agreement'; an aide to Hussein said the Sharif merely had 'a hasty perusal and explanation (with little opportunity given him to think it over or criticize)'.[23] However, it makes no difference: either way, Hussein knew of the Sykes–Picot Agreement's existence and its main provisions, meaning that his later claim of having heard nothing about the agreement until its disclosure by the Bolsheviks in November 1917 was a falsehood.

Contradiction between Sykes–Picot and the
Hussein–McMahon correspondence

The charge of a fundamental contradiction between the provisions of
the Sykes–Picot Agreement and those of the Hussein–McMahon correspondence overlooks the crucial fact that both agreements recognized
the Arab right to self-determination and provided for the establishment
of a large Arab state. Their alleged incompatibility becomes a matter of
degree rather than of substance, namely, the conformity between their
territorial delineation of the prospective Arab Empire. Moreover, it
should be borne in mind that the McMahon–Hussein correspondence
never culminated in an official and legally binding agreement, or for
that matter, in any agreement whatsoever. It was an intricate process of
bargaining in which both parties pitched for the highest possible prize:
Hussein for the largest empire he could secure for himself and his family; McMahon for harnessing the entire 'Arab Nation' to the Allied
cause. Neither of them accepted the other's offers as final and both tried
to improve on them until the territorial haggling was dropped without
agreement. As far as the British were concerned, McMahon's tentative
promises were nothing but a general statement of intent that had to be
subjected to detailed scrutiny during the postwar negotiations. On 20
October 1915, the British Foreign Secretary, Sir Edward Grey,
instructed McMahon to avoid concrete territorial pledges to Hussein
unless these were absolutely necessary, only to be ignored by the latter
who believed that his promises were equivocal enough to leave 'as free a
hand as possible to His Majesty's Government in the future' and sufficiently definite to exclude those areas which involved British and
French interests.[24] The problem was that it was precisely this equivoca-
tion which was to give rise to the longstanding charge of British perfidy.

Actually, if any one was perfidious, it was Sharif Hussein and the
Hashemites, who initiated negotiations with Britain's Cairo Office on
the false claim that they represented the 'whole of the Arab Nation
without any exception'. In addition, they fantastically inflated their military strength and made a string of promises (notably to detach the Arab
forces in the Ottoman Army from their imperial master) they knew full
well they could never make good. They also secretly double-dealt with
the Ottomans behind Britain's back, both before the declaration of the
revolt and in the late stages of the war.[25]

Had Cairo officialdom recognized the Sharif's meagre political and
military power base, it undoubtedly would have spurned his grandiose
demands. Also, while the British did fall for Hussein's false pretences,
they made their territorial and financial largesse contingent on his

harnessing the entire 'Arab Nation' to the Entente's cause. In McMahon's words:

> It is most essential that you should spare no effort to attach all the Arab peoples to our united cause and urge them to afford no assistance to our enemies. It is on the success of these efforts and on the more active measures which the Arabs may hereafter take in support of our cause, when the time for action comes, that the permanence and the strength of our agreement must depend.[26]

Needless to say, the Hashemites never came close to fulfilling this fundamental condition on which the entire deal was predicated, as most Arabs remained loyal to their Ottoman suzerain to the very end. Yet the Hashemite failure to deliver their part of the bargain did not prevent them from censuring the British for foul play nor from enjoying the deal's abundant fruits.

To be sure, the attribution of spheres of privileged economic treatment to Great Britain and France reflected their paternalistic attitudes, but this was fully in line with the spirit and custom of the day. Hussein himself viewed British economic prerogatives in his kingdom as indispensable: already in his first letter to McMahon he proposed that 'England shall have the preference in all economic enterprises in the Arab countries whenever conditions of enterprises are otherwise equal' and that it would act as a protector of the newly-established Arab State.[27] Hence, the Anglo-French 'priority of right of enterprise and local loans' and their exclusive right 'to supply advisers or foreign functionaries at the request of the Arab State', both stipulated by the Sykes–Picot Agreement, were fully commensurate with Arab independence as envisaged by the Hussein–McMahon correspondence, the only difference being that France would also enjoy these prerogatives; and even this modification was cleared with Hussein's Cairo representative, Lieutenant Muhammad Faruqi.[28]

This ostensible discrepancy notwithstanding, there was no real contradiction between the Sykes–Picot Agreement and the territorial qualifications made by McMahon in his correspondence with the Sharif. Broadly speaking, these qualifications rested on four interconnected grounds; the first of which was Britain's existing treaties with other Arab chiefs, such as the sheikhs of Kuwait and Muhammarah, al–Idrisi and Ibn Saud. These, in turn, excluded much of the Arabian Peninsula from the prospective Arab Empire, something that Hussein could never bring himself to accept. He repeatedly pleaded with Britain to goad these potentates into recognizing his supreme authority, albeit to no avail; none of them was willing to come under the Hashemite wing, and Ibn Saud eventually kicked the Hashemites out of the Hijaz.

Second, the British had to consider their Indian interests, which focused by and large on securing the British position in Mesopotamia. This was presented by McMahon to Hussein as follows:

> With regard to the *vilayets* [*sic*] of Baghdad and Basra, the Arabs will recognize that the established position and interests of Great Britain necessitates certain administrative arrangements in order to secure these territories from foreign aggression, to promote the welfare of the local populations and to safeguard our mutual economic interests.

When Hussein contested this provision, McMahon reiterated the importance of a 'friendly and stable administration in the vilayet of Baghdad' for British interests and suggested leaving the issue for the time being since 'the adequate safeguarding of these interests calls for a much fuller and more detailed consideration than the present situation and the urgency of these negotiations permit'.[29]

In other words, not only was Hussein *not* promised the whole of Mesopotamia, the future of which remained open-ended, but he was informed of the extent of British interest in this area. In this respect the Sykes–Picot Agreement did little more than delineate those areas of British interests intimated by McMahon to Hussein.

Third, the British excluded areas that were not purely Arab, defined by McMahon as 'the two districts of Mersina and Alexandretta and portions of Syria lying to the west of the districts of Damascus, Homs, Hama and Aleppo [which] cannot be said to be purely Arab'.[30] This vague geographical expression was to become the central bone of Anglo-Arab contention with regard to the compatibility of the Sykes–Picot Agreement with the Hussein–McMahon correspondence in general, and the exclusion of Palestine from the area of the prospective Arab Empire in particular. According to a standard British interpretation, first articulated in 1920, Palestine was indeed excluded from the territory of such an empire owing to its position west of the Ottoman district, or *velayet*, of Damascus which at the time included the area that was to become the Emirate of Transjordan.[31]

The weakness of this contention, as Emir Faisal pointed out at a meeting in London in March 1921, in what was to become the standard pan-Arab claim, was that:

> If His Majesty's Government relied upon the strict interpretation of the word 'vilayet', as applied to Damascus, they must also

interpret the word to mean the same with regard to Homs and Hama. There was not, and never had been, a vilayet of Homs and Hama...[Hence] as the Arabic stood, it would clearly be interpreted by any Arab, and had been so interpreted by King Hussein, to refer to the four towns and their immediate surroundings. Palestine did not lie to the west of the four towns, and was therefore in his opinion, included in the area for which His Majesty's Government had given pledges to his father.[32]

Declassified documents in the British archives confirm that contemporary officialdom in Cairo and London did indeed interpret McMahon's four 'districts' as meaning 'towns', but *not* in the expansive geographical sense claimed by Arab partisans. Quite the reverse in fact: *they viewed the four towns as synonymous with the entire territory of the prospective Arab Empire in Syria*; *ipso facto* this excluded Palestine from the territory of this empire. Indeed, even Faisal, in his above meeting, while contesting the British interpretation of McMahon's promises, said that 'he was quite prepared to accept...that it had been the original intention of His Majesty's Government to exclude Palestine'.[33]

The last, and probably the most important, reason McMahon was hesitant in his correspondence with the Sharif related to Britain's keen awareness of French interests in the Levant. In his letter of 24 October 1915, McMahon excluded from the area of the Arab Empire all those regions in which Great Britain was not 'free to act without detriment to the interests of her ally, France'.[34] He did not go beyond this general formulation because he had no definite idea 'of the extent of French claims in Syria, nor of how far His Majesty's Government have agreed to recognize them'; but he claimed to have 'endeavoured to provide for possible French pretensions to those places' by his general reservation.[35]

It was a matter of common knowledge at the time, however, that the French had a keen interest in, and a deep emotional attachment to, Syria, 'in which latter term they included Palestine and the Christian Holy Places'.[36] Indeed, in his reply to McMahon's promises, Hussein agreed to exclude the two *velayets* of Mersina and Adana from the Arab Kingdom, but insisted that 'the two *vilayets* of Aleppo and Beirut and their sea coasts are purely Arab *vilayets*'.[37]

Since Palestine at the time did not exist as a unified political or administrative entity, but rather was divided into two separate units: the northern part, extending nearly to Jaffa, belonged to the *velayet* of Beirut, and the southern part was defined as the independent sanjak of Jerusalem. In his letter of 24 October, McMahon avoided a specific definition both of the areas which 'cannot be said to be purely Arab' and of those in which Britain was not 'free to act without detriment to the interests of her ally, France'. Had Hussein let this ambiguity stand, he could have later disowned any precise idea of its territorial delimitation. In choosing to interpret McMahon's vague reservation as including the *velayet* of Beirut, however, the Sharif explicitly acknowledged its application to the northern half of Palestine, and implicitly – to the entire country. Hence, the exclusion of the northern part of Palestine from the area of the Arab Empire by the Sykes–Picot Agreement could not have come as a surprise to Hussein; the southern part of Palestine, or much of the sanjak of Jerusalem, was in any event awarded by this agreement to the independent Arab Empire.

All this means that the Antonius quote at the beginning of this section could not be further from the truth: the Hashemites misled their British interlocutors, rather than the other way round; the Sykes–Picot Agreement served as a catalyst of Arab unification, not fragmentation; and no fundamental contradiction existed between the territorial provisions of the Sykes–Picot Agreement and those of the Hussein–McMahon correspondence.

Unite and Rule

The Hashemites demanded of Britain not self-determination for Arabic-speaking Ottomans but a successor empire that would include Arabs, Turks, Armenians, Kurds, Assyrians and Jews. This expectation created a serious dilemma for British decision-makers. As imperialists themselves, they had no compunction about substituting a Hashemite Empire for the Ottoman, especially if the latter fell under British tutelage. However, they worried about its feasibility. Could the Hashemites muster the necessary support? Effective propaganda by the Hashemites and their partisans in London and in the Middle East, not least 'Lawrence of Arabia', allayed this doubt. Even so, the British continued to wonder about the Hashemite project. Lawrence himself acknowledged in 1915 that 'no national feeling' existed at all among the Arabic-speakers. Years later, he termed Arab unity 'a madman's notion – for this century or next, probably...I am sure I never dreamed of uniting even the Hijaz and Syria. My conception was of a number of small states.'[38]

This, however, was not how post-First World War British policy-makers attempted to resolve the tension between their instinctive imperialist support for pan-Arab unity and their recognition that this goal was but a mirage. Contrary to the conventional wisdom, Britain's 'original sin', if such was indeed committed, lay not in the breaking-up of Middle Eastern unity but in its attempted over-unification. As Winston Churchill, then the Colonial Secretary, told the House of Commons on 14 June 1921, shortly after presiding over the establishment of the states of Iraq and Transjordan, and the effective limitation of Palestine to the territory between River Jordan and the Mediterranean:

> Broadly speaking, there are two policies which can be adopted towards the Arab race. One is the policy of keeping them divided, of discouraging their national aspirations, of setting up administrations of local notables in each particular province or city, and exerting an influence through the jealousies of one tribe against another. That was largely, in many cases, the Turkish policy before the War, and cynical as it was, it undoubtedly achieved a certain measure of success.
>
> The other policy, and the one which, I think, is alone compatible with the sincere fulfilment of the pledges we gave during the War to the Arab race and to the Arab leaders, is an attempt to build up around the ancient capital of Baghdad, in a form friendly to Britain and to her Allies, an Arab state which can revive and embody the old culture and glories of the Arab race, and which, at any rate, will have a full and fair opportunity of doing so if the Arab race shows itself capable of profiting by it. Of these two policies we have definitely chosen the latter.[39]

Between Nation and Empire

The notion of the West's original sin in the Middle East has become nearly universal. Even sceptics who otherwise reject the received wisdom regarding Britain's bad faith and duplicity accept Western culpability for the Middle East's notorious volatility. They ascribe this to the region's unwitting importation of ideologies at variance with older traditions, notably those of nationalism and statehood. In the words of Elie Kedourie:

> A curse the West has indeed brought to the East, but – and here lies the tragedy – not intentionally; indeed the curse was considered – and still is by many – a precious boon, the most precious that the West could confer on the East in expiation of its supposed sins; and the curse itself is as potent in its maleficence in the West as it is in the East. A rash, a malady, an infection spreading from western

Europe through the Balkans, the Ottoman Empire, India, the Far East and Africa, eating up the fabric of settled society to leave it weakened and defenceless before ignorant and unscrupulous adventurers, for further horror and atrocity: such are the terms to describe what the West has done to the rest of the world, not wilfully, not knowingly, but mostly out of excellent intentions and by example of its prestige and prosperity.[40]

Kedourie's lamentation evokes a wider tendency to view nationalism as the scourge of international relations, the primary source of inter-state conflict and war; a tendency which has gained considerable currency following the end of the Cold War and the bloody wars of dissolution in the former Yugoslavia and several former Soviet Asiatic republics.

This historical diagnosis raises the question of cause and effect. There is nothing inherently violent about nationalism when it results from the desire of a specific group which shares a common descent, language, culture, tradition and history, and which seeks self-rule in a specific and bounded territory. Nationalism goes hand in hand with inter-state violence only when the quest for self-rule is hindered by another party or when it leads to aggression against a foreign territory – in which case it crosses the line from a nationalist to an imperialist policy. In other words, imperialism, not nationalism, has constituted the foremost generator of violence in modern world history. The desire to dominate foreigners, to occupy external territories, contains the seeds of inevitable violence.

Given that almost no empire voluntarily sheds its colonies, the disintegration of empires has rarely been a peaceful process, as evidenced by the Ottoman collapse. During the nineteenth century, its European provinces were the most violent part of the Continent as subject peoples vied for their freedom; but the Middle Eastern provinces were also rife with mayhem: Wahhabi raids in Mesopotamia and the Levant in the first decade, the Lebanese civil strife of the 1840s to 1860s, and the national awakening of the Armenians in the 1890s.

Violence, then, was not imported to the Middle East as a by-product of European nationalism; it was integral to the region's political culture well before the European powers entered. Nor did this violence result from a connection to Islam, as is sometimes suggested. Rather, it followed from the Middle East's millenarian imperial traditions. In this respect, Europe has had little to teach the Middle East. From the ancient great empires of the Mediterranean and the Fertile Crescent (for example, Egypt, Greece, Rome, Carthage, Persia, Assyria, Babylon, etc.), through the early Muslim empires, to the Ottoman Empire, the story of the Middle East has been the story of the rise and fall of universal empires and imperial dreams. Politics in this region has been characterized by a constant struggle for regional mastery; the dominant power seeks to subdue, and even to eliminate, all potential challengers, so as to bring the entire region under its domination. Such ambitions have remained largely unsatisfied thanks to the equally formidable forces of fragmentation and degeneration. The result has been a wide gap between delusions of grandeur and the stark realities of weakness, between the imperial dream and the centrifugal forces of parochialism. These forces gained momentum during the last phases of the Ottoman Empire – culminating in its disastrous decision to enter the war on the losing side and the resultant creation of a new imperial dream that would survive the Ottoman demise to haunt Middle Eastern politics for generations to come.[41]

Conclusions

This analysis does not suggest that actions by the Great Powers in the Middle East were driven by the noblest of motives, nor does it condone their interference in that region, nor absolve them of some responsibility for the region's present misfortunes. It does establish that, contrary to conventional wisdom, the history of the region since the First World War is no less the making of local actors than it is of the Great Powers. The Ottoman Empire was not a hapless victim of European imperialism but rather an active participant in the Great Power game; the destruction of this empire was largely self-inflicted; the European powers did not break the Middle East's political unity but rather over-unified the region; Britain neither misled its Arab allies nor made simultaneous contradictory promises regarding the post-war settlement in the Middle East; and there was no national 'Arab awakening' before or during the First World War.

Ottoman behaviour set a number of patterns that have been much emulated. First, it established a pattern of pragmatic co-operation in the face of verbal opposition with the 'infidel' West. This became a regular attribute of Middle Eastern politics and remains so to this very day. Just as the Ottoman Empire used the great European Powers to gain a long lease of life, subsequent rulers have had few qualms about seeking the support of the 'infidel' powers they vilify – even against fellow Muslims – whenever this suits their interests. Religious, nationalistic and anti-imperialist rhetoric aside, Sharif Hussein fought alongside the British 'infidels' against his Muslim suzerain to promote his imperialist ambitions. His great-grandson, King Hussein of Jordan, repeatedly relied on British, American and Israeli support to prop up his throne. Egyptian President Gamal Abdel Nasser, who had made his reputation by standing up to 'Western imperialism', introduced large numbers of Soviet troops into Egypt when confronted with an unmanageable Israeli threat. Ayatollah Ruhollah Khomeini, the high priest of radical Islam, was not deterred from acquiring weapons from the 'Great Satan' by way of saving the Islamic Republic. Even Saddam Hussein managed to survive his eight-year war against Islamic Iran through heavy reliance on Western and Soviet military and economic support. There has been no 'clash of civilizations' between the Middle East and the West during the past two centuries but rather a pattern of pragmatic co-operation and conflict.

NOTES

The author would like to thank Inari Karsh and Daniel Pipes for their incisive comments on an earlier draft.

1. See, for example, Arnold Toynbee, 'The Present Situation in Palestine', *International Affairs* (1931), p. 40; Bernard Lewis, *The Middle East: 2000 Years of History from the Rise of Christianity to the Present Day* (London, 1995), pp. 342–3; George Lenczowski, *The Middle East in World Affairs*, 4th edn (Ithaca, NY, 1980), pp. 58–9, 79–87; Roger Owen, *State, Power and Politics in the Making of the Modern Middle East* (London, 1992), especially Chapters 1 and 4; André Raymond, 'The Ottoman Legacy in Arab Political Boundaries', in Carl L. Brown (ed.), *Imperial Legacy: The Ottoman Imprint on the Balkans and the Middle East* (New York, 1996), pp. 115–28; David Fromkin, *A Peace to End All Peace: The Fall of the Ottoman Empire and the Creation of the Modern Middle East* (New York, 1990), pp. 17, 19, 565.

2. George Antonius, *The Arab Awakening* (London, 1938); Amin Said, *al-Thawra al-Arabiyya al-Kubra* (Cairo, 1951); Suleiman Musa, *al-Haraka al-Arabiyya: Sirat al-Marhala al-Ula li-l-Nahda al-Arabiyya al-Haditha, 1908–1924* (Beirut, 1970); Abu Khaldun Sati al-Husri, *Yawm Maisalun: Safha min Tarikh al-Arab al-Hadith*, rev. edn (Beirut, 1964); Zaki Hazem Nuseibeh, *The Ideas of Arab Nationalism* (Ithaca, NY, 1956); Zeine N. Zeine, *The Emergence of Arab Nationalism with a Background Study of Arab–Turkish Relations in the Near East* (2nd rev. edn) (Beirut, 1966); Edward W. Said, *Orientalism: Western Conceptions of the Orient* (reprinted with a new Afterword) (London, 1995), p. 220.

3. L. Carl Brown, *International Politics and the Middle East* (London, 1984), p. 5.

4. For further discussion of this issue see Chapter 2 in this volume.

5. For an elaborate discussion of the Ottoman Empire's entry into the First World War see Chapter 3 in this volume.

6. As evidenced most notably by the recommendations of the interdepartmental committee, headed by Sir Maurice de Bunsen of the Foreign Office, which regarded the preservation of a decentralized and largely intact Ottoman Empire as the most desirable option.

7. Eliezer Tauber, *The Emergence of the Arab Movements* (London, 1993), Chapter 28. Tauber's exhaustive study of pre-First World War Arab societies is among the more generous in terms of the total number of Arab activists. Ernest Dawn put their total number at 126 in *From Ottomanism to Arabism: Essays on the Origins of Arab Nationalism* (Urbana, IL, 1973), pp. 152–3.

8. Ernest Dawn, 'The Origins of Arab Nationalism', in Rashid Khalidi, Lisa Anderson, Muhammad Muslih and Reeva S. Simon (eds), *The Origins of Arab Nationalism* (New York, 1991), p. 13.

9. 'Correspondence between Sir Henry McMahon, His Majesty's High Commissioner at Cairo, and the Sherif of Mecca July 1915–March 1916, presented by the Secretary of State for Foreign Affairs to Parliament by Command of His Majesty', Cmd. 5957, London, 1939, p. 3 (hereinafter 'Hussein–McMahon Correspondence').

10. *Arab Bulletin*, 23 June 1916, p. 47, and 6 February 1917, pp. 57–8, FO 882/25; McMahon to Grey, 20 October 1915, FO 371/2486/154423; 'Intelligence Report', 28 December 1916, FO 686/6, p. 176.

11. *See*, for example, *Arab Bulletin*, No. 7, 30 June 1916, pp. 57–8; No. 9, 9 July 1916, pp. 78–80; note by Captain G.S. Symes, 'Egypt and the Arab Movement', 14 August 1917, FO 141/783/5317.

12. *Arab Bulletin*, No. 15, 10 August 1916, p. 157; No. 22, 19 September 1916, pp. 279–81; No. 25, 7 October 1916, pp. 338–9; No. 26, 16 October 1916, p. 373; Colonel Hamilton (Political Agent in Kuwait), 'Ibn Saud and His Neighbours', *Arab Bulletin*, No. 92, 11 June 1918, pp. 187–92; Report by Sir Percy Cox, 23 December 1917, IOR L/P & S/10/388 (P5140), p. 14 (India Office).

13. 'Report on the Existing Political Condition in Palestine and Contiguous Areas' by the Political Officer in Charge of the Zionist Commission, 27 August 1918, FO 371/3395/147225, p. 5 (231).

14. *Arab Bulletin*, No. 53, 14 June 1917, p. 263; T.E. Lawrence, *Secret Despatches from Arabia* (London, 1939), pp. 39–40; Joyce to Rees Mogg, 12 December 1916, Joyce Collection, Liddell Hart Military Archives, King's College London.

15. 'Statements made on behalf of His Majesty's Government during the year 1918 in regard to the future status of certain parts of the Ottoman Empire', Cmd. 5964, London, 1939, p. 4.

16. Report by T.E. Lawrence, 30 July 1917, FO 686/8.

17. This set of ideas, to be sure, had been articulated before the First World War, most notably by the Syrian political exiles Abd al-Rahman al-Kawakibi (1854–1902) and Najib Azuri (1873–1916), as well as by some of the secret Arab societies. However, the pan-Arab ideal was inculcated in the wider Arab masses only after the Hashemites had been given control over the newly established Arab states in the wake of the war and gained access to the Great Power decision-making process as representatives of the 'Arab Nation'. With this, it transcended the Hashemite imperial dream.

18. Antonius, *The Arab Awakening*, pp. 248–9.

19. For the text of the Sykes–Picot agreement, as well as a memorandum by its two authors accompanying the draft agreement see CAB 42/11/9. *See also* E.L. Woodward and R. Butler (eds), *Documents on British Foreign Policy 1919–1939*, First Series, Vol. 4 (London, 1960), pp. 241–51 (hereinafter *DBFP*).

20. Elie Kedourie, *In the Anglo–Arab Labyrinth: The McMahon–Husayn Correspondence and Its Interpretations, 1914–1939* (Cambridge, 1976), p. 155.

21. Sykes to War Office, 30 April 1917, FO 882/16. For Picot's report of the meeting, *see* his telegram of 2 May 1917, MAE, Guerre 1914–18, Vol. 877.

22. For accounts of these meetings, *see* Wingate to Foreign Office, 7 May 1917, reporting Sykes's telegram from Jeddah of the previous day, FO 371/3054/93335; *Arab Bulletin*, No. 50, 13 May 1917, p. 207; Sykes's telegram of 24 May 1917, FO 371/3054/104269; 'Note by Sheikh Fuad El Khatib taken down by Lt-Col. Newcombe', FO 882/16; Picot's telegram of 24 May 1917, MAE, Guerre 1914–18, Vol. 877.

23. Memorandum by Sir Mark Sykes, June 1918, FO 371/3381/107379; 'Note by Sheikh Fuad El Khatib'.

24. McMahon to Grey, 26 October 1915, FO 371/2486/163832.

25. For further discussion of this issue, *see* Efraim and Inari Karsh, 'Myth in the Desert, or Not the Great Arab Revolt', *Middle Eastern Studies* (1997), pp. 267–312.

26. McMahon's letter of 14 December 1915, 'Hussein–McMahon Correspondence', p. 12. *See also* his letter of 25 January 1916: 'We are greatly pleased to hear of the action you are taking to win all the Arabs over to our joint cause, and to dissuade them from giving any assistance to our enemies'. *Ibid.*, p. 14.

27. Hussein's letter to McMahon of 14 July 1915, 'Hussein–McMahon Correspondence', pp. 3–4.

28. On Faruqi's role in extracting McMahon's promises to Hussein *see* Karsh and Karsh, 'Myth in the Desert', pp. 282–7.

29. McMahon's letters of 14 October and 24 December 1915, 'Hussein–McMahon Correspondence', pp. 8, 14.

30. McMahon's letter of 24 October 1915, *ibid.*, p. 8.

31. H.W. Young, 'Foreign Office Memorandum on Possible Negotiations with the Hedjaz', 29 November 1920, FO 371/5066/14959, especially paragraphs 9–12.

32. 'Report of Conversation between Mr R.C. Lindsay, CVO, representing the Secretary of State for Foreign Affairs, and His Highness the Emir Feisal, representing the King of the Hedjaz'. (Held at the Foreign Office on Thursday, 20 January 1921), CO 732/3, fol. 366. Faisal's reasoning was incorporated into Antonius's *The Arab Awakening*, p. 178, almost verbatim.

33. CO 732/3, fol. 366. For further discussion of this issue, *see* Efraim and Inari Karsh, *Empires of the Sand: the Struggle for Mastery in the Middle East, 1789–1923* (Cambridge, MA, 1999), pp. 238–41.

34. 'Hussein–McMahon Correspondence', p. 8.

35. McMahon to Grey, 26 October 1915, FO 371/2486/163832.

36. 'Report of the Committee on Asiatic Turkey', p. 3.

37. Hussein's letter of 5 November 1915, 'Hussein–McMahon Correspondence', p. 8.

38. T.E. Lawrence, 'Syria: the Raw Material', *Arab Bulletin*, No. 44, 12 March 1917, FO/882/26 [written early in 1915 but not circulated]; *T.E. Lawrence to his Biographers Robert Graves and Liddell Hart* (London, 1963), p. 101.

39. Martin Gilbert, *Churchill*, Vol. 4, *1916–1922* (London, 1975), p. 596.

40. Elie Kedourie, *The Chatham House Version and Other Middle Eastern Studies* (London, 1970), p. 10; Elie Kedourie, 'The Nation-State in the Middle East', *The Jerusalem Journal of International Relations*, 9 (1987), p. 3.

41. For further discussion of this issue, *see* Chapter 1 in this volume.

5

Cold War, Post-Cold War:
Does it Make a Difference for the
Middle East?[1]

While the euphoric predictions of a 'new world order' and the 'end of history' have been buried in the alleys of Sarajevo and the killing fields of Rwanda, the end of the Cold War still constitutes the primary prism through which world affairs in general, and Middle Eastern events in particular, are observed. Stemming from the premise that 'international rather than regional powers wielded most of the power and did most of the manipulation most of the time',[2] this system-dominant approach has reduced the indigenous actors to meaningless entities who, at best, exercise a limited control over their own fate and, at worst, are malleable objects in the hands of omnipotent superpowers.

This chapter adopts the opposite approach. It will argue that not only does the Cold War fail to provide an adequate analytical framework for understanding contemporary Middle Eastern affairs, but it ignores the main impetus behind regional developments: the local actors. Hence, the end of the Cold War is bound to have only a limited impact on the international politics of the Middle East.

There are three principal reasons for this assertion:

First, none of the Middle Eastern conflicts or schisms owed its origins to the Cold War; they were all deeply rooted in the indigenous soil and some of them – notably the Arab–Israeli and the Iran–Iraq disputes – predated the advent of the Cold War and have outlived its demise; consequently, as long as these protagonists do not view the resolutions of their conflicts as being in their best interest, no major breakthrough in this direction is likely to ensue.

Second, superpower policy towards the Middle East was not exclusively motivated by Cold War considerations. This was particularly pertinent in the case of the Soviet Union, which viewed the Middle East in predominantly regional terms by virtue of its being part of the Soviet borderland, like Eastern Europe, Finland or China; and it was only during Mikhail Gorbachev's tenure that the Soviets came to subordinate their regional interests to global considerations.[3] Western interest in the

Middle East was more globally oriented; but this had never precluded the existence of other weighty interests which had nothing to with the Cold War, not least the need for Middle Eastern oil and the lucrative trade in arms; these considerations are certain to persist in the wake of the Cold War, as demonstrated by the 1990–91 Gulf Conflict.

This state of affairs also made superpower rivalry in the Middle East more complex and nuanced than the standard black/white Cold War dichotomy, particularly since superpower alignments and loyalties often cut across local divides and vice versa. The Shah's Iran, for example, America's foremost Middle Eastern ally, developed a good working relationship with the Soviet Union, while Saddam's Iraq counterbalanced its alignment with Moscow through a network of relationships with the West Europeans. Even the Arab–Israeli conflict has never fallen into the all-too-often misconceived pattern of an Israeli–Western axis versus a Soviet–Arab one. Western association with many Arab regimes (Saudi Arabia, Transjordan, Iraq, etc.) predated the establishment of the State of Israel and persisted during the entire Cold War era; some pro-Western regimes (that is, Iraq) were lost to Moscow, but equally prominent former Soviet allies were gained, most notably post-1973 Egypt.

Finally, the Cold War had nothing to do with Francis Fukuyama's idealized vision of a Manichean struggle between liberal democracy and communism. Although in Europe the line between liberal and popular democracy was clearly drawn, there was no great demand in the Middle East for either form of government, especially liberal democracy; this in turn made superpower rivalry in that region an opportunistic struggle for assets and allies, devoid of ideological convictions or high moral grounds. A mutually beneficial interdependence between the superpowers and their Middle Eastern allies thus emerged, favouring each partner in accordance with the vicissitudes of regional and global affairs, but on the whole kinder to the junior than to the senior partner. Far from being the hapless objects of policy, undertaking political initiative 'with an eye to the reaction of the outside world',[4] Middle Eastern states have been active and enterprising free agents, doggedly pursuing their own national interests, often in disregard of superpower wishes.

By way of substantiating this argument, I will first outline the pattern of relations between the superpowers and their Middle Eastern allies during the Cold War, then demonstrate its persistence into the 'New World Order' as manifested by the two most outstanding Middle Eastern developments in the post-Cold War era: the 1990–91 Gulf Conflict and the Israeli–Palestinian Declaration of Principles of 1993.

Great Powers and Small States

Analyses of international politics in general, and Great Power/small state relationships in particular, often fall within one of the two paradigms: 'the patron-client relationship' and the 'tail wags the dog' (or 'the power of the weak', to borrow Arnold Wolfers' term).[5] The first paradigm argues that relationships between actors of unequal power and status favour, by and large, the senior actor, whose bargaining position is by definition superior to that of its junior partner. Such relationships may range from a more-or-less symbiotic interaction to a situation of unilateral exploitation, and are based on reciprocity in the exchange of material goods or protection for services, loyalty, and deference to the patron.[6]

Conversely, the tail-wags-the-dog paradigm views Great Power rivalry, an inherent trait of international politics, as advantageous for the small state. This applies not only to the Cold War system, where interbloc polarization and the nuclear balance of terror significantly enhanced the bargaining power of the small states *vis-à-vis* the great powers,[7] but also to earlier international systems in which 'no state has ever been strong enough to eat up all the rest; and the mutual jealousy of the Great Powers has preserved even the small states, which could not have preserved themselves'.[8]

Moreover, the 'power of the weak' is not a mere extension of Great Power rivalry. Small states possess coercive power assets of their own, at times very formidable ones indeed:

> One such asset is the solidarity that usually prevails among the small states and which makes all of them sensitive to what they see as 'bullying' one of them. The potential hostility of a large number of smaller states, some of which may be allies or close friends, is a cost that any nation setting out to impose its will on a weaker country must take into consideration. Further power accrues to a weak country if it can credibly threaten to switch its allegiance from one side to another. The mere belief on the part of the great power that such a shift would be detrimental to its interests gives the weak state a far-from-negligible coercive asset, sometimes called 'the power of blackmail'.[9]

Indeed, if there is one aspect of their Middle Eastern experience that both superpowers would rather forget it is the negative correlation between the magnitude of their investment in smaller states and the amount of influence gained. For all their exertions, neither the United States nor the Soviet Union had a decisive say in their smaller allies' grand strategies, and they found themselves time and again forced to give a retrospective blessing to actions with which they were in total disagreement.

This is not to say that the superpowers were slavishly trailing the wishes of their junior partners, or that their impact was not critical at times; yet successful intervention was largely due to its convergence with indigenous dynamics that had made the local players more receptive to external influence. The superpowers managed to reinforce existing regional trends and even to bring some of them to fruition; but they neither swayed the Middle East in new directions, nor changed existing currents of flow. It was the shock of the October War in 1973 that made Israelis painfully aware of their vulnerability and allowed the US Administration to mediate the historic Egyptian–Israeli Disengagement Agreement of 1975, and it was the sheer determination of the Egyptian President, Anwar Sadat and the Israeli Prime Minister, Menachem Begin, to end the longstanding enmity between their peoples that rendered American mediation effective. Had either been implacably opposed to the idea of a bilateral peace, there would have been practically nothing that President Carter could have done about it, for all his naive enthusiasm.

It was on the cardinal issues of war and peace that superpower influence was most constrained. Just as the United States could not force its Arab allies and Israel to accept its position on a political settlement, so the Soviets failed to convince most of their Arab partners to disavow their total rejection of Israel. Just as Israel launched the 1967 Six Day War without Washington's blessing when it deemed its existence to lie in the balance, so the Egyptian War of Attrition (1969–70), the October War (1973), the Syrian military intervention in Lebanon (1976) and the Iraqi invasions of Iran (1980) and Kuwait (1990) took place against Soviet wishes and advice. The only place where superpower intervention seemed to carry weight was in the sphere of war termination, and even this was more limited than met the eye: the superpowers were normally successful in preventing Israel from carrying military victory to its natural conclusion (for example, in 1967, 1973 and 1982), but far less so in bringing other combatants to stop fighting when the going was good. The Soviets failed to convince Sadat to accept a ceasefire on the first day of the October War, or to force Asad to stop his offensive against the PLO in the summer of 1976. Both superpowers toiled for about a year to bring Iran to accept a UN ceasefire resolution, and even then the Iranian decision was more a result of the total collapse of national morale and a string of successful Iraqi offensives than of superpower pressure.

Soviet–Arab Disputes

Take, for example, Soviet–Arab discourses on the role of armed force in resolving the Arab–Israeli conflict. During the 25-year period from the Six Day War to the disintegration of the Soviet Union in January 1992, the Russians sought to convince their Arab allies of the merits of a peaceful resolution to the conflict, predicated on Security Council Resolution 242 of November 1967 and negotiated under the auspices of the United Nations and the active supervision of the two superpowers,[10] but their pleas fell on deaf ears. Violently opposed to Israel's right to exist, Syria and the PLO dismissed the idea of a political settlement altogether and voiced their commitment to the continuation of the 'armed struggle'.[11] Even Egypt, Moscow's foremost Middle Eastern ally, though accepting Resolution 242, launched a war of attrition against Israel in April 1969.

The Soviets pleaded with Nasser to forgo the use of force and, once hostilities broke out, to stop fighting and reach a negotiated settlement; they even threatened him with military sanctions – to no avail.[12] Not only did these pressures fail to impress Nasser, but on a secret visit to Moscow at the end of January 1970 he managed to implicate the Soviets in his war by threatening to step down in favour of a pro-American president unless Soviet air defence units were immediately sent to Egypt to neutralize Israel's overwhelming air supremacy.[13] The power of blackmail was exploited to the full.

An even more pronounced demonstration of the limits of Soviet influence was afforded by the outbreak of the October 1973 War. When Anwar Sadat, who in the autumn of 1970 assumed the presidency following Nasser's premature demise, began threatening Israel with war unless there was progress towards a negotiated settlement, the Soviets were greatly alarmed. For over a year they denied Egypt vital arms supplies, thus frustrating its war preparations and forcing Sadat to postpone his campaign. The Egyptian retribution was ominous: in July 1972 Sadat ordered the immediate departure of all Soviet units placed in Egypt in 1970 at Nasser's request.

This move caught the Soviets off guard. Notwithstanding their reluctance to introduce these units into Egypt in the first place, and their consequent unease about keeping them there, this was certainly not the way they envisaged their departure. They therefore tried to cut their losses by resuming arms deliveries to Egypt, though not of the scope or at the pace desired by Sadat. At the same time they sustained their efforts to forestall a regional conflagration. Only now they resorted to friendly persuasion rather than arm-twisting tactics, trying to show the Arabs the hazards of war and the benefits of a negotiated settlement. A special effort was made to alert the US Administration to the inflammability of the Middle East situation through a steady stream of public and private warnings, in the hope that the Americans would be sufficiently alarmed to lean more heavily on Israel, or alternatively, that the Israelis would recognize the severity of the situation and accept some of the Arab demands. An exceptionally stark warning was conveyed to President Richard Nixon by Secretary-General Leonid Breshnev during their summit meeting in California in June 1973;[14] similar warnings were made by Foreign Minister Andrei Gromyko in his address to the UN General Assembly on 25 September 1973, and during his meeting with Nixon in the White House three days later.[15] When all their warnings were ignored by the Americans, the Soviets made a last-ditch attempt to alert the Israelis to the impending war by withdrawing their civilian dependants from Egypt and Syria in a massive air and sea-lift on 4 October, two days before the actual outbreak of hostilities.

This move was drastic enough to enrage Sadat – who feared that his meticulously prepared war would be jeopardized at the last moment – and to raise a few eyebrows among the Israeli intelligence community. Yet, since the Israelis believed that the Soviets would most probably alert the Americans to an impending war (which they in fact did), and that the Americans would in turn warn Israel (which they did not), they concluded, albeit with considerable misgivings, that the Soviet action signified another rupture in Arab–Soviet relations, of the sort that had taken place in Egypt in July 1972.[16]

The Soviets were no more successful in bringing their Arab allies to the negotiating table than they had been in preventing them from waging war. Convinced that the key to a political settlement lay in Washington, not in Moscow, Sadat began extricating Egypt from the Soviet orbit already in the early 1970s. The breach between the two countries rapidly widened in the wake of the October War, as Egypt tied its political, economic and military fortunes to those of the United States, and was made absolute in March 1976 when Egypt unilaterally abrogated its 1971 Friendship and Co-operation Treaty with the Soviet Union and terminated the latter's naval services in Egyptian ports.

Syria, by now Moscow's foremost Middle Eastern ally, proved no more co-operative a partner. Ignoring repeated Soviet pleas, it refused to attend the Arab–Israeli peace conference convened in Geneva in December 1973. Shortly afterwards, much to Soviet dismay, it opted for an American-sponsored disengagement agreement with Israel and, moreover, accompanied the negotiation process with a war of attrition on the Golan Heights.

Although the Syrians would eventually drop their objection to the Geneva framework and adopt the preferred Soviet way to a settlement, namely, an international peace conference, they would remain adamantly opposed to Moscow's perception of the essence of such a settlement, which was predicated on the right of all regional states, Israel included, to a secure existence. As a result, a delicate 'balance of tolerance' evolved from the mid-1970s onwards, whereby the two allies agreed to disagree. The Syrians supported the convocation of an international conference on the Middle East but continued to reject Israel's right to exist. For their part the Soviets made no bones about their acceptance of Israel, yet refrained from exerting overt pressure to drive Syria to accept this position; they reluctantly signed a bilateral treaty with Syria in October 1980, yet told Damascus not to interpret it, or for that matter their military and political support, as an endorsement of its political stance.[17]

Even Mikhail Gorbachev, the first Soviet leader to attempt an even-handed approach to the Middle East conflict, which put the Arab and the Israeli cases on a par and called for a solution based on a 'balance of interests among all sides',[18] was forced to recognize the limits of Soviet influence. He went to far greater lengths than his predecessors in opposing Syria's intransigence: he repeatedly declined its requests for state-of-the-art weaponry; sought to isolate it in the Arab World by supporting conservative Arab regimes; restored diplomatic relations with Israel (severed since the 1967 War); and allowed a mass exodus of Soviet Jews to Israel. When Asad questioned the prudence of these actions he was bluntly told to seek a peaceful solution with Israel since 'reliance on military force in settling the Arab–Israeli conflict has completely lost credibility'. The quest for 'strategic parity' with Israel, the cornerstone of Syria's regional policy since the mid-1970s, drew a particularly scathing criticism for 'diverting attention from the question of achieving security and peace in the Middle East'.[19]

While there is little doubt that this approach heightened Asad's sense of vulnerability, it also intensified his hostility towards Gorbachev and left him impervious to the latter's wishes. For example, when in 1988 the PLO implicitly recognized Israel's existence and declared Palestinian independence, Syria denounced this move as a sell-out and refused to recognize the proclaimed Palestinian state; its response to the 1993 Israel–PLO Declaration of Principles was equally scathing.

The Limits of American Influence

The United States' relationship with its Middle Eastern allies was no simpler. Neither its most spectacular success in the post-1967 era (the winning over of Egypt from Moscow) nor the most disastrous setback (the fall of the Shah and the consequent loss of Iran) was primarily of its own making. It was Sadat's deep animosity towards the Soviet Union (significantly exacerbated by its attempts to forestall the October War) and his belief in the United States' leverage over Israel and ability to relieve Egypt's economic plight that produced his change of heart, and it was he who was the driving force behind the improving relations. He first nodded in the American direction in July 1972, when he expelled the Soviet units from Egypt; he did so again in February 1973, by sending his national security adviser, Hafiz Ismail, for talks with Nixon and Kissinger. As the administration would not bite the bait, Foreign Minister Ismail Fahmy turned up in Washington shortly after the October War with the explicit message that Sadat meant business. To underscore Egypt's strategic and political value to its would-be ally, Sadat gave the green light for the ending of the Arab oil embargo that had been imposed on the United States and several West European states during the October War. As architect and direct beneficiary of the embargo, he sought to cash in on its suspension once his brainchild had outlived its usefulness.

Another example of a mutually beneficial alignment in which the junior partner called most of the shots, with the benevolent consent of his senior counterpart, was afforded by the US–Iranian relationship in the decade preceding the Islamic revolution. Though Iran was a long-time associate of the United States, it was only in the late 1960s and the early 1970s that it established itself as America's closest Middle Eastern ally. The process started during the Johnson presidency, when Iran began receiving large quantities of sophisticated weaponry, and gained considerable momentum in 1972, when Nixon gave the Shah a blank cheque to buy whatever conventional weaponry he wished.[20] As the latter took the administration at its word, Iran evolved into the most lucrative market for American military and civilian goods. Between 1972 and the Shah's downfall in January 1979, the value of United States military sales to Iran amounted to some $20 billion, including the highly advanced F-14 aircraft, attack helicopters, M-60A main battle tanks and various types of missiles. In the summer of 1976 the two countries worked out a five-year trade programme that provided for the purchase of $50 billion worth of American goods, including $10 billion worth of military equipment. On the eve of the revolution, the number of Americans working in Iran exceeded 27,000.[21]

This state of affairs gave the Shah an ever-growing leverage over the United States. He was no longer the young malleable ruler of 1953, re-instated through Western cloak-and-dagger operations, but rather a confident autocrat, keeping his subjects in permanent awe, pursuing grand ambitions; a player on the world stage courted by West and East alike. While the Shah's grand aspirations would have been less tenable without American aid and support, his dependence on the United States was more than matched by Washington's need for Iran. As early as 1967, Secretary of Defense McNamara wrote to President Johnson that 'our sales have created about 1.4 million man-years of employment in the US and over $1 billion in profits to American industry over the last five years'.[22] As bilateral trade would soon enter the multi-billion dollar sphere, the stability and well-being of Iran, or more precisely, of the Pahlavi dynasty, would become an American concern of the first order.

However, this was not all. Iran's unique geopolitical location, with the Soviet Union to the north and the world's large oil deposits in the south, made it invaluable to American strategic interests. As the Americans desperately sought to extricate themselves from the Vietnam quagmire, and to avoid similar future entanglements, they appreciated any local power that could protect US interests in this part of the world. In July 1969, during a visit to the island of Guam, Nixon announced what came to be known as the Nixon Doctrine. He reaffirmed America's unwavering commitment to its treaty obligations, but made clear that 'as far as the problems of international security are concerned... the United States is going to encourage and has a right to expect that this problem will be increasingly handled by, and the responsibility for it taken by, the Asian nations themselves'.[23]

As an astute politician, well versed in the art of political survival, the Shah exploited this doctrine for his own ends. He supported American allies and actions worldwide and cultivated a well-oiled lobby in the United States to convince the American public of Iran's strategic importance. At the same time, he did not shy away from exploiting America's Achilles heel – its obsessive fear of Soviet penetration. In June 1965, the Shah made a state visit to Moscow, which culminated in a large-scale commercial agreement, and, no less important, a $110 million arms deal. In the next few years, Iran's relations with the Soviet Union and Communist Bloc countries improved further, lending greater credence to the Shah's occasional threats to seek Soviet arms and military equipment. And even if some American officials doubted the Shah's 'Soviet option', they could not ignore his threat to take his business elsewhere in the West. The United States was, after all, Iran's foremost, but not exclusive, arms supplier. Large quantities of British, French and Italian weapons poured into the Iranian armed forces. Were the United States to reduce its share in Iran's military buildup, its Western competitors were certain to fill the void.

In these circumstances the Americans were happy to allow the Shah to dictate the general direction of the bilateral relationship. They ignored virulent anti-American attacks by Iran's domestic media on account of the Shah's vocal international support for American policies; they tolerated the Shah's persistent striving for higher oil prices, lauding instead his refusal to participate in the 1973–74 Arab oil embargo and his attempts to preserve stability in the world oil market; they conveniently overlooked their own long-standing opposition to nuclear non-proliferation and agreed to sell Iran eight large nuclear power plants for civilian purposes; and they supported the Shah's subversive activities in Iraq in the early 1970s through the Kurdish uprising in the north of the country, and then looked the other way when the Shah betrayed the Kurds to the Iraqi regime once they had outlived their usefulness to him.[24]

Losing Iran

So pervasive was the Iranian–American symbiosis that successive administrations came to view Iranian interests as indistinguishable from their own. The Shah was seen as a permanent part of the Middle Eastern political landscape, something that had always been there – and always would. No writing on the wall, however ominous, was allowed to shatter this illusion.[25]

Upon entering the White House in January 1977, Jimmy Carter was presented with a rosy picture of the domestic situation in Iran. 'At age 57, in fine health, and protected by an absolute security apparatus', read a Department of State memorandum, 'the Shah has an excellent chance to rule for a dozen or more years, at which time he indicated that the Crown Prince would assume the throne.'[26] Actually the Shah's health was anything but fine. He was suffering from terminal cancer, diagnosed a few years earlier by French physicians. However, what had been known to the French for quite some time remained unknown to the American intelligence and foreign affairs community, despite the Shah's importance for United States national interests.[27] No wonder that the administration remained largely oblivious to the gathering storm in Iran until it was too late.

In a memorandum to the secretary of state, Cyrus Vance, in July 1977, his assistant for Near Eastern and South Asian Affairs, Roy Atherton, assessed that 'there is less chance of a dramatic shift in direction in Iran than in most other countries'.[28] Reports by the Central Intelligence Agency (CIA) throughout the summer and autumn of 1977 were similarly sanguine. They anticipated 'no radical change in Iranian political behaviour in the near future' and estimated that, if anything, 'we are looking at evolution not revolution'. In line with the standard fallacy of attributing Middle Eastern developments to external influences, rather than to indigenous dynamics, these assessments struck an exceedingly optimistic line:

> The Shah seems to have no health or political problems at present that will prevent him from being the dominant figure in Iran into and possibly throughout the 1980s. His style of rule and his general policies will probably remain the same unless dramatic developments in the international environment force him to make a change.[29]

It was only on 9 November 1978 that the US Ambassador to Iran, William Sullivan, sent Washington a dramatic memorandum urging his superiors to start 'thinking the unthinkable', namely, what was to be done in the event of the Shah's collapse.[30] This view was shared by a handful of State Department analysts while the CIA reached the same conclusion a fortnight later.[31] Yet others remained hopeful almost to the bitter end. Secretary of State Vance, for example, could not bring himself to admit that the game was over. On 16 November, when the Shah declared martial law in a last-ditch attempt to arrest the avalanche, the Department of State endorsed the move on the understanding that 'military rule is only temporary and he [the Shah] intends as rapidly as possible to move the country towards free elections and a new civilian-directed government'. Zbigniew Brzezinski and his National Security Council staff were equally unaware of the real nature of the Iranian upheaval. Until the situation exploded in their faces in January 1979, they were convinced that a tough 'no-nonsense' policy, either by the Shah or by a successor military government, could save the day.[32] At no stage of the crisis, not even when all was over, did the administration realize that what had just happened in front of its very eyes was a revolution in the grand style of the French or the Russian, not merely turbulence on a large scale.

As a tearful Shah fled Iran on 16 January 1979 and a buoyant Ayatollah Khomeini made a triumphant return home after 16 years of exile, the pre-eminence of indigenous dynamics in Middle Eastern affairs and the limits of superpower influence had been confirmed yet again. While the Carter administration no doubt mismanaged the Iran crisis on a grand scale, the fact is that the United States was reacting to events that were not of its own making and over which it had but limited control. The Iranian revolution was a volcanic eruption of long-suppressed popular passions and desires. Putting this genie back into the bottle was well beyond America's power. All the administration could realistically do was to try to limit the damage to American interests to the barest minimum. As things were, the perennial constraints on superpower regional policy came to the fore in a particularly devastating way: excessive Cold War mentality, competing international priorities, bureaucratic infighting, inability to transcend cultural barriers – all these coalesced to produce a setback that even a decade of bitter regional conflict (the Iran–Iraq War, that is) and momentous global changes would fail to redress.

A Post-Cold War Blunder: The Iraqi Invasion of Kuwait

American post-Cold War pre-eminence could also not prevent the repetition of similarly catastrophic blunders. As a superpower with a global array of interests, yet with a limited capacity for comprehending the social, cultural and political underpinnings of these interests, the United States had often failed to identify unfavourable regional developments before their escalation into fully fledged conflicts; this tendency has not disappeared following the end of the Cold War, as was starkly demonstrated by the 11 September 2001 terrorist attacks on New York and Washington.

As Iraqi troops were massing along the Kuwaiti border during July 1990, after a year of sustained pressure on the emirate to help finance Iraq's rehabilitation from the Iran–Iraq War, the Americans were fixated with Europe. They had been so since the revolutions of 1989 which brought the East European communist regimes tumbling down. Now they were busy working with the Europeans to construct a new set of security arrangements that would allow conflicts on the Continent to be handled in a sensitive and efficient manner. The general mood was euphoric. A brave new world was around the corner. No minor disputes between Third World autocrats could cloud this moment of festivity.

This is not to say that the administration was completely mindless of the mounting tensions in the Gulf. American spy satellites picked up the movement of Iraqi troops towards the Kuwaiti border almost immediately, but it was believed that their purpose was intimidation rather than imminent action.[33] When Ambassador April Glaspie reported back to Washington after her disastrous meeting with Saddam on 25 July and stated that 'his emphasis that he wants a peaceful settlement is surely sincere', there was a general sigh of relief and the United States returned to other business. The view was that the crisis had abated. So confident was Glaspie of Saddam's peaceful intentions that she decided to revive her holiday plans, which she had shelved when the crisis erupted, and returned to Washington on 30 July.

These rosy assessments were hardly supported by developments on the ground. Intelligence reports continued to tell of a rapidly expanding military build-up. By 27 July, eight divisions of some 100,000 men from the best Iraqi units were poised on the joint border. Senior officials in Washington still judged this to be more consistent with intimidation than with preparations for an actual invasion, which would have required far heavier communications traffic and a more substantial artillery stocks, munitions and logistics 'tail'. This view was reinforced by a personal message from the Egyptian President, Husni Mubarak, to George Bush, assuring the administration that there was no problem and encouraging the United States to keep a low profile. A message was thus sent from Bush to Saddam, ensuring him of US affability and asking for an Iraqi *quid pro quo*. The Americans also toned down their own remarks and heeded Arab advice to keep themselves detached from a problem that the Arabs now intended to solve among themselves.

As news filtered out that Iraq had relaxed neither its demands nor its military pressure, a ready explanation was found. On 27 July a meeting of Organization of Petroleum Exporting Countries (OPEC) ministers was beginning in Geneva. There the Iraqi oil minister set out to raise the current price from $18 a barrel to $25. This went against both prevailing market conditions, as there was still a glut, and Saudi determination to keep the price at a 'reasonable' level that would not trigger Western inflation. Working closely with its former adversary (Iran), Iraq allowed itself to be pulled down to a lower price only reluctantly, first to $23 and finally to $21. In return it achieved what was assumed to be a critical agreement on OPEC's overall production quotas (of 22.5 million barrels a day) and promises of firm enforcement.

When this agreement was achieved on 28 July it was widely assumed that the Iraqis had been rather clever in imposing some discipline into the cartel's affairs and had obtained a better OPEC agreement than they could have otherwise expected. However, it soon transpired that Saddam was increasing the military pressure on Kuwait by moving forward his artillery, logistics support and aircraft. This apparently indicated that Saddam had already made up his mind to invade, come what may. His public readiness to continue a dialogue with Kuwait was largely a smokescreen aimed at gaining international legitimacy for the impending military action. Indeed, in conversation with the Arab League Secretary-General, Chadly Klibi, the Iraqi Foreign Minister, Tariq Aziz, unequivocally stated that the Kuwaiti royal family must go.

Unfortunately, this was treated in Washington with the disbelief that commonly accompanies a warning that another government is about to break a basic international rule. The prevailing view – shared by the Kuwaitis, the other Arabs, the British and even Israeli intelligence, which had long been cautioning against Saddam's aggressive intentions – was that Iraq's objective was still intimidation and that, if military action was taken, it would probably be confined to seizing part of the disputed Rumaila oilfield or possibly the strategically located Warba and Bubiyan islands which Iraq had long coveted. It was assumed that Saddam would pull back from Kuwait once the islands were secured. A compelling strategic case was constructed concerning the reasons why Iraq badly needed the islands.

The only problem with the analysis was that this objective had never figured prominently in Saddam's public or private utterances, where the immediate Iraqi demand was cash. Nevertheless, this notion of a limited strike was critical to American policy. If it had been appreciated that the logic of Iraqi military action had been to take all of Kuwait, that might have required a firm American response; the thought that it was geared only to wounding produced more reticence.

However, even if the United States had wished to take stronger action, which apparently was not the case, it was still dependent on its regional allies. The Egyptians and the Saudis were relying on the impending meeting between Iraq and Kuwait in the Saudi city of Jeddah and wanted the Americans to do nothing that might undermine its success. There were limits to how far Washington could go ahead of its major Arab allies. Moreover, its coercive options were also constrained. Without local support it could not send ground troops into the area and, anyway, they would take weeks to arrive.

All the ambiguities and constraints in American policy towards the Middle East and towards Iraq itself were now surfacing. The administration could not ignore the Iraqi pressure on Kuwait, but it did not want to jettison its policy of placating Baghdad, which it had been pursuing since the mid-1980s. It still wanted to obtain Saddam's help in opposing terrorism and in promoting a moderate view on the Arab–Israeli dispute. Saddam's unpredictability and ruthlessness were recognized, yet there was hope that he would be rational in his basic calculations.

Until Iraqi forces crossed the Kuwaiti border in strength on 2 August, the administration remained hopeful that the crisis would be peacefully resolved. When on 27 July the Senate voted 80 to 16 to impose economic sanctions on Iraq, the administration still objected. On 31 July, when Congressman Lee Hamilton asked what the administration's response to an Iraqi invasion of Kuwait would be, John Kelly, assistant secretary of state for South Asian and Near Eastern Affairs, refused 'to venture into the realms of hypothesis'. The following day, after a telephone conversation between President Bush and King Fahd, the United States issued a statement hoping that the next meeting between Iraq and Kuwait would be more successful. Less than 24 hours later, Kuwait was no more.

Could the United States, and the West in general, have prevented the invasion? Probably not. The intensity of Saddam's anxiety over the future of his personal rule and his conviction that the incorporation of Kuwait's wealth into the Iraqi coffers provided the best guarantee for his political survival meant that only a recognition that an invasion would lead to his certain undoing could have averted such a move. Since the Americans and the Europeans failed to grasp Saddam's predicament in the first place, the need for such drastic measures did not even cross their minds. Yet, even if they had interpreted the situation correctly they would have still been dependent on their key regional allies such as Saudi Arabia and Egypt. The administration therefore had little choice but to take its cues from those most directly involved with efforts at mediation, who also failed to identify the nature of the problem at hand. The result was an incoherent and ineffectual policy combining mild warnings to Iraq with attempts to sustain good relations with a state which, on the most favourable interpretation, was engaged in extortion and in opposition to a number of major American foreign policy goals. The unfortunate message this conveyed was one of indifference and infirmity which, in turn, encouraged Saddam to believe that he could invade Kuwait with impunity.

Failing to Bring About a Peaceful Iraqi Withdrawal

Just as America's position as 'the only remaining superpower' did not deter Saddam from invading Kuwait, so it failed to induce him to withdraw peacefully from the Emirate. Given the depth of Saddam's economic plight, and the commitment that he had made by the invasion, Iraq's peaceful withdrawal from Kuwait was never a viable option. It was infinitely more difficult for him to withdraw than it would have been for him not to invade. An unconditional withdrawal, or even withdrawal with a face-saving formula that did not involve the retention of the invasion's financial and economic gains, was totally unacceptable because not only would it have failed to redress the difficult economic problems which drove Saddam into Kuwait, and which were then made worse by the international sanctions against Iraq, but it would have also constituted an enormous loss of face which Saddam felt unable to afford. Only the credible threat that the retention of Kuwait would lead to his certain demise could have driven Saddam out of Kuwait without war; but this was a message the United States, as leader of a variegated international coalition, could not convey.

The various carrots offered to Saddam, some of them by the US Administration itself, did not do the trick either. Four basic types of concessions were on offer: a possible change of regime in Kuwait; serious negotiations with the Kuwaitis on economic and territorial questions; progress on other regional issues, such as the Arab–Israeli conflict; and a promise that Iraq would not be attacked and that American forces would leave the region following the evacuation of Kuwait. For example, on 24 September, French President François Mitterrand implicitly recognized the legitimacy of some of Iraq's territorial claims to Kuwait and suggested that the resolution of the Kuwait crisis be followed by a comprehensive peace conference on the Middle East. In the following months, France would offer Saddam several ladders for a climb-down; the last such attempt was made on 15 January 1991, a few hours before the expiry of the UN ultimatum to Iraq to leave Kuwait, only to be contemptuously rebuffed by Saddam. A request by Jacques Poos, Luxembourg's Foreign Minister and the European Community's rotating President, to come to Baghdad in January 1991 on behalf of the Community was similarly dismissed out of hand, as was his suggestion to meet Foreign Minister Aziz in Algeria. The UN Secretary-General, Javier Pérez de Cuéllar, discovered no greater Iraqi flexibility, either in his meeting with Aziz in August 1990 or in a subsequent meeting with Saddam in January 1991. Even the Americans were showing signs of flexibility. In September 1990 Under-Secretary of State Robert Kimmitt hinted that the United States would not be opposed to Kuwait being forced to negotiate away its differences with Iraq, once the latter had withdrawn. Later that month, in his address to the General Assembly, President Bush stated that Iraq's unconditional withdrawal from Kuwait would pave the way 'for all the states and peoples of the region to settle the conflict that divides Arabs from Israel'. Moreover, in an about-face in America's longstanding opposition to an international conference on the Middle East, on 5 December 1990 the US Ambassador to the UN, Thomas Pickering, indicated his government's readiness to consider such a conference, should Iraq withdraw from Kuwait.

That Saddam failed to pick up these offers of concession, and many others of the same kind, was a clear indication of both his lack of interest in a withdrawal and the weakness of the international anti-Iraq coalition. Saddam wanted a political solution all right; but only one that would allow him to retain the financial and economic fruits of his aggression. Had the international coalition acquiesced in Iraq's *complete* satellization of Kuwait – the invasion's original objective – Saddam might well have withdrawn, even though this process would inevitably have taken an exceedingly prolonged period of time. Since this was a non-starter even for the most appeasing members of the coalition, an Iraqi withdrawal was not on the cards: the gap between the two sides was simply too wide to bridge. A worldwide coalition thus failed to coerce a local dictator into reneging on his aggression and was forced to resort to arms to this end; and even though the war ended in a resounding victory, its very occurrence, not to speak of Saddam's survival, underscored the limits of American, and for that matter Great Power, influence in the 'New World Order'.

The Origins of the 1993 Israel–PLO Deal

In a vitriolic attack on the Israeli–Palestinian peace accord of September 1993, Edward William Said (of Columbia University) sneered at 'the fashion-show vulgarities of the White House ceremony' and castigated his own President, Bill Clinton, for acting as 'a twentieth-century Roman emperor shepherding two vassal kings through rituals of reconciliation and obeisance'.[34] What this hyped-up rhetoric failed to mention is that the agreement was reached in secret negotiations in the Norwegian capital, Oslo, at a time when the formal and highly publicized peace process under the auspices and good offices of the United States, launched at the 1991 Madrid Conference, was virtually stalemated. Not only was the US Administration conspicuously absent from the Oslo talks, but it was barely aware of their existence. When news of the agreement broke, Secretary of State Warren Christopher was stunned (just as he had incidentally been on the occasion of Sadat's Jerusalem visit 17 years earlier, then as Deputy Secretary of State), while President Clinton sought to capitalize on the event to boost his flagging popularity by holding the signing ceremony in the White House. If there was anyone who was shepherded to the White House lawn, it was the host of the party, not his two guests. Far from being the personal whim of Clinton over two subservient vassals, the Israeli–Palestinian deal was the culminating point of a long and tortuous process of disillusionment, mainly among Israelis but also among some Arabs, with the continuation of the conflict.

This process began with the 1967 Six Day War, which dealt militant pan-Arabism a mortal blow and disabused some Arabs of their hopes of destroying the State of Israel. It continued with the 1973 October War, which was to Israel what 1967 had been to the Arabs: a great 'shocker'. The complacency that had gained hold over the Israeli psyche following the astounding 1967 victory was irrevocably shattered. The Israel that emerged from the 1973 trauma was a different nation: sober, mellowed, scarred in many lasting ways. It was still distrustful of its neighbours, it is true, yet was better tuned to potential signs of regional moderation; highly apprehensive of the security risks attending territorial concessions yet aware that land could not buy absolute security. Indeed, successive opinion polls in the wake of the October War showed a steady growth in public support for the 'territory for peace' formula offered by Security Council Resolution 242 of November 1967. Even at the time of the 1977 elections, when Labour lost power to Menachem Begin's right-wing Likud, three out of four Israelis were ready to trade all or part of the occupied territories in return for peace.

This means that the 1977 elections were less of a victory for Likud, let alone for its territorial maximalism, than a vote of no confidence by a young and angry generation of Israelis against Labour's growing incompetence and corruption. This was later vividly illustrated by the fact that only some 200,000 Israelis – a mere four per cent of Israel's Jewish population – made their home in the occupied territories, and the fact that the Israeli leadership was allowed to trade the Sinai Peninsula for contractual peace in 1979.

The advent of the Islamic Republic in Iran in 1979 and the eruption of the Iran–Iraq War a year later were yet another eye-opener to many Arabs. Tehran's relentless commitment to the substitution of its militant brand of Islamic order for the existing *status quo*; its reluctance to end the war before the overthrow of the Ba'th regime in Baghdad; and its subversive and terrorist campaign against the Arab monarchies of the Gulf, all proved to the Gulf states that the Iranian threat exceeded by far the Israeli danger and that there was no adequate substitute for Egypt at the helm of the Arab world. Hence, before 1980 was out, President Saddam Hussein, who a year earlier had triumphantly hosted the Baghdad Summit which expelled Egypt from the Arab League for its peace with Israel, was pleading with the excommunicated Sadat for military support. As Egypt developed into an important military and economic provider – with more than a million Egyptians servicing the over-extended Iraqi economy – Saddam would tirelessly toil to pave the way for its reincorporation into the Arab fold, regardless of its peace treaty with Israel. By the end of the 1980s, Egypt had already regained its focal role in the Arab world, with its moderate policy becoming the mainstream Arab line and its former detractors seeking its friendship and protection. In May 1989 Egypt took part in the all-Arab summit in Casablanca for the first time since its expulsion from the Arab League a decade earlier. Four months later, Libya's radical ruler, Muammar Gaddafi, paid an official visit to Egypt, and in December 1989 President Hafiz Asad of Syria, who for more than a decade had spearheaded the Arab campaign against the separate Egyptian–Israeli peace, swallowed his pride and restored full diplomatic relations with Egypt.

A no less profound process of disillusionment took place in Israel as a result of the protracted and futile Lebanon War (1982–85). While the Israeli public was willing to support the destruction of the PLO's military infrastructure in South Lebanon as a means to bring 'Peace to the Galilee', it would not back the ambitious plan of Defence Minister Ariel Sharon and his Chief-of-Staff, Lieutenant General Rafael Eitan, to eliminate the PLO as an independent political actor; weaken Syria and neutralize it as a threat to Israel; install a friendly regime in Lebanon under the Christian leader Bashir Gemayel; and strengthen cooperation with the United States while further undermining Soviet influence.[35] To most Israelis, therefore, the Lebanese entanglement discredited the notion of 'war by choice' (as Prime Minister Begin so proudly called the war), and provided additional proof that there was no military solution to the Arab–Israeli conflict.

At the same time, the war had a sobering impact on the Palestinian national movement. By destroying the PLO's military infrastructure in Lebanon and denying it a territorial base for attacks on Israel, the Lebanon War drove the organization towards a political path. This culminated in the PLO's apparent change of strategy in November and December 1988, from vociferous commitment to Israel's destruction to *ostensible* acceptance of a two-state solution: Israel and a Palestinian state on the West Bank and the Gaza Strip.

A strong impetus to these decisions was provided by the eruption of the *intifada* in December 1987. This popular uprising did more to redeem Palestinian dignity and self-esteem than two and a half decades of armed struggle by the PLO. Frustrated with the long-standing neglect and manipulation of their cause by Arabs and Israelis alike, the Palestinians proved capable of becoming self-reliant and resisting the Israeli occupation in a fashion they had never done before. This, in turn, brought the Palestinian problem to the fore in the Arab–Israeli conflict and enabled Yasser Arafat to overcome his more dogmatic opponents within the PLO. With the Palestinians in the territories anxious to see progress on the diplomatic front that would make their sacrifice worthwhile, the PLO could hardly afford to remain entrenched in the rejectionist posture that had led it nowhere.

It was at this juncture that the evolving regional pragmatism received a further boost by the end of the Cold War. Both Arabs and Israelis were naturally wary of this development which they feared would constrain their capacity for action. Special dissatisfaction with the thaw in superpower relations was voiced in Damascus, which did not attempt to conceal its abhorrence of Mikhail Gorbachev's readiness to sacrifice Soviet regional interests – and allies – for the sake of superpower détente.

With this trend reinforced by the crumbling of the East European regimes, and more so by the disintegration of the Soviet Union, the radical regimes in the Middle East concluded that the region had been left to the mercy of the only remaining superpower, the United States, and its 'lackeys', first and foremost, Israel. This gloomy assessment led to the further weakening of the militant Arab camp, illustrated most vividly by the completion of Egypt's reincorporation into the Arab fold and the formation of the (apparently) moderate Arab Co-operation Council (ACC) in 1989, with the participation of Egypt, Jordan, North Yemen and Iraq. In 1989, Israel's right-wing Prime Minister, Yitzhak Shamir, at the head of a National Unity Government, proposed elections in the occupied territories to choose representatives who would then discuss some future form of self-government as a first stage towards a comprehensive settlement. This alarmed elements within Shamir's own party, the Likud, and he began to backtrack. As a result, the coalition with the Labour Party collapsed and Shamir formed the most right-wing government in Israel's history.

The Gulf Conflict and the Arab–Israeli Peace Process

Significantly enough, the final nail in the coffin of regional rejectionism was a result, not of the momentous events on the European continent, but rather of a cataclysmic indigenous event: the Iraqi invasion of Kuwait and the ensuing 1991 Gulf War. Contrary to the standard perception, this episode was no confirmation of American post-Cold War omnipotence. Rather, as noted earlier, the 'only remaining superpower' was surprised by an act of aggression by a local actor, which it deemed detrimental to its vital interests and which it was unable to reverse without resort to arms. Had it not been for the active support of the main Arab States and Saudi Arabia's consent to the use of its territory as a springboard for a military action against Iraq, the United States would have never been able to orchestrate the anti-Iraq coalition, let alone to muster the necessary political support to wage war. Much as the Arabs needed American help to remove a lethal regional threat, the United States needed the Arabs to assist it to secure its political and economic interests.

More importantly, Israelis and Arabs found themselves in the same boat, as Saddam sought to legitimize his predatory move by portraying it as a noble attempt to promote the liberation of Palestine from 'Zionist occupation'. While the falsehood of this pretence was eminently transparent, the widespread emotional outburst it aroused, particularly when Saddam began firing his missiles at Israel, underscored the explosiveness of the Israeli–Palestinian conflict. This exceptional convergence of destinies led to a tacit collaboration between Israel and the Arab members of the anti-Iraq coalition during the conflict: the former kept the lowest possible profile, even refraining from retaliating against Iraq's missile attacks, while the latter highlighted the hollowness of Saddam's Palestinian pretensions and participated in the war operations against Iraq. This, in turn, made it much easier for US Secretary of State, James Baker, to kick off the Madrid peace process shortly after the war.

More than America's newly gained pre-eminence, it was the trauma attending the Iraqi invasion of Kuwait and Saddam's survival that brought Syrian President Asad to Madrid. Contrary to conventional belief, Asad had never viewed the evolving New World Order as necessitating a fundamental revision of his long-standing rejection of Israel's existence, as illustrated by his acrimonious relations with Gorbachev and his venomous attacks on the PLO's begrudging recognition of Israel in 1988. Yet once his mortal enemy, Saddam Hussein, had swallowed Kuwait, Asad could not allow the Iraqi action to stand, for fear that he would be Saddam's next victim. Hence his immediate enrolment in the anti–Iraq coalition; hence Syria's participation in the liberation of Kuwait and its outspoken opposition to ending the war before the physical elimination of Saddam Hussein.[36]

Paradoxically, the PLO's folly of siding with Saddam gave an important boost to Arab–Israeli reconciliation. The Gulf monarchies were neither forgiving nor forgetful of what they considered an act of Palestinian betrayal of their hospitality. This state of mind was illustrated not only by the harsh treatment of Palestinians in liberated Kuwait: within a month of the end of the war Saudi financial support for the PLO had been cut off, driving the organization to the verge of bankruptcy.

Starved of financial resources, marginalized at the Madrid peace process launched in October 1991, increasingly outshone in the occupied territories by the Hamas militant Islamic movement; and beset by growing internal fighting, the PLO was desperate for political rehabilitation – and Yasser Arafat for a personal comeback. Fortunately for him, Prime Minister Yitzhak Rabin was becoming increasingly exasperated with the inconclusive peace process under US auspices. Returning to power in June 1992, the 70-year-old former chief-of-staff, who had masterminded Israel's 1967 victory, was keenly aware that this was his last chance to go down in history as Israel's greatest peacemaker and he was determined to seize the moment come what may. If this meant breaking the taboo to which he had previously subscribed and recognizing the PLO as the sole representative of the Palestinian people, so be it. With the convergence of these Palestinian and Israeli undercurrents, against the backdrop of their long mutual disillusionment, the road to the September 1993 Declaration of Principles was short.

Conclusions

Whether they would admit it or not – and Middle Easterners have always found it easier to blame others for their misfortunes – the main responsibility for the region's unhappy lot lies with the local players. That Arabs have been fighting Jews, Iranians, Kurds and fellow Arabs for decades has had nothing to do with Cold War politics, but rather has had to do with the tangled web of conflicting national aspirations, ethnic cleavages, religious militancy, and economic and territorial greed. Similarly, superpower failure to stop the regional bloodletting and bring about a general reconciliation had less to do with Soviet or American machinations than with their limited leverage over the smaller regional states. To a certain extent this was a corollary of the political and ideological polarization that dominated superpower relations during the Cold War, where one's gain was (all-too-often erroneously) seen as the other's loss; at the same time it reflected the fundamental asymmetry inherent in any Great Power/small state relationship, regardless of the structure of the international system. The small state's parochial outlook and localized interests make it better tuned to the threats and opportunities in its immediate environment than the Great Power whose global range of interests precludes *ipso facto* full and lasting concentration on specific regional problems. To the small actors, regional developments are an absolute; to the Great Power they are one of many problems competing for attention and resources. This, in turn, gives the local actors the ability to manipulate Great Power weighting of the overall balance of forces and interests in their favour; and though it would be somewhat premature to gauge the full consequences of the end of the Cold War, there is sufficient evidence that this relative advantage is likely to change, not to disappear, with the demise of the Cold War.

The global balance of power and international rules of the game have of course changed, but not to the extent of reducing the regional actors to malleable objects in the hands of 'the only remaining superpower'. The void left by the diminution in superpower rivalry has already been filled by a host of domestic and international concerns such as greater US preoccupation with economic recovery and social malaise at home; the expansion and integration of the European Union; economic and political restructuring in the former Communist states; and across-the-board humanitarian and political intervention. With Great Power attention vacillating among these competing issues in accordance with shifts in their acuteness, local states are bound to take advantage of the situation to promote their self-serving objectives.

Against this backdrop, the forceful eviction of Iraq from Kuwait may prove to be the exception rather than the rule in the 'New World Order'; the unique historical juncture that made Operation Desert Storm possible is unlikely to recur in the foreseeable future, as vividly evidenced by the muddled Western response to a string of local conflicts, from Yugoslavia, to Rwanda, to Somalia, to Chechnya.

It would be advisable, therefore, for Great Powers and Middle Easterners alike to reconcile themselves, fully and unreservedly, to this reality. Just as a horse can be brought to water but cannot be forced to drink, so regional peace and reconciliation depends overwhelmingly on the local players; no external power will be able to perform miracles in the absence of indigenous will. The American mediation of the

Egyptian–Israeli peace treaty of 1979 was effective only because the Egyptian and Israeli political leaderships were bent upon making peace; but when the administration attempted to sustain the momentum and implement self-governing rule in the West Bank and Gaza, as stipulated by the Camp David Accords, it ran into a brick wall: the PLO, committed as it was to the destruction of Israel, refused to join the process.[37]

Similarly, when following the 1993 Accords, the PLO gained control over almost the entire Palestinian population of the West Bank and Gaza and nearly half of this territory, the Western Powers failed to convince it to take the extra mile towards a comprehensive peace with Israel. Reluctant to shed his long-standing commitment to Israel's destruction, despite having pretended to do so for over a decade, in the summer of 2000 Arafat declined far-reaching territorial concessions by Prime Minister Ehud Barak and launched a prolonged war of attrition against Israel. President Clinton's desperate attempts to lure the Palestinians into stopping the war, in the form of further territorial concessions, were to no avail; so were the strenuous efforts of the Bush Administration.

The final proof of the 'sub-system dominance' of Middle Eastern politics, if such is at all needed at this stage, was afforded by the terrorist atrocities of 11 September 2001 when, at the height of its international pre-eminence, the United States suffered the worst ever attack on its territory. Also, even though the administration swiftly toppled the militant Afghan Government that had harboured the culpable terrorist organization, and dealt a heavy blow to this organization, it nevertheless failed to destroy it altogether and has remained embroiled in an anti-terrorist campaign for quite some time. Moreover, even the operation against the Afghan Government did not start before securing the support or acquiescence of a wide range of regional actors, from Pakistan, to Turkestan, Tajikistan, to the main Arab states; and the reluctance to alienate these local actors has greatly constrained US ability to widen its self-proclaimed 'war on terrorism' from Afghanistan to the main sponsors of international terrorism such as Iran, Iraq, Syria and the Palestinian organizations.

NOTES

1. Reprinted from *Review of International Studies* (1997), by permission of Cambridge University Press; all rights reserved.
2. Avi Shlaim, *War and Peace in the Middle East* (New York, 1994), p. 5.
3. Surprisingly enough, most Western analysts tended to overlook Moscow's predominantly regional perspective on the Middle East and to cling to the erroneous belief that Soviet policy towards this region had always been primarily motivated by global considerations. *See*, for example, Robert O. Freedman, *Soviet Policy toward the Middle*

East since 1970 (New York, 1982); Alvin Z. Rubinstein, *Red Star on the Nile* (Princeton, NJ, 1977); Galia Golan, *Yom Kippur and After* (Cambridge, 1977); Adam Ulam, *Dangerous Relations: The Soviet Union in World Politics* (New York, 1983), pp. 40, 114–15, 182–3; Walter Z. Laqueur 'Soviet Dilemmas in the Middle East', and Roman Kolkowitz, 'Soviet Policy in the Middle East', in Michael Confino and Shimon Shamir (eds), *The USSR and the Middle East* (New York, 1973), pp. 77–89; Henry A. Kissinger, *White House Years* (Boston, MA, 1979), Chapters 10, 14, 15, 30.

4. L. Carl Brown, *International Politics and the Middle East* (Princeton, NJ, 1984), p. 16.

5. Arnold Wolfers, *Discord and Collaboration* (Baltimore, MD, 1962), p. 111.

6. M. Handel, *Weak States in the International System* (London, 1971), pp. 132–5. There are those who, by adopting the so-called client-centric approach, emphasize the bargaining power of the client *vis-à-vis* the patron and go so far as to include cases of unilateral dependence of the patron on the client within the patron–client paradigm. Such views, nevertheless, fail to comprehend the essence and inner meaning of the concept of patron (or alternatively, client) which, originating in the Latin *pater* implies preponderance, authority and seniority. Hence, any interrelationship clearly favouring the weaker partner *ipso facto* falls within the boundaries of the 'power of the weak', or the 'tail-wags-the-dog' paradigm.

7. Stanley Hoffmann succinctly described this interrelationship: 'When the eagle's claws are clipped the dove can save its life.' *See* his: *Gulliver's Troubles, Or the Setting of American Foreign Policy* (New York, 1968), p. 53.

8. A.J.P. Taylor, *The Struggle for Mastery in Europe, 1848–1918* (Oxford, 1971), p. xix.

9. Wolfers, *Discord and Collaboration*, p. 112.

10. *See*, for example, *Pravda*, 18 February 1968, 6 and 21 June 1968, and 19 August 1968; *Izvestiya*, 2 February 1968; Soviet Government Statement on the Middle East, Tass, 28 April 1976; 'Soviet proposal concerning a Middle East settlement', Tass, 1 October 1976.

11. *See*, for example, Damascus Radio, 22 February, 8 March 1971; Asad's interview with the Bulgarian Communist Party organ *Robotnichenko Delo*, 2 February 1971, and with *al-Anwar* (Beirut), 10 August 1972.

12. Mahmoud Riad, *The Struggle for Peace in the Middle East* (London, 1981), p. 102; Muhammad Heikal, *The Sphinx and the Commissar* (London, 1978), Chapter 11; Jean Lacoutier, *Nasser: A Biography* (London, 1973), pp. 330–1.

13. Muhammad Heikal, *The Rood to Ramadan* (New York, 1975), pp. 79–83.

14. For the June 1973 summit, see Richard Nixon, *RN: The Memoirs of Richard Nixon* (New York, 1990), pp. 884–5; Henry Kissinger, *Years of Upheaval* (Boston, MA, 1982), pp. 297–9.

15. *Pravda*, 26 September 1973; Kissinger, *Years of Upheaval*, p. 463.

16. *See*, for example, Hanoch Bartov, *Dado*, Vol. 1 (Tel Aviv, 1978), p. 314; Chaim Herzog, *The War of Atonement* (Boston, MA, 1975), pp. 48–50.

17. Efraim Karsh, *Soviet Policy Towards Syria: The Asad Years* (London, 1991), Chapter 1.

18. *See*, for example, *Pravda*, 21 July 1988, *Izvestiya*, 8 September 1989; *Literaturnaya Gazeta*, 31 May 1989; Tass, 5 September 1988. *See also* interview with Vladimir Poliakov (Head of the Near East Department in the Soviet Foreign Office), in *Le Quotidien de Paris*, 13 October 1988, and in *Izvestiya*, 8 September 1989.

19. Tass, 19 June 1985, 29 October 1988 and 1 November 1988; *Pravda*, 20 June 1985; *Krasnaya Zvezda*, 1 and 3 November 1988; *Moscow Radio*, 24 April 1987; *al-Anba* (Kuwait), interview with Konstantin Geyvendov (*Izvestiya*'s Middle Eastern commentator), 12 September 1987.

20. Secret Memorandum, Executive Office of the President: from Henry A. Kissinger to the Secretary of State and Secretary of Defense, 'Follow Up on the President's Talk with the Shah of Iran', 15 June 1972.

21. John D. Stempel, *Inside the Iranian Revolution* (Bloomington, IL, 1981), pp. 72–4; James A. Bill, *The Eagle and the Lion: The Tragedy of American–Iranian Relations* (New Haven, CT, 1988), pp. 202–9.

22. Bill, *The Eagle and the Lion*, p. 173.

23. Kissinger, *White House Years*, p. 224.

24. House Select Committee of Intelligence Report (The Pike Report) on American Involvement in the Kurdish Insurrection, as reprinted in the *Village Voice* (New York), 26 January 1976. The main findings of the report also formed the basis for two articles by William Safire: 'Mr Ford's Secret Sell-Out', *New York Times*, 5 February 1976; 'Son of Secret Sell-Out', *New York Times*, 12 February 1976.

25. There were of course occasional warnings of the risks attending the Shah's ambitious development programmes, some of which even questioned the prudence of predicating American national interests on the fortunes of one person, however powerful. Yet even these manifested self-doubts would normally conclude on a positive note, emphasizing the remoteness of the identified threats and the effective control exercised by the Shah. *See*, for example, 'Religious Circles', US Embassy, Iran, 15 May 1972; 'The Conduct of Relations with Iran', secret report by the Department Of State, Office of the Inspector General, October 1974; 'Iran: An Overview of the Shah's Economy', confidential memorandum, CIA, 16 October 1974; 'Iran's Modernizing Monarchy: A Political Assessment', secret aerogram from Helms Richard to United States Department of State, 8 July 1976.

26. 'The Future of Iran', Department of State, Bureau of Intelligence and Research, drafted by Franklin P. Huddle, 28 January 1977.

27. *See*, for example, 'Iran in the 1980s', secret report, CIA, 5 October 1977; William H. Sullivan, *Mission to Iran* (New York, 1981), p. 155.

28. 'Your appearance before the House International Relations Committee, Thursday, 18 July, 10 a.m. on the Sale of AWACS to Iran'. Memorandum to Cyrus Vance from Alfred Roy Atherton, 27 July 1977.

29. 'Iran in the 1980s', Secret Report, CIA, August 1977; 'Iran in the 1980s', Secret Report, CIA, 5 October 1977.

30. Cyrus Vance, *Hard Choices: Critical Years in America's Foreign Policy* (New York, 1983), pp. 325, 329.

31. *See*, for example,'Pessimism about Iranian Stability', Confidential Memorandum by Theodore H. Moran, Consultant to Policy Planning Staff, to Department of State, 4 October 1978; 'Iran: Political Assessment', Secret Briefing, Department of State, drafted by Precht Henry, 18 October 1978; 'The Policies of Ayatollah Khomeini', Intelligence Memorandum, CIA, 20 November 1978; 'Iran Update on Moharram', Secret Alert Memorandum, CIA, 5 December 1978.

32. Zbigniew Brzezinski, *Power and Principle: Memoirs of the National Security Adviser, 1977–1981* (London, 1983), pp. 371–82; Bill, *The Eagle and the Lion*, pp. 249–57.

33. The analysis in this section draws on Lawrence Freedman and Efraim Karsh, *The Gulf Conflict, 1990–1991: Diplomacy and War in the New World Order* (Princeton, NJ, 1993).

34. Edward Said, 'The Morning After', *London Review of Books*, 21 October 1993, p. 3.

35. Zeev Schiff and Ehud Ya'ari, *Israel's Lebanon War* (London, 1984), p. 304.

36. *See*, for example, *Damascus Radio*, 4, 8 and 10 March 1991.

37. *See*, for example, Said, 'The Morning After', p. 3.

6

The Long Trail of Arab
Anti-Semitism[1]

I

For anyone still disposed to credit the standard Muslim-Arab contention that, so far as Palestine is concerned, Arabs have never had anything against Judaism or Jews but only against Zionism and Zionists, the anti-Israel war launched by the Palestinian Authority in October 2000 should have gone far to dispel any remaining illusions. If not the violence itself, or the wanton destruction of ancient Jewish sites in Nablus and Jericho, then the words accompanying them; and if not the words shouted by frenzied mobs, then the presumably more reflective words articulated by leaders and dignitaries.

To pluck but one example from the flood of high-level, anti-Jewish invective, here are a few snippets from a sermon delivered on 13 October 2000 by Ahmad Abu Halabiya, former acting rector of the Islamic University in Gaza. The sermon, given the day after the barbaric lynching of two Israeli soldiers in the West Bank city of Ramallah, was broadcast live on the official television channel of Yasser Arafat's Palestine Authority:

> Have no mercy on the Jews, *no matter where they are, in any country* [emphasis added]. Fight them, wherever you are. Wherever you meet them, kill them. Wherever you are, kill those Jews and those Americans who are like them and those who stand by them. They are all in one trench against the Arabs and the Muslims because they established Israel here, in the beating heart of the Arab world, in Palestine.

Of course, it has long been a staple of Arab diplomacy that such sentiments themselves are to be understood as an expression of frustration with Zionism, not with Jews or Judaism. After all, did not Arabs and Jews co-exist harmoniously for centuries prior to the advent of the Zionist movement? As Fayez A. Sayegh, the Kuwaiti representative,

told the United Nations General Assembly during the debate over the
'Zionism-is-racism' resolution in November 1975:

> We in the Arab world showed hospitality to Jews who came fleeing
> from persecution in Europe when European anti-Semitism was
> driving them into our arms... it was only when the Zionists came
> that, despite our hospitality to the Jew, we showed hostility to the
> Zionist.

However, this idyllic picture is at odds with the historical record.
True, persecution of Jews in the Islamic world never reached the scale
of Christian Europe. But that did not spare the 'Jews of Islam' (to use
the phrase of the historian Bernard Lewis) from centuries of legally
institutionalized inferiority, humiliating social restrictions and the spo-
radic rapacity of local officials and the Muslim population at large. In
pre-Zionist Palestine itself, Arab peasants, revolting in the 1830s against
a military conscription imposed by Egyptian authorities, took the occasion to ravage the Jewish communities of Safed and Jerusalem, and
when Arab forces arrived from Egypt to quell the insurrection, they, in
turn, slaughtered the Jews of Hebron. A century later, in June 1941, following an abortive pro-Nazi coup in Iraq, the Jews of Baghdad were
subjected to a horrendous massacre in which hundreds perished... and
so forth.

The truth of the matter is that, for all their protestations to the contrary, Arabs have never really distinguished between Zionists, Israelis
and Jews, and often use these terms interchangeably. As Anis Mansur,
one of Egypt's foremost journalists and a one-time confidant of
President Anwar Sadat, put it in a moment of candour: 'There is no
such thing in the world as Jew and Israeli. Every Jew is an Israeli. No
doubt about that.'

Indeed, the fact that Arab anti-Zionism has invariably reflected a
hatred well beyond the 'normal' level of hostility to be expected of a
prolonged and bitter conflict would seem to suggest that, rather than
being a response to Zionist activity, it is rather a manifestation of long-
standing prejudice that has been brought out into the open by the vicissitudes of the Arab–Israel conflict.

This is hardly to deny the clash of destinies between two national
groups. However, it is precisely because Zionism was construed as epit-
omizing the worst characteristics traditionally associated with Jews in
the Muslim-Arab mind that the Zionist enterprise could be portrayed in
so lurid a light by politicians and intellectuals alike. As Lutfi Abd al-
Azim, the editor of a prestigious Egyptian weekly, wrote in 1982, three

years *after* the conclusion of an Egyptian–Israeli peace treaty:

> A Jew is a Jew, and hasn't changed for thousands of years. He is base, contemptible, scorns all moral values, gnaws on live flesh and sucks blood for a pittance. The Jewish Merchant of Venice is no different from the arch-executioners of Deir Yasin and those at the [Palestinian] refugee camps. Both are similar models of inhuman depravity.

II

Where do such vicious stereotypes come from? It has been rightly observed that modern, ideological anti-Semitism is an invention of nineteenth-century Europe, and that traditionally the Islamic world was by and large free of such 'doctrinaire refinements' (in the phrase of the late Elie Kedourie). But the ease and rapidity with which the precepts of European anti-Semitism were assimilated by the Muslim-Arab world testify to the pre-existence of a deep anti-Jewish bigotry. This bigotry dates back to Islam's earliest days, and indeed to the Qur'an itself.

Reflecting the Prophet Muhammad's outrage over the rejection of his religious message by the contemporary Jewish community, both the Qur'an and later biographical traditions of the Prophet abound with negative depictions of Jews. In these works they are portrayed as a deceitful, evil and treacherous people who in their insatiable urge for domination would readily betray an ally and swindle a non-Jew; and who tampered with the Holy Scriptures, spurned God's divine message, and persecuted His messenger Muhammad just as they had done to previous prophets, including Jesus of Nazareth. For this perfidy, they will incur a string of retributions, both in the afterlife, when they will burn in hell, and here on earth where they have been justly condemned to an existence of wretchedness and humiliation.

As this summary suggests, the traits associated with Jews make a paradoxical mixture: they are seen as both domineering and wretched, both haughty and low. However, such is the age-old Muslim stereotype – as it is, *mutatis mutandis*, the Christian. Coming to know Jews as a small subject community in their midst, most Muslims held them in the contempt reserved for the powerless. 'I never saw the curse denounced against the children of Israel more fully brought to bear than in the East', wrote an early-nineteenth-century Western traveller to the Ottoman Empire, 'where they are considered rather as a link between animals and human beings than as men possessed by the same attributes.' To another contemporary visitor to the region, the Jews' 'pusillanimity is so excessive, that they flee before the uplifted hand of a child'. That was one side of the picture. As for the other, even Egypt's President Sadat, the man who would go farther than any other Middle Eastern leader in accepting the existence of a sovereign Jewish state, could remind his people in April 1972 of *why* the Jews had been brought so low, and why their power was still to be feared:

> They were the neighbours of the Prophet in Medina. They were his neighbours, and he negotiated with them and reached an agreement with them. But in the end they proved that they were men of deceit and treachery, since they concluded a treaty with his enemies, so as to strike him in Medina and attack him from within...They are a nation of traitors and liars, contrivers of plots, a people born for deeds of treachery.

Given the depth of anti-Jewish feeling in the Arab Middle East, it is hardly surprising that some of the hoariest and most bizarre themes of European anti-Semitism should have struck a responsive chord when they made their way there over the course of the centuries. Thus, special derision is reserved in Arab writings (as in Christian ones) for the biblical notion of the chosen people, seen in Anis Mansur's words as the quintessence of 'Judaism's perception of the Jews as ... masters of the universe – its peoples, lands, and skies ... to whom all other peoples are but servants, undeserving of belief in the Jewish God'. To this doctrine is attributed, in turn, the licence Jews supposedly take in mistreating non-Jews, with the Talmud characterized as not only condoning but actually requiring acts like the swindling of Gentiles and the 'rape of women of other religions'.

Then there is the 'blood libel', that medieval Christian fabrication according to which Jews use Gentile blood, and particularly the blood of children, for ritual purposes. Imported to the Ottoman Empire by Christians in the fifteenth century, this fantastical charge acquired a mythic status, reaching a peak of popularity in the nineteenth century. Among the numerous places in which the libel surfaced, and local Jews were made to suffer for it, were: Aleppo (1810, 1850, 1875); Antioch (1826); Beirut (1824, 1862, 1874); Damascus (1840, 1848, 1890); Deir al-Qamar (1847); Homs (1829); Tripoli (1834); Jerusalem (1847); Alexandria (1870, 1882, 1901–1902); Port Said (1903, 1908); and Cairo (1844, 1890, 1901–1902).

Although most of these incidents were of Christian manufacture, and although Ottoman authorities often extended help to the persecuted

Jews, the libel itself was quickly internalized in the Muslim imagination, where it remains firmly implanted to this day. Thus, in August 1972 King Faisal of Saudi Arabia could confide to the mass-circulation Egyptian magazine *al-Musawwar* that,

> ...while I was in Paris on a visit, the police discovered five murdered children. Their blood had been drained, and it turned out that some Jews had murdered them in order to take their blood and mix it with the bread that they eat on that day.

The blood libel is not only kept alive by avowed anti-Semites (like King Faisal). Rather, it is prevalent even among scholars and intellectuals. In *Israeli Religious Thought: Stages and Sects* – published by a respectable Egyptian academic press, Dr Hasan Zaza, a professor of Hebrew at Ein Shams University in Cairo, accepts the veracity of the blood libel despite his awareness that Jewish religious law specifically forbids the eating of anything containing blood. For how is it possible, he asks rhetorically, that a charge that has been levelled time and again all over the world for so many generations could be just an unsubstantiated rumour?

Perhaps the most successful anti-Semitic import of all to the Muslim-Arab world is the theory of an organized Jewish conspiracy to achieve world domination, particularly as spelled out in the notorious *Protocols of the Elders of Zion*. This virulent anti-Semitic tract, which was fabricated by the Russian secret police at the turn of the twentieth century, made its appearance in western Europe during and immediately after the First World War. As early as 1918, Chaim Weizmann, travelling in Palestine with the Zionist Commission, was presented with copies of the *Protocols* by his Arab interlocutors. Translated into Arabic in the mid-1920s, the work has retained its popular appeal to this day, and been published in numerous editions and in several different translations, including one by the brother of Egyptian president Gamal Abdel Nasser. (Nasser himself would recommend the pamphlet as a useful guide to the 'Jewish mind', as would his successor Anwar Sadat, and King Faisal of Saudi Arabia, and Mu'ammar Gaddafi of Libya, among many others.)

As with the blood libel, the astounding popularity of the *Protocols* is directly related to the millennial disparagement of Jews as treacherous and grasping. According to one venerable strand of the Muslim-Arab thought on the subject, what lies behind the supremacist concept of the chosen people is, in fact, a perverse inferiority complex that dates back to biblical times. When the ancient Jewish kingdoms were destroyed,

this inferiority complex was transmogrified from a will to occupy neighbouring lands into a determination to exert financial, economic and
political control *wherever* Jews lived – an objective that was in fact
achieved in many Western countries. Modern Zionism could thus be
seen as a reversion to the original form of this same impulse – the
impulse, that is, to occupy foreign lands and subjugate their peoples,
and to justify doing so by invoking biblical promises.

When, moreover, the Zionists managed to harness international support for their enterprise – in the form of the Balfour Declaration and an
endorsement of its pledges by the League of Nations – they utilized (so
the argument runs) the same foul methods used against the Prophet
Muhammad and other victims of ancient Jewish aggression. 'We have
known the Jews to be most tyrannical and despotic', the Jaffa Muslim–
Christian Society complained in May 1920 to the district's British military governor, reminding him:

> ...of the deeds perpetrated by their forefathers; of the persecution
> and ill-treatment they mete out to their contemporaries; of what
> they did to Jesus and Muhammad (peace be upon them); [and] of
> what they had been meditating towards the Muslim and Christian
> nations.

During the 1920s and the 1930s, these and other traditional Islamic per-
ceptions coalesced with themes articulated in the *Protocols* to create a
distinctly Middle Eastern version of the theory of a worldwide Jewish
conspiracy. Thus, the prominent Palestinian educator Khalil Sakakini,
an Orthodox Christian fully conversant with the surrounding Muslim
society, could equate the Zionist enterprise with the murder of Jesus and
Muhammad – and also float the newer stereotype of Jewish domination
of the Great Powers, whether the Romans at the time of Jesus or, now,
the British. 'There is little doubt that the British government is [morally
and politically] bankrupt,' Sakakini wrote in the 1930s. 'Who can have
high regard for a government which is totally under the Jewish sway, like
a slave?' On another occasion he said: 'Isn't there a single European
country loathing to be an instrument in Jewish hands?'

Similarly, the Palestinian politician Rashid Hajj Ibrahim warned in
the late 1940s that Jewish ambitions ran well beyond Palestine to
encompass the entire Middle East. 'The Jews covet Egypt,' he argued:

> because this is Moses' place of origin; they desire Syria and
> Lebanon - because their Temple was built from Lebanon's cedars;
> they have set their sights both on Iraq, the birthplace of Abraham
> the Patriarch, and the Hijaz – Ishmael's birthplace; and they want

to have Transjordan because it is a part of Palestine and used to be a part of Solomon's kingdom.

Muhammad Nimr al-Khatib, who wrote an account of the 1948 Arab–Israeli war, ascribed the Arabs' defeat in that conflict to their failure to recognize that Jews now exercised worldwide dominion. 'The old generation perceived the Jews ... as a cowardly, avaricious, and submissive group which we could easily throw into the sea', he lamented, but in the modern era the Arabs face an organized evil with tentacles all over the world. 'We are not fighting the Jews you know', he went on, but rather 'the powers that defeated Hitler and Japan; we are fighting world Zionism, which exploits Truman, enslaves Churchill and Attlee, and dominates London, New York, and Washington'.

Forty years later, in 1988, Syrian President Hafiz al-Asad would express the same sentiment in no less explicit terms:

> The ambitions of racist Zionism are as clear as the sun...They do not want Palestine alone or a piece of land here or there. They do not want only another Arab country. They want ... to impose their hegemony beyond that until it covers the entire world.

III

Have there been any signs of a diminishment of Arab anti-Semitism as, in the last decade, Israel and its Arab neighbours have ostensibly drawn closer? None whatsoever. Quite to the contrary: Egypt, at peace with Israel for over two decades, may be, today, the world's most prolific producer of anti-Semitic ideas and attitudes. These ideas and attitudes are voiced openly by the extreme Islamist press, by the establishment media, and even by supporters of peace with Israel like Anis Mansur. In numerous articles, scholarly writings, books, cartoons and public statements, Jews are painted in the blackest terms imaginable.

The traditional blood libel is still in wide circulation in today's Egypt, together with a string of other canards whose tenor may be glimpsed in the title of an 1890 tract recently reprinted by, of all places, the Egyptian Ministry of Education: *Human Sacrifice in the Talmud*. Jews have been accused of everything from exporting infected seeds, plants and cattle in order to destroy Egyptian agriculture, to corrupting Egyptian society through the spread of venereal diseases and the distribution of drugs. Similarly popular are the *Protocols of the Elders of Zion*, which may be in wider distribution in Egypt than anywhere in the world. In the fashion of the *Protocols*, the hand of 'world Jewry' is seen behind everything from the destruction of Russian society to the downfall of former German chancellor Helmut Kohl, to the control of world public opinion through the film industry. 'We cannot watch a single American movie that does not include dialogue commending the Jews and their beliefs', complains Muhammad Abd al-Mun'im, chief editor of the influential weekly *Ruz al-Yussef*. 'They have transgressed their limits and reached the point of saying that they are superman-creatures and the best to be born on this planet from all of history.'

Other Arab parties engaged in negotiations with Israel have done their best to keep up with Egypt's example. In Syria, whose late president supposedly made 'a strategic choice' for peace in the mid-1990s, anti-Semitism remains an integral part of political and intellectual discourse. Particularly popular in Syria is Holocaust denial, another staple of Arab anti-Semitism that is sometimes coupled with overt sympathy for Nazi Germany. Only in the summer of 2000, just as Syrian and Israeli leaders were about to meet in Washington for crucial talks, the official newspaper *Tishrin* published an article by its editor denying the murder of six million Jews by the Nazis. President Bashar Asad himself, in stark contradiction to earlier high hopes of a modernizing, liberal ruler, misses no public opportunity to voice the vilest anti-Semitic prejudice.

The same can be said of Yasser Arafat and his Palestinian Authority (PA). Indeed, the seemingly sudden and spontaneous outburst of naked racial and religious hatred since October 2000 is perfectly in line with the PA's systematic effort – flagrantly violating its obligations under Oslo – to instill in its people, and particularly in its young people, an ineradicable enmity not only for the state of Israel but for Jews and Judaism.

As part of this effort, Palestinians have been informed of the most outlandish Jewish plots to corrupt and ruin them – outlandish, but wholly congruent with the medieval myth of Jews as secret destroyers and poisoners of wells. Thus, the PA Minister of Health, Riad al-Za'anun, has charged Israeli doctors with using 'Palestinian patients for experimental medicines', while the Palestinian representative to the Human Rights Commission in Geneva accused them of injecting Palestinian children with the AIDS virus. For his part, the PA Minister of Ecology, Yusuf Abu Safiyyah, indicted Israel for 'dumping liquid waste ... in Palestinian areas in the West Bank and Gaza' – a charge famously amplified by Suha Arafat when, in the presence of Hillary Clinton, she told an attentive audience in Gaza in November 1999 that 'our people have been subjected to the daily and extensive use of poisonous gas by the Israeli forces, which has led to an increase in cancer cases among women and children'. Even Yasser Arafat himself has repeatedly charged Israel with using ammunition containing depleted uranium against hapless Palestinians.

In their schoolbooks, Palestinian children learn about an evil Jewish persona, traceable to biblical times, which accounts for the worldwide persecution of the Jews through the ages. They are indoctrinated with the idea that Jews are, and always have been, implacable enemies of Islam, people who 'called Muhammad a liar and denied him, [who] fought against his religion in all ways and by all means, a war that has not yet ended until today'. The Bible and the Talmud come in for special abuse as the principal sources of Jewish moral depravity, the Bible being 'full of texts that support the Jews' tendency to racial and religious zealotry', and the Talmud a racist treatise obliging the Jews to seclude themselves from others even as they infiltrate and ruin the societies in which they live. As one such textbook, *The New History of the Arabs and the World*, puts it with malignant inventiveness:

> It is said in the Talmud: 'We [the Jews] are God's people on earth...[God] forced upon the human animal and upon all nations and races that they serve us, and He spread us through the world to ride on them and hold their reins. We must marry our beautiful daughters with kings, ministers, and lords and enter our sons into the various religions, for thus we will have the final word in managing the countries. We should cheat [non-Jews] and arouse quarrels among them, then they will fight each other...Non-Jews are pigs whom God created in the shape of man in order that they be fit for service for the Jews, and God created the world for [the Jews].

IV

What then of the future? On occasion, it is true, Arab anti-Semitism has coexisted with or even led to a desire to reach an accommodation with the Jews. King Abdallah Ibn Hussein, founder of the Hashemite Kingdom of Transjordan and the grandfather of Jordan's late King Hussein, was keen to incorporate the Jewish community in Palestine into his realm, precisely in order to benefit from the Jews' (perceived) worldwide political influence. Anwar Sadat's anti-Jewish prejudice did not prevent him from signing the first-ever Arab peace treaty with Israel.

In most instances, however, Arab anti-Semitism has served rather to exacerbate distrust and hatred of Israel, thus rendering the possibility of real reconciliation ever more remote. The smallest incident can suffice to pierce the thin veneer of official 'anti-Zionism', resulting in a torrent of abuse directed not just against Israel and its leaders but against Jews pure and simple – a people, in the words of the Egyptian government daily *al-Akhbar*, who 'should not be trusted because they are a nation of vagabonds filled with hatred towards the entire world'.

That such reprehensible lies, and much worse, can appear in the official newspaper of a government at peace with Israel for two decades suggests how deeply anti-Semitic bigotry is entrenched in Arab societies. Whatever happens in the specific conflict between Palestinian Arabs and Israel in the coming days and months, for the foreseeable future Muslim-Arab lands seem destined to remain the only regions in today's world where anti-Semitism – *not* anti-Zionism – still constitutes state policy. These are the 'partners' with whom Israel is expected to forge a lasting peace.

NOTE

1. Reprinted from *Commentary* (December 2000), by permission; all rights reserved.

7

The Collusion that Never Was: King Abdallah, the Jewish Agency and the Partition of Palestine[1]

One of the more enduring conspiracy theories in the historiography of the Arab–Israeli conflict relates to the existence of a Jewish–Hashemite collusion to carve up Palestine between themselves following the termination of the British Mandate. Dating back to the late 1950s or the early 1960s,[2] and unanimously accepted by both mainstream and 'revisionist' historians,[3] this theory claims that the collusion was hatched at a secret meeting on 17 November 1947 between King Abdallah of Transjordan and the Acting Head of the Jewish Agency's Political Department, Golda Meir, and was 'consciously and deliberately intended to frustrate the will of the international community, as expressed through the United Nations General Assembly, in favour of creating an independent Arab state in part of Palestine'.[4] 'The common ground for the agreement was a mutual objection to the creation of a Palestinian state,' runs the conspiracy theory. 'The Jewish Agency in particular abhorred such a possibility, asserting that the creation of a Palestinian state would perpetuate the ideological conflict in Palestine.'[5]

This conventional wisdom could not be further from the truth. There was *not* and could not have been a Jewish–Transjordanian collusion to divide Palestine in contravention of the UN Partition Resolution for the simple reason that the goals of these two parties were mutually exclusive: Abdallah viewed Palestine as an integral part of his kingdom while the Zionist movement considered it the site of a prospective Jewish State in line with the UN Resolution. More concretely:

- A careful examination of the two documents on which the collusion theory hinges - reports by Ezra Danin and Eliyahu Sasson, two Zionist officials who attended the Meir–Abdallah meeting – proves that Meir was implacably opposed to any agreement that would violate the letter and spirit of the Partition Resolution that was about to be passed 12 days later. In no way did she consent to Transjordan's annexation of the Arab areas of Mandatory Palestine.
- Meir's own verbal account of her conversation with Abdallah, oddly

overlooked by all historians, further proves that Mandatory Palestine was *not* divided on 17 November 1947.

- As mere Acting Head of the Jewish Agency's Political Department, Meir was in no position to commit her movement to a binding deal with King Abdallah, especially since that deal would run counter to the Jewish Agency's sustained exertions on behalf of partition.

- Meir's conversation with Abdallah was never discussed by the Jewish Agency Executive, the effective government of the Yishuv (the Jewish community in Mandatory Palestine). The Yishuv's military operations during the 1947–49 war show not a trace of the alleged deal in either planning or execution. To the contrary, the Zionist leadership remained deeply suspicious of Abdallah's expansionist ambitions up to the pan-Arab invasion of the newly-established State of Israel in mid-May 1948.

- While the Jewish Agency undoubtedly preferred Abdallah to the former Jerusalem Mufti, Hajj Amin al-Husseini, this by no means implied rejection of an independent Palestinian State. Quite the reverse, well after the Abdallah–Meir meeting the foremost Israeli policy-makers – Prime Minister David Ben-Gurion and Foreign Minister Moshe Sharett – still preferred such a state to Transjordan's annexation of the Arab parts of Mandatory Palestine.

- Abdallah viewed Palestine as an integral part of the vast empire he had been seeking to establish throughout his political career, and its Jewish community as an autonomous subject province rather than an independent nation-state.

The Abdallah–Meir Meeting: The Documentary Evidence

As noted earlier, Danin's and Sasson's reports constitute the foremost, indeed the only source used to substantiate the collusion theory. However, do they actually prove the clinching of such a deal? Let these two accounts speak for themselves, starting with Danin's far more elaborate report:

> … [Abdallah] got right to the point. He stressed that our conversation should be viewed as an exercise in thinking aloud. 'At the time we talked about partition, and now I would like to know your opinion…I agree to partition that will not shame me before the Arab world when I come out to defend it. Let me seize this opportunity to suggest to you the idea, for future consideration, of an independent Hebrew Republic in part of Palestine within a

Transjordan state that would include both banks of the Jordan, with me at its head, and in which the economy, the army and the legislature will be joint.'

The emphasis was on the assumption that it would not be *under* Transjordanian rule, but within a Transjordanian monarchy. He did not press for an answer, but explained that in the event of the creation of such a state he would be able to expand the territoriy of his state to embrace G[reater] S[yria] and even Saudi Arabia. When we explained to him that our case was being discussed at the United Nations, that we hoped that it would be decided there to establish two states, one Jewish and one Arab, and that we wished to talk now about an agreement with him [i.e., Abdallah] based on these resolutions, he said that he understood this, and that it would be desirable to meet again immediately after the adoption of the UN resolution to discuss ways of co-operating in the light of that decision.

At this point he went on to ask what our attitude would be to an attempt by him to seize the Arab part of the country? We replied that we would look favourably on it, especially if it did not obstruct us in the establishment of our state, did not lead to a confrontation between us and his forces, and, particularly if this action were accompanied by a declaration that the seizure was solely aimed at ensuring order and keeping the peace until the United Nations could establish a government in that part [of Palestine]. To this he retorted: 'But I want that part for myself in order to annex it to my state, and I do not want to create a new Arab state which will upset my plans and allow the Arabs "to ride on me". I want to be the rider, not the horse.' He did not accept our suggestion that he arrange for this in a different manner, namely a referendum in which his influence would be decisive.

... At the end he reiterated that concrete matters could only be discussed after the UN had passed its resolution, and said that we must meet again immediately afterwards.[6]

Eliyahu Sasson's much shorter report reads as follows:

Golda [Meir], Ezra [Danin], [and] myself met Meir [code-name for Abdallah] Monday. Stated will not allow his forces to collide with us nor co-operate with any other force against us. Belittled military power [of] Arab states believed would not dare break into Palestine. In case he will decide [to] invade Palestine [he] will concentrate [on] Arab area with a view to prevent bloodshed, keep

law [and] order, forestall Mufti. Prepared [to] co-operate with us
[in] this matter... ready [to] sign written agreement with us
provided we agree [to] assist attach Arab part to Transjordan.
Replied [that] we [would be] prepared [to] give every assistance
within [the] frame [of the] UN Charter. Agreed [to] meet again
after UN decision.[7]

Between them the two reports prove the following points:

- As stated by Abdallah at the outset, the conversation was seen as a
  joint exercise in 'thinking aloud' about the general principles of a
  possible Hashemite–Jewish understanding, not as one designed to
  produce a concrete agreement. Hence his avoidance of pressing for an
  answer to his ideas; and hence his concluding remarks that no concrete
  issues could be discussed before the passing of the UN Resolution as
  well as his suggestion for a follow-up meeting.
- In Abdallah's thinking, partition 'that will not shame me before the
  Arab world' meant an autonomous Jewish province within a kingdom
  stretching on both sides of the Jordan River. As we shall see later, these
  were not hollow words but rather the gist of Abdallah's thinking on
  the Palestine Question since the early 1920s.
- Most importantly, in no way, shape, or form did Golda Meir give
  Abdallah a 'green light' to annex the Arab part of Mandatory Palestine
  to his kingdom. Quite the contrary. While quiescent in his possible
  capture – but by no means annexation! – of this area, 'especially if it
  did not obstruct us in the establishment of our state [and] did not lead
  to a confrontation between us and his forces', she made it eminently
  clear that:
  1. Any Jewish–Hashemite arrangement would have to be compatible
     with the imminent UN Resolution. In Danin's words: 'We
     explained to him that our case was being discussed at the United
     Nations, that we hoped that it would be decided there to establish
     two states, one Jewish and one Arab, and that we wished to talk now
     about an agreement with him based on these resolutions.' In
     Sasson's words: 'Replied [that] we [would be] prepared [to] give
     every assistance within [the] frame [of the] UN Charter.'[8]
  2. The *sole purpose* of Transjordan's intervention in post-Mandatory
     Palestine would be to ensure law and order 'until the United
     Nations could establish a government in that part',[9] namely, a short-
     lived law-enforcement operation aimed at facilitating the establish-
     ment of a legitimate Palestinian government.

Were Abdallah to gain Palestinian, Arab and international support
for his territorial ambitions, the Zionist movement might go along;

hence Meir's suggestion for a referendum that would legitimize Abdallah's claim to rule this area. However, the distance from this to approval of Abdallah's annexation of western Palestine to his kingdom is very great indeed.

In other words, it was the Jewish representative who defended the political rights of the Palestinian Arabs by insisting on the ephemerality of the Transjordanian seizure of the Arab parts of Mandatory Palestine as a means to facilitate the establishment of a legitimate government there in accordance with the Partition Resolution. It was the Arab leader who insisted on annexing the area to his kingdom rather than creating 'a new Arab state which will upset my plans and allow the Arabs "to ride on me"'. The gap between these two positions was too wide to bridge, and neither Abdallah nor Meir tried to do so.

The Overlooked Document: Meir's Verbal Report

Meir presented no official report to the Jewish Agency Executive (JAE) on her conversation with Abdallah, which indicates that she deemed it to contain no concrete agreement that needed to be discussed and approved by this highest decision-making institution of the Zionist movement. It was only six months later, on 12 May 1948, in a verbal report to the Provisional State Council (which succeeded the JAE as the Yishuv's effective government) on a second meeting with Abdallah (held the previous day) that Meir gave her own account of the November 1947 conversation:

> I do not know whether all present here are aware that several months ago, about ten days before the [passing of the] UN Resolution, a meeting with King Abdallah took place with the participation on our part of Sasson, Danin, and myself. The meeting was in Transjordan, though on Jewish territory, that is – he came from Amman to see us. The meeting was conducted on the basis that there was an arrangement and an understanding as to what both of us wanted and that our interests did not collide.
>
> For our part we told him then that *we could not promise to help his incursion into the country [i.e., Mandatory Palestine], since we would be obliged to observe the UN Resolution which, as we already reckoned at the time, would provide for the establishment of two states in Palestine.* We said that we could not therefore give active support to the violation of this resolution. If he was prepared and willing to confront the world and us with a *fait accompli* – the tradition of

friendship between us would continue and we would certainly find a common language on settling those matters that were of interest to both parties.

He then promised us that his friendship towards us still existed and that there could be no confrontation between us. He spoke on his friends and on the other [Arab] states and especially on the Mufti; he dismissed the strength of the other neighbouring states and agreed with us that if we were attacked by Arabs it went without saying that we had to respond.

The meeting was conducted very amicably and without any arguments. During the conversation he said, as if by passing, two things that raised some suspicion, apprehension. But the meeting ended on the understanding that we would meet again after the UN Resolution. The two things that raised suspicion were:

a. He wanted to know what we thought about the possible inclusion of the Jewish State (the 'Jewish Republic' as he called it) within the Transjordanian Kingdom;

b. He hoped to have a partition that would not disgrace him [in front of the Arabs].

These two things raised, as already noted, our apprehension, and we thought that in due course we would discuss the matter.10

As is clearly evidenced by Meir's account, Mandatory Palestine was *not* divided in November 1947. There was mutual recognition of the lack of enthusiasm on either side for military confrontation and of the existence of a certain convergence of interests. However, no definitive agreement on the country's future was reached. To the contrary, as Meir saw it, Abdallah was made to understand that the decision on whether to confront the world with a *fait accompli* by annexing the Arab parts of Palestine to his kingdom was exclusively his, and that he could expect no Jewish support whatsoever for such a move.

Misconception of the Decision-making Process

Misreading of historical documents and overlooking vital evidence are the more obvious flaws of the collusion theory. The misconception that such critical decisions as the making of war and peace or the division of foreign lands can be made in the course of a single conversation between state officials without consultations or extended bargaining reflects a fundamental lack of understanding of the nature of foreign policy-

making in general and of the Zionist decision-making process in particular. Whether regular or irregular, direct or indirect, overt or covert,
political relations among nations are routinely maintained through
foreign-policy establishments – diplomats, officials and politicians –
without necessarily informing, at every single twist and turn, the state's
ruling institution (be it a Cabinet or a 'Revolutionary Command
Council' of sorts); yet, on the whole, they operate within the broad lines
set out by the state leadership. Resourceful bureaucrats can, of course,
find ways and means to influence their ministers, just as powerful
foreign secretaries can sidestep their own officialdom and manipulate, or
even deceive the Cabinet. Conversely, heads of state can, and at times
do, circumvent their foreign-policy establishments. Yet in democratic
societies there are clear limits to what the most powerful foreign
secretaries, or even heads of state, can do without Cabinet or, at times,
parliamentary approval: they cannot commit their countries to binding
agreements in the course of a single conversation, let alone to such a far-
reaching undertaking as that alleged by the collusion theory.

This state of affairs was fully applicable to the Zionist movement.
The lion's share of its secret contacts with King Abdallah, among other
Arab leaders, was maintained by the Jewish Agency's Political
Department, headed since 1933 by Moshe Sharett, and more concretely
by the Department's Arab Section, headed since 1939 by Eliyahu
Sasson. By way of doing so, the Political Department enjoyed a wide
latitude, but it nevertheless remained bound by the policy guidelines set
by the Zionist movement's governing bodies and institutions.

Indeed, the main source of strength of the Jewish national movement
had been its ability to organize itself from an early stage as a 'state in the
making' based on democratic-parliamentary principles:

> It was all there, set up and running, within a year or two of the call-
> ing of the first Congress of Zionists in 1897: free elections on a
> constituency basis; universal suffrage (i.e., men and women voting
> and members of the Congress itself); a fully representative assem-
> bly; a political leadership responsible to that assembly; open debate
> on all major issues; and, before long, what might usefully be called
> a loyal opposition too.[11]

As Jewish presence in Mandatory Palestine grew rapidly during the
1930s and the centre of gravity of Zionist activities shifted from Europe
to Mandatory Palestine, the Jewish Agency Executive evolved into the
foremost decision-making body of the Zionist movement and the *de
facto* 'government' of the Yishuv, managing its affairs, from the more

mundane aspects of daily life to the critical political issues of the day, such as the various British proposals on the future of Palestine, Jewish–Arab relations in the prospective Jewish State, and so on.

It is inconceivable therefore for the Zionist movement to have reached any binding agreement with Abdallah, not to speak of such a far-reaching understanding on the division of Palestine and the incorporation of its Arab parts into Transjordan, without the matter being thoroughly discussed and approved by the JAE. This is all the more pertinent to this specific case since the alleged deal would have run counter to the Zionists' own contemporary efforts to bring about a UN resolution on partition. That Meir's conversation with Abdallah was not discussed by the JAE – either prior to its occurrence or in its aftermath – indicates that it involved no binding agreement. During the six fateful months between November 1947 and May 1948, when it was superseded by a 13-member Provisional State Council, the JAE discussed numerous critical issues pertaining to the Yishuv's ability to weather both the war waged by the Palestinian Arabs following the Partition Resolution, and the pan-Arab attack that was bound to come if a Jewish state were to be proclaimed upon the end of the Mandate: the alleged Meir–Abdallah agreement was not one of them. Rather, as will be shown shortly, the isolated references to Abdallah revealed deep uncertainty as to the King's future agenda.[12] This in turn leads to the conclusion that, for all its significance, the Meir–Abdallah meeting was both an immediate effort to weaken Arab opposition to partition and to prevent the outbreak of an Arab–Jewish war, and yet another link in the chain of intermittent Jewish–Hashemite secret contacts aimed at forging the widest possible common denominator between the two parties. Nothing more, nothing less.

The Jewish Agency and the Partition it Had Never Approved

If Palestine was indeed divided on 17 November 1947, which it most certainly was not, then the Jewish Agency that was an alleged party to this deal displayed no awareness whatsoever of its existence. Not only had such a partition never been discussed by the JAE, but the Yishuv's military operations during the 1948–49 war show not a trace of its existence. To the contrary, as is clearly borne out by Meir's verbal report, the meeting left her and the Zionist leadership deeply suspicious of Abdallah's expansionist ambitions, the precise nature of which were to be gauged in a follow-up meeting after the passing of the UN

Resolution. In the event, this meeting did not take place until 11 May 1948, and Jewish suspicions of Abdallah's real agenda remained unabated up to the Arab attack on the newly-established State of Israel, in which Transjordan's Arab Legion played a pivotal role.

The Jewish Agency's distrust of Abdallah was vividly demonstrated by its vehement opposition to the presence of Transjordan's British-led Arab Legion in Mandatory Palestine, and its tireless efforts to bring about its departure.[13] Thus, for example, at a discussion on security issues on 16 November 1947, a day before Meir's meeting with Abdallah, JAE Chairman David Ben-Gurion warned his colleagues that the Arab Legion's presence in Palestine constituted a potential security threat. 'It is true that it is headed by a person who is not our enemy', he said, 'but we must brace ourselves for all trouble.'[14] The Abdallah–Meir meeting did nothing to allay these apprehensions. On 7 December 1947 Ben-Gurion reiterated his apprehensions about the deployment of the Arab Legion in Palestine. 'The Government claims that this is their force', he reported on a meeting with the British High Commissioner, General Sir Alan Cunningham, in which he had protested on this point. 'But this is an Arab Legion.'[15] Two days later, Ben-Gurion expressed doubts over Abdallah's political standing. 'All evidence points to the fact that the Mufti has gained control over the Arab community in the country [Mandatory Palestine]', he told a JAE meeting. 'King Abdallah is isolated.'[16] In a cable to Sharett in New York he was equally puzzled about Abdallah's intentions, if slightly more optimistic: '"The King" is still defiant – does not lend a hand to the Mufti or the League; it is not clear to me whether he will stay his course, but there is a chance for this.'[17]

By January 1948 this guarded optimism was all but gone. 'There have been some news recently which may change our view of the king', Ben-Gurion recorded in his diary on 1 January 1948:

> It is said that the Arab Legion will operate [in Palestine] and the neighbouring Arab states will send a symbolic force. This may be correct. According to this information, the Legion will occupy *the whole* of Palestine, though without entering the populated areas, and will force the Jews to negotiate on the [Arab] League's terms: autonomy for the Jewish community under a single [Arab] regime for the whole country; Palestine within the League. Sasson recalled what [the King] said during the [November 1947] meeting in Naharaim: 'A partition that will not disgrace me in front of the Arabs. What do you think about a small republic [within my kingdom]?' This proves that the idea resides in the king's heart and is not of recent origin.[18]

Later that day Ben-Gurion dined with Avraham Rutenberg, in whose house the Meir–Abdallah meeting took place, and who now tried to convince Ben-Gurion to persuade the United Nations to introduce the King into the Arab parts of Palestine. 'We have to examine whether this is desirable – because Abdallah means Iraq',[19] was Ben-Gurion's cautious response, reflecting the lack of any agreed deal on the partition of Palestine. Two days later, he received a warning from Eliyahu Epstein (Eilath), the Jewish Agency's delegate in the United States, of Abdallah's intention to employ the Arab Legion in Palestine on behalf of the Arab League. 'In the entire country?', the puzzled Ben-Gurion jotted to himself. 'In the Arab area?'[20]

This scepticism was not confined to the leader of the Zionist movement. Contemporary documents are replete with deep-seated suspicions of Abdallah held by both Zionist officialdom and such leaders as Moshe Sharett, all of whom were totally unaware of the alleged agreement with the King on the division of Mandatory Palestine. Early in January 1948 Sharett opined that if it transpired that Abdallah were capable of gaining control over the Arab parts of Palestine, either directly or by proxy, then the Zionist movement should make serious efforts to support him. Yet he profoundly feared that 'the King will deceive and cheat us'.[21] In other words, two months after Meir's meeting with Abdallah, her direct superior and the head of the department that had maintained secret contacts with the King for well over a decade was unaware of the alleged deal to divide Mandatory Palestine, despite receiving Sasson's report on the conversation three days after the meeting.

Even Sasson who participated in the Meir–Abdallah meeting did not behave as if there existed any firm agreement with the King. Instead, as Palestinian–Jewish fighting intensified he increasingly lost trust in Abdallah's ability to stay his course. On 9 February 1948 he told Ben-Gurion that the King would most probably have to play along with the Arab League's plan. Sasson still believed in Abdallah's sincerity; however, given his dependence on the British and his limited power base, he thought that the King could no longer be relied upon.[22] A month later Sasson told Ben-Gurion of the need to establish a secret dialogue with the governments of Egypt, Lebanon, and Syria in an attempt to reach an understanding that would prevent an all-out war. 'Have you despaired of your King?', Ben-Gurion asked, apparently surprised at Abdallah's glaring absence from the list. 'No, but he is helpless', Sasson answered. 'I despaired of the King since the British had surrendered him', added Reuben Shiloah, Ben-Gurion's adviser, and founding father of the Mossad, who attended the meeting.[23]

If anything, one need not look further than Sasson's impassioned appeal on 5 December 1947 to the Secretary-General of the Arab League, Abd al-Rahman Azzam, imploring him to accept the UN Partition Resolution, to realize that no Hashemite–Jewish deal had been struck: had Palestine been actually divided between Abdallah and the Jewish Agency on 17 November, then there would have been no need for such an appeal in the first place.[24] That the Zionist movement sought a mutually-agreed solution with the Arab League, which Abdallah so intensely detested, three weeks after his meeting with Meir, indicated that all options were open.

Transjordanian Annexation or an Independent Palestinian State?

Indeed, the Zionist preference for Abdallah over the Mufti as its direct neighbour did not *ipso facto* preclude the possibility of an independent Palestinian State that would not be headed by this arch enemy of the Jewish national cause. As far as the Zionist movement was concerned, a Jewish state was to be established in part of Mandatory Palestine; what happened to the rest of the country, as noted by Moshe Sharett, 'is not for us but rather for them [the Arabs] to decide, whether it would be merged [with Transjordan] or separated'.[25] Since all Zionist efforts during the 1930s to reach an understanding with the Palestinian leadership came to nought,[26] and since there was no 'Palestinian Option' in the late 1940s due to the extreme fragmentation of Palestinian society and the unwavering intransigence of its leadership, the Zionists sought to win to the cause of partition whichever Arab partners they could find. King Abdallah figured prominently in these efforts given his intermittant contacts with the Zionist movement since the early 1930s, but he was by no means the only one. In 1946, the Zionists managed to convince the Egyptian Prime Minister, Ismail Sidqi, to try to persuade the Arab World of the desirability of partition, with its attendant Palestinian State, but this success was aborted by Sidqi's fall from power in the autumn of 1946.[27]

On 15 September 1947, a couple of months before the passing of the Partition Resolution, the Jewish Agency made yet another attempt to convince the Arab World of the merits of partition. At a secret meeting with Azzam in London, Aubrey (Abba) Eban and David Horovitz, the Jewish Agency's liaison officers with the newly-created United Nations Special Commission for Palestine (UNSCOP), tried to convince the

Arab League's General-Secretary that 'once agreement had been reached on a practical compromise such as that suggested by UNSCOP, it should not be difficult to convince the Arab world that it had nothing to fear from Jewish development, and that no threat of Jewish expansion would exist'. Azzam remained unimpressed. 'The Arab world is not at all in a compromising mood,' he said:

> You will achieve nothing with talk of compromise or peace. You may perhaps achieve something by force of your arms. We will try to rout you. I am not sure we will succeed, but we will try. We succeeded in expelling the Crusaders, but lost Spain and Persia, and may lose Palestine. But it is too late for a peaceable solution.[28]

Then came Sasson's above-noted plea to Azzam to accept the idea of partition and to forego recourse to violence, to which the latter did not even bother to reply.

That the Zionist movement was not averse to the possibility of a Palestinian State, as envisaged by the Partition Resolution, was also evidenced by Meir's refusal to condone Abdallah's annexation of the Arab parts of Palestine and her insistence on the temporary nature of Transjordan's occupation 'until the United Nations could establish a government in that part [of Palestine]'. It was further underscored by Foreign Minister Moshe Sharett at the Israeli Cabinet meeting of 16 June 1948. Those were the days of the first armistice after the pan-Arab invasion of Israel the previous month. Fighting was about to resume in three weeks; several political solutions revising the Partition Resolution were being contrived, especially by the British Government; and Sharett briefed his fellow ministers on the various options confronting Israel. 'At a certain stage we committed ourselves *vis-à-vis* the international community to a specific arrangement – that of the 29th of November,' he said:

> We gave our partial and explicit agreement to a specific arrangement, and now we are being asked in England and America: 'Do you wash your hands of it? But you would be reneging on your commitment!' It seems to me that it should be clear, which is precisely what I have said at a press conference and advised colleagues to speak in a similar vein: the 29 November Resolution is an arrangement comprising several components, which together constitute one whole. When there was a chance for this 'package deal' to be implemented – we accepted it. And if it is still feasible – we would not renege on our undertaking. But when changes are being introduced, and should certain components of this arrange-

ment be changed – then our hands are free, and there would be a renegotiation of the entire arrangement.

There are four such components [in the 'package deal']: (a) a Jewish state in a certain part of Palestine within specific borders; (b) a separate Arab state, unattached to Transjordan, let alone Syria, but rather a separate Arab–Palestinian state in a specific territory of Palestine and within specific borders; (c) an international Jerusalem having an efficient international regime based on certain elements, such as ensuring equality and free access to holy sites etc; (d) an economic alliance *unifying* these three elements – the Jewish state, the Arab state, and International Jerusalem – into a single economic entity, thus *preserving* the country's unity and the interrelationship between those parts. This is what we have agreed to.

'I assume, therefore, that it is our [i.e., the Cabinet's] unanimous view that an Arab Palestine is here to stay', Sharett concluded, reflecting the general reluctance within the Israeli leadership to condone Transjordan's annexation of the Arab areas of Mandatory Palestine:

> And there is a more concrete question of Arab Palestine, namely the question of Abdallah. I do not think that on this issue we can determine the course of events in one way or the other, but we should have a prepared position for all possible contingencies.
>
> If Arab Palestine goes to Abdallah, this means unification with Transjordan; and a possible linkage with Iraq. And if this Palestine is a separate state, standing on its own – it is a wholly different issue. In the former case [i.e., unification with Transjordan] – an economic alliance is impossible. This is not to say that no economic alliance would be feasible – but not the economic alliance [envisaged by the UN Partition Resolution] in which we would pay tax [to the Palestinian State], and which would comprise joint customs, an international regime, as well as shared use of the railway system and the port of Haifa. All this will be inconceivable. We undertook to associate ourselves with a specific partner, and we are prepared to negotiate with it. But not with another partner.[29]

Two months later, in a telegram to Bechor Shalom Shitrit, Minister of Police and Minorities in the Israeli Government, Sharett was equally opposed to Transjordan annexing the Arab areas of Mandatory Palestine:

> We should strive for contact and mutual understanding with people and groups among our opponents who carry weight in Arab

public life and who are today prepared for co-operation with us, whether on the basis of recognizing the State of Israel within its borders or in order to establish independent rule in the Arab part of Western Palestine.

Without being able to totally remove from the agenda the possibility of the annexation of the Arab part of Western Palestine to Transjordan, we must prefer the establishment of an independent Arab state within Western Palestine. In any event we must endeavour to explore this possibility and to underscore its desirability in our eyes over the annexation proposal.[30]

Similarly, in a conversation in early December 1948 with the British Ambassador to Transjordan, Sir Alec Kirkbride, Ralph Bunche, the UN Acting Mediator for Palestine, claimed that,

The Jews had practically abandoned their original idea of insisting on the Arab areas of Palestine being formed into an independent state because he, Bunche, had convinced them that it was as likely as not to fall under the influence of Haj Amin el Husseini and to be an endless source of friction and disorder.[31]

In other words, more than a year after Palestine had allegedly been divided by Abdallah and Meir, Israeli leaders still needed to be convinced of the merits of Transjordan's annexation of the Arab parts of Palestine. Even a cursory examination of Ben-Gurion's war diary would easily reveal divergencies within the Israeli leadership over the future status of the Arab areas of Palestine: an independent state or part of Transjordan.[32] It is true that Bunche was somewhat self-complimentary in crediting himself with this attitudinal change. On the one hand, the Israelis needed no reminder of the hazards of a Mufti-dominated state; and they were painfully aware of the slim prospects of the emergence of a viable moderate Palestinian leadership. On the other hand, Bunche failed to convince the most important Israeli leaders of the merits of Transjordanian annexation. 'While we may still expect two more [military] operations, our main objective now is peace', Ben-Gurion told a meeting of foreign policy officials and experts on Arab affairs on 18 December 1948:

Aliya requires the end of war, our future necessitates peace and friendship with Arabs. Therefore I support talking to Abdallah, though I doubt to what extent the British will allow him to make peace. But we should clarify [to Abdallah] from the outset that, apart from a truce, there is not yet any agreement between us, and that the discussion is on the basis of a *tabula rasa*. *We will not be able to agree lightly to the annexation of [the Arab] parts of Palestine to Transjordan*, because of (1) Israel's security: *an Arab State in Western Palestine is less dangerous than a state that is tied to Transjordan*, and tomorrow – probably to Iraq; (2) Why should we vainly antagonize the Russians? (3) Why should we do this [i.e., agree to Transjordan's annexation of Western Palestine] against the [wishes of the] rest of the Arab states? This does not mean that we may not agree under any circumstances – but only in the context of a general arrangement.[33]

In line with this view, Ben-Gurion instructed the Israeli delegation to the truce talks with Transjordan 'to remain non-committal for the time being, while avoiding [outright] objection; to explain the difficulties (England, the Arab states, Russia); to express sympathy; to say that there is not yet a government decision on this issue'.[34]

Abdallah and the Jews: Independence or Subject Status?

Just as the Zionist movement would not concede to Abdallah what he considered to be his, so the King was totally impervious to the essence of Zionist aspirations: national self-determination. As a product of the Ottoman imperial system, where religion constituted the linchpin of the socio-political order of things, Abdallah had no real grasp of Jewish nationalism, or, for that matter, of the phenomenon of nationalism *per se*. True, he had been the moving spirit behind his father's decision to launch the so-called 'Great Arab Revolt' against the Ottoman Empire in 1916. However, the revolt had far less to do with the desire to free the 'Arab Nation' from the shackles of Ottoman captivity than with the ambition to substitute a Hashemite Empire, extending well beyond the predominantly Arabic-speaking territories, for that of the Ottomans.[35] It was only after he had been elbowed out by his younger brother, Faisal, from what he considered to be his prospective kingdom, i.e. Iraq, that Abdallah turned his sights to Transjordan as a springboard for an alternative empire embracing Syria, Palestine, and possibly Iraq and Saudi Arabia.

Hence, when in March 1921 the British Colonial Secretary, Winston Churchill, suggested that Transjordan be constituted as an Arab province of Palestine, under an Arab governor amenable to him and subordinate to the High Commissioner for Palestine, Abdallah demurred. If a certain territory had to be incorporated into another as a

province, then it should be Palestine into Transjordan, under his headship, and not the other way round:

> If His Majesty's Government could agree that there should be an
> Arab Emir over Palestine and Transjordania in the same relation
> with the High Commissioner for Palestine as that of the Emir
> Faisal with the High Commissioner for Mesopotamia, he was
> convinced that the present difficulties between Arabs and Jews
> would be most easily overcome.

Churchill's explanation that there was a fundamental difference between
Mesopotamia, which had been provisionally recognized as an independent state, and Palestine, which had been entrusted to the administration
of a Mandatory Government, failed to impress Abdallah.

> His Majesty's Government proposed to have his brother Faisal in
> Mesopotamia with a High Commissioner or a mandate, or what-
> ever term they might like to employ. He felt strongly that a similar
> régime should be adopted for Palestine and Transjordania.[36]

This was an ambition that Abdallah was to nurture until the late
1940s, when it was dealt a mortal blow by the establishment of the State
of Israel and its ability to withstand the pan-Arab assault of May 1948,
and he never tired of reiterating it to successive British and Zionist
interlocutors. Because of his Ottoman education and his own imperial
ambitions he viewed Jews, like other non-Muslim minorities, as
members of a tolerated religious community [*millet*], deserving protection and autonomy in the practice of their religious affairs – but not a
state of their own. Given his perception of Jews as an influential, affluent and technologically advanced community, he was keen to incorporate them into his kingdom – as subjects. As the Transjordanian Prime
Minister, Samir al-Rifai, told Brigadier I.N. Clayton of the British
Middle East Office (BMEO) in Cairo on 11 December 1947: 'The
enlarged Transjordan State with the support of Jewish economy would
become the most influential State in the Arab Middle East.'[37]

It is in this light that Abdallah's acquiescence in the idea of partition,
first raised as a concrete political option by the 1937 Royal Peel
Commission, should be seen: not acceptance of the partition of
Mandatory Palestine into independent Jewish and Palestinian states but
rather the incorporation of these two communities into his kingdom.
This is what he repeatedly communicated to the Zionist movement in
the 1930s – before, during, and after the Peel Commission;[38] this is what
he told the follow-up Woodhead Commission of Inquiry (1938);[39] and

this is what he told Jewish leaders well after the Second World War,[40] including Golda Meir in their meeting on 17 November 1947,

As shown earlier, it was only upon realizing that this solution was totally unacceptable to Meir that Abdallah opted for the lesser choice of incorporating the Arab areas of Mandatory Palestine into his kingdom. However, even then he did not view this option as final, but rather as a tactical withdrawal on the road of his strategic goal: in early December 1947, shortly after the passing of the Partition Resolution and a fort-night after his secret meeting with Meir, Abdallah sought to convince the Arab League to finance Transjordan's occupation of Palestine which he was prepared to undertake.[41] As his Arab partners were no warmer to the idea than his Jewish interlocutors, Abdallah renewed his efforts to convince the Jewish Agency to cede him some of the territory awarded to them by the UN or even to forego the idea of an independent state altogether and to become an autonomous province in his kingdom.

The last such attempt was made in Abdallah's second meeting with Golda Meir on 11 May 1948, a mere three days before the establishment of the State of Israel and its subsequent invasion by the Arab states. Through his personal envoy, Muhammad Zubeiti, Abdallah had already communicated to his Jewish interlocutors his envisaged solution to the Palestine question: 'the country would remain undivided, with auton-omy for the areas in which the Jews constituted the majority, such as Tel Aviv. This arrangement would last one year, after which the country would be incorporated into Transjordan.' Meir's categoric rejection of the idea at their meeting on 11 May 1948 failed to discourage Abdallah. He had always been for peace, he argued, but now the only way to avoid war was to accept his proposal. In any event, why were the Jews in such a hurry to proclaim their own state? Even as his guests were taking their leave, Abdallah reiterated his request to consider his offer:

> And if the reply were affirmative, it had to be given before 15 May. He would invite his Palestinian backers and the moderate Arabs, and ask us [i.e., the Jews] to send moderate representatives too – and then the matter could be settled. He also said: 'There is no need to fear that the Government will include extremist Arabs, Jew-haters, but only moderate Arabs.'[42]

Meir dismissed the idea out of hand.

Conclusions

The above discussion proves that the 'collusion theory' has no credence, for the simple reason that Abdallah and the Zionist movement were talking at cross purposes: the former wished to see the Jews as prospective subjects of his expanded kingdom and kept on pressing the idea up to the proclamation of the State of Israel; the latter strove to establish their own independent state, free of foreign control and subjugation. These two positions were mutually exclusive, and in their two decades of intermittent contacts Abdallah and the Jewish Agency never came even close to transcending this divide.

Whenever the Jewish interlocutors pointed to the glaring contradiction between Abdallah's apparent support for the partition of Palestine and his advocacy of a unified Transjordanian–Palestinian kingdom, or 'federation', under his headship, the King would either indulge in vague generalities (for example, his 12 August 1946 meeting with Sasson) or resort to a 'salami tactic' (for example, his November 1947 conversation with Meir) of trying to harness Jewish support to certain parts of his imperial dream while leaving its ultimate implementation to a later date.

However, as conclusively shown both by the account of the latter meeting by all its Jewish participants (Meir, Danin and Sasson), and by Jewish political and military activities in the wake of the meeting, even Abdallah's interim goal of annexing the Arab parts of Palestine to his kingdom was unacceptable to the Zionist leadership. They were prepared to acquiesce in his capture of these areas – but only as a temporary law-enforcement measure to prevent bloodshed and facilitate the establishment of a legitimate Palestinian government in accordance with the Partition Resolution. They were not, however, prepared to condone the annexation of these territories to Transjordan for a number of interconnected reasons: (1) lingering doubts over whether Abdallah would be amenable to most Palestinians; (2) fears of Abdallah's imperial ambitions and mistrust of his promises; (3) the belief that a Palestinian State in part of Western Palestine was far less dangerous a neighbour than an expanded Transjordanian Kingdom.

NOTES

1. Reprinted from *Journal of Contemporary History* (1999), by permission of SAGE Publishers; all rights reserved.
2. *See*, for example, Abdallah al-Tall, *Karithat Filastin: Mudhakkirat Abdallah al-Tall, Qa'id Ma'rakat al-Quds* (Cairo, 1959); A. Sayegh, *al-Hashemiyun wa-Qadiyat Filastin* (Sidon, 1964), pp. 261–5; Israel Baer, *Bithon Israel: Etmol, Ha-yom, Mahar* (Tel Aviv, 1966), pp. 125–35; Jon Kimche and David Kimche, *Both Sides of the Hill* (London, 1960), p. 60; Marie Syrkin, *Golda Meir: Woman with a Cause* (London, 1964), pp. 195–202.

3. For mainstream subscription to the theory *see*, for example: Neil Caplan, *Futile Diplomacy*, Vol. II: *Arab-Zionist Negotiations and the End of the Mandate* (London, 1986); Mary Wilson, *King Abdullah, Britain and the Making of Jordan* (Cambridge, 1987), pp. 161–7, 214; Yoav Gelber, *Jewish–Transjordanian Relations, 1921–1948* (London, 1997); Dan Schueftan, *Optsia Yardenit: Israel, Yarden, Veha-palestinaim* (Tel Aviv, 1986).

   For the 'revisionist' approach *see*, for example: Simha Flapan, *The Birth of Israel: Myth and Realities* (New York, 1987), pp. 8, 42–4, 142–4, 167–8; Avi Shlaim, *Collusion Across the Jordan: King Abdullah, the Zionist Movement, and the Partition of Palestine* (Oxford, 1988); Avi Shlaim, *The Politics of Partition* (Oxford, 1990) (an abridged and slightly revised edition of *Collusion*).

4. Shlaim, *Collusion*, p. 1; Shlaim, *The Politics of Partition*, p. viii.

5. Ilan Pappé, *The Making of the Arab–Israeli Conflict, 1947–1951*, (London, 1992), p. 118.

6. Ezra Danin, 'Siha Im Abdallah, 17 November 1947', Central Zionist Archives (hereinafter CZA) S25/4004.

7. Eliyahu Sasson to Moshe Shertok [Sharett], 20 November 1947, CZA, S25/1699.

8. Danin, 'Siha Im Abdallah'; Sasson to Shertok.

9. Danin, 'Siha Im Abdallah'.

10. Golda Meir's verbal report to the Provisional State Council on 12 May 1948. Israel State Archives, *Provisional State Council: Protocols, 18 April–13 May 1948* (Jerusalem, 1978), p. 40 (emphasis added).

11. David Vital, 'Some of the Forks in the Road', in Efraim Karsh and Gregory Mahler (eds), *Israel at the Crossroads* (London, 1994), pp. 9–10.

12. *See*, for example, protocols of the meetings of the Zionist Agency Executive meetings of 2, 9, 16, 23 and 30 November 1947, 7 and 9 December 1947, CZA.

13. *See*, for example, Meir's meeting with Sir Alan Cunningham, 17 December 1947, and her letter to him from the same day, State of Israel, ISA and World Zionist Organization, CZA, *Teudot Mediniot Ve-diplomatiot, December 1947–May 1948* (Jerusalem, 1979) (hereinafter, *Israel Documents*), pp. 83–4; a meeting in London between representatives of the Jewish Agency and the Colonial Secretary, Arthur Creech-Jones, on 23 December 1947, *ibid.*, pp. 96–7.

14. CZA, Jewish Agency Executive meeting of 16 November 1947, p. 4 (12697).

15. CZA, Jewish Agency Executive meeting of 7 December 1947, protocol 13, p. 2 (12717), protocol 14, p. 1 (12724).

16. CZA, Protocols of the JAE meeting of 9 January 1948, p. 1 (12740). In his diary Ben-Gurion made the point in similar terms: 'Opposition [to the Mufti among the Palestine Arabs] is feeble...According to Sasson the Mufti has gained control over all the Palestine Arabs. The King is isolated and cannot be trusted.' David Ben-Gurion [9 December 1947], *Yoman Ha-milhama, Tashah-Tashat*, Vol. 1 (Tel Aviv, 1982), p. 28.

17. *Israel Documents*, p. 60.

18. Ben-Gurion, *Yoman Ha-milhama* [1 January 1948], Vol. 1, pp. 100–1 (emphasis in the original).

19. *Ibid.*, p. 103. As late as 16 April 1948 Ben-Gurion warned a JAE meeting that 'we should not be lured into a sense of relief, there may be various mishaps, for example if the Arab Legion will go into action' (p. 3, 12562).

20. *Ibid*, [3 January 1948], p. 107.

21. E. Danin to E. Sasson, 4 January 1948, *Israel Documents*, p. 127. In the same cable Danin also reported David Horowitz's great fear that Abdallah 'will cheat and fail us'.

22. Ben-Gurion, *Yoman Ha-milhama* [9 February 1948], Vol. 1, pp. 224–5.

23. *Ibid.*, 7 March 1948, p. 284.
24. *Israel Documents*, p. 30.
25. Shertok to Sasson, 18 August 1946, CZA, S25/10015.
26. *See*, for example, David Ben-Gurion, *My Talks with Arab Leaders* (Jerusalem, 1972); Caplan, *Futile Diplomacy*, Vol. 2; Avraham Sela, 'Talks and Contacts between Zionist Leaders and Palestinian-Arab Leaders, 1933–1939', *Ha-mizrah Ha-hadash*, 22 (1972), pp. 401–23 (part 1); 23 (1973), pp. 1–21 (part 2).
27. Shlaim, *Collusion*, pp. 76, 80–1.
28. A.S. Eban, 'Note of Conversation with Abd al-Rahman Azzam Pasha, London, 15 September 1947', CZA, S25/9020, brought in Caplan, *Futile Diplomacy*, pp. 274–6; Aharon Cohen, *Israel and the Arab World*, London, 1970, p. 381, citing Horovitz's account.
29. Israel's State Archives, 'Protocol of the Provisional Government Meeting of 16 June 1948', pp. 12–13, 23–24 (emphasis in the original).
30. Sharett to Shitrit, 8 August 1948, in Yehoshua Freindlich (ed.), *Teudot Mediniot Ve-diplomatiot, May-September 1948* (Jerusalem, 1981), p. 498.
31. Kirkbride to Bernard Burrows, 10 December 1948, FO 371/68603/E16265.
32. Ben-Gurion, *Yoman Ha-milhama* [29 December 1948], Vol. 3, p. 910.
33. *Ibid.*, 18 December 1948, p. 885 (emphasis added).
34. *Ibid.*, 4 January 1949, p. 927.
35. *See* Efraim and Inari Karsh, 'Myth in the Desert, or Not the Great Arab Revolt', *Middle Eastern Studies*, 33, 2 (1997), pp. 267–312.
36. 'First Conversation on Trans-Jordania, Held at Government House, Jerusalem, March 28, 1921', FO 371/6343, fols 99–101.
37. Clayton to Foreign Office, 12 December 1947, telegram 67, FO 371/62226/E11928.
38. *See*, for example, B. Joseph, 'Note of Talk with Salim Ayoub, 20 May 1936' and 'Note of Talk with S.A., M. al-Unsi and Fr. N.', 5 June 1936, CZA, S25/10093; Lourie to Shertok (Sharett), 25 May 1936, S25/6325; Shertok to Abdallah, 30 April 1936 and Abdallah to Shertok, 6 May 1936, S25/3243; Yehoshua Porath, *Mi-mehumot Li-mrida: Ha-tnu'a Ha-arvit-Ha-Palestinit, 1929–1939* (Tel Aviv, 1978), pp. 97–8.
39. *See*, for example, 'Text of the Proposal for the Solution of the Palestine Problem Sent to the British Government' (i.e., to the Woodhead Commission, May 1938), in King Abdallah of Jordan, *My Memoirs Completed: 'al-Takmilah'* (London, 1951), pp. 89–90.
40. *See*, for example, Sasson's reports on his two meetings in August 1946 with Abdallah: CZA, S25/9036; Sasson, *Ba-derekh el Ha-shalom: Igrot Ve-shihot* (Tel Aviv, 1978), pp. 367–72.
41. Haza al-Majali, *Mudhakkirati* (Beirut, 1960), p. 63.
42. Meir's verbal report to the Provisional State Council on 12 May 1948.

Were the Palestinians
Expelled?[1]

I

Since the birth of the Jewish State in 1948, there have been two Arab–
Israeli conflicts. The first one was, and is, military in nature. Played out
on the battlefield, it has had more than its share of heroes, villains, mar-
tyrs and victims. The second, less bloody but no less incendiary, has
been the battle over the historical culpability for the 1948 War and the
accompanying dispersion of large numbers of Palestinian Arabs.

The Israeli 'narrative' of this episode sees the Palestinian tragedy as
primarily self-inflicted, a direct result of the vehement Palestinian/Arab
rejection of the United Nations resolution of 29 November 1947 calling
for the establishment of two states in Palestine, and the violent attempt
by the Arab nations of the region to abort the Jewish State at birth. By
contrast, Palestinians view themselves as the hapless victims of a Zionist
grand design to dispossess them from their patrimony.

For much of the last half-century, this second battle lay in the background as Israel struggled for survival and the Arab world continued to
nourish, and from time to time act upon, its hope for the Jewish State's
extinction by military means. However, the focus of confrontation has
now shifted. As the possibility looms of some political resolution to the
century-long conflict between Israel and the Palestinians, the latter have
adamantly insisted on reintroducing into debate the events surrounding
the 1948 War and the birth of Israel. In the words of the prominent
Palestinian politician Hanan Ashrawi:

> They [the Israelis] cannot wipe the slate clean and say: 'Now we
> will deal with history in another way. The political process is a new
> process and must not be taken back'....What we need is, first of all,
> a genuine recognition, an admission of guilt and culpability by
> Israel; the real authentic narrative of the Palestinians has to come
> out, to be acknowledged, to be recognized.

Ashrawi is not invoking history for history's sake. Hers is a clear and far-reaching political agenda: first, to rewrite the history of the 1948 War in a manner that stains Israel politically and morally; then, to force Israel to measure up to its 'original sin' – the allegedly forcible dispossession of native Palestinians – both by permitting the return of refugees to parts of the territory that is now Israel and by compensating them monetarily for their sufferings.

For the first time since 1948, this objective seems to be within reach. Fatigued by decades of fighting, and yearning for normality, most Israelis, while still nominally opposed to the return of Palestinian refugees, have effectively conceded defeat in the factual battle over their past. Not only have substantial elements of the Palestinian narrative – championed within Israel itself by a group of revisionist 'new historians' – become the received wisdom in the country's academic and intellectual circles, but this same view of the past has also made inroads into public consciousness. A number of new high-school textbooks, introduced recently into the Israeli curriculum, repudiate many well-documented and long-established facts about the 1948 War in favour of standard Arab/Palestinian claims, including the charge that substantial numbers of Palestinians were expelled during the war and that Israel bears sole responsibility for their ongoing status as refugees.

'Only ten years ago, much of this was taboo', the Israeli author of one of the new ninth-grade textbooks boasted to the *New York Times*. 'Now we can deal with this the way Americans deal with the Indians and black enslavement.' That is precisely how the Palestinians plan to deal with it as well: that is, through Israel's acknowledgement of guilt and the implementation of the Palestinian 'right of return'.

The city of Haifa, on Israel's north-west coast, has come to epitomize this demand for 'rectification' (to use Hanan Ashrawi's term). It is not difficult to understand why. In 1948, Haifa's Arab population was second in size only to that of Jaffa. No less significantly, Haifa then constituted the main socio-economic and administrative centre in northern Palestine for both Arabs and Jews. It was one of the primary ports of the eastern Mediterranean, the hub of Palestine's railway system, the site of the country's oil refinery, and a formidable industrial centre.

When hostilities between Arabs and Jews broke out in 1947, there were 62,500–66,000 Arabs in Haifa;[2] by May 1948, all but a few were gone, accounting for fully a tenth of the total Palestinian dispersion. Little wonder, then, that Haifa has acquired a mythical place in Palestinian collective memory, greater than Jaffa's or even Jerusalem's. As the prominent Palestinian author and political activist, Fawaz Turki, himself a native of Haifa, has put it:

> You [Israelis] owe me. And you owe me big. You robbed me of my
> city and my property. You owe me reparations (which I know that
> you, or your children, will one day have to pay, and under duress if
> need be) for all the pain and unspeakable suffering you have put
> me, my family, and my fellow exiles through.

But what exactly happened in Haifa? Was there 'an act of expulsion', as
the Palestinians and Israeli 'new historians' have argued? Or was the
older Israeli contention correct – namely, that the Arabs who fled the
city in 1947–48 did so of their own volition, and/or at the behest of their
leaders? During the past decade, as it happens, Israeli and Western state
archives have declassified millions of records, including invaluable contemporary Arab and Palestinian documents, relating to the 1948 war
and the creation of the Palestinian refugee problem. These make it possible to establish the truth about what happened in Haifa – and by extension, elsewhere in Palestine.

II

As the British Mandate in Palestine neared its end in 1947–48, a struggle broke out for control of the city of Haifa. The hostilities, which pitted Arab fighters recruited locally as well as from neighbouring Arab
countries against soldiers of the Jewish military force known as the
Hagana, would reach their peak on 21–22 April 1948, when the British
suddenly decided to evacuate the town and the Hagana moved in
quickly to capture the Arab quarters and assert control. However, the
first thing the documents show is that Arab flight from Haifa began well
before the outbreak of these hostilities, and even before the UN's 29
November 1947 Partition Resolution.

On 23 October, over a month earlier, a British intelligence brief was
already noting that 'leading Arab personalities are acting on the assumption that disturbances are near at hand, and have already evacuated their
families to neighbouring Arab countries'.[3] By 21 November, as the
General Assembly was getting ready to vote, not just 'leading Arab personalities' but 'many Arabs of Haifa' were reported to be removing their
families.[4] As the violent Arab reaction to the UN resolution built up,
eradicating any hope of its peaceful enforcement, this stream of refugees
turned into a flood.

Thus it was that, by mid-December 1947, some 15,000–20,000

people, almost a third of the city's Arab population, had fled,[5] creating severe adversity for those remaining. Economic and commercial activity ground to a halt as the wealthier classes converted their assets to gold or US dollars and transferred them abroad. Merchants and industrialists moved their businesses to Egypt, Syria or Lebanon, causing both unemployment and shortages in basic necessities. Entire areas were emptied of their residents.

These difficulties were exacerbated by deep cleavages within the Arab community itself. The town's Christian Arabs – erecting clear boundaries between themselves and Muslims – refused to feed the Syrian, Lebanese and Iraqi recruits arriving to wrest the city from the Jews, asserted their determination not to attack Jewish forces unless attacked first, and established a special guard to protect themselves from Muslim violence. Added to this was a growing lawlessness, including pandemic looting of deserted properties.[6]

At the time, the official leadership of Haifa Arabs was a 15-member body called the National Committee, headed by Rashid Hajj Ibrahim, a scion of a respected family of North African origins, whose public activity dated back to Ottoman days. Although the Committee strove to curb the mass flight, urging Haifa's Arabs to stay put and castigating those who fled – occasionally, these warnings were backed by the torching of escapees' belongings – its remonstrations proved of no avail.

To be sure, the Committee itself hardly constituted a model of commitment or self-sacrifice: not only were its own ranks being depleted by the flight of some of its members, but scarcely a meeting was attended by all those who remained. Moreover, affluent though they were, Committee members, while taking care to reimburse themselves for the smallest expense, rarely contributed financially to the national struggle. Transcripts of the Committee's meetings do not exactly convey a grasp of the severity of the situation: they tend to be taken up instead with trivialities, from the placement of an office partition to the payment to a certain individual of £1.29 in travel expenses.[7]

Even when the Committee did try to deal with the cycle of violence in which the town was embroiled, its efforts were repeatedly undermined by the sheer number of armed groups operating in defiance of its authority, by infighting between its own pragmatists and militants, and by the total lack of co-ordination, if not outright hostility, between the Committee and its parent body, the Arab Higher Committee (AHC). The latter, the effective government of all the Arabs in Palestine, was headed by the former Mufti of Jerusalem, Hajj Amin al-Husseini, now resident in Cairo. Giving his own terrorists free rein in Haifa, the Mufti turned a deaf ear to the Committee's requests and recommendations.

Not that the National Committee was amenable to Haifa's inclusion within the prospective Jewish State, as envisaged by the Partition Resolution, or eschewed violence as a means to abort this eventuality. Yet it felt that it needed a breathing space in order to get external support and organize the Haifa Arab community for the tough struggle that lay ahead. As well-informed Haifa Arabs told the British: 'Hajj Ibrahim advocates the policy of conserving the Arab effort until the British withdrawal, or until a favourable opportunity for a full scale attack should present itself.'[8] Indeed, when on 12 December 1947 Haifa's Jewish mayor, Shabtai Levy, suggested the issue of a joint Arab–Jewish proclamation urging the population to forego any acts of violence, and expressing his readiness, as a representative of the Jewish community, to negotiate the details of such an agreement with an authorized Arab body, the Committee rejected this proposal. 'We have been toiling day and night to maintain [peace and] quiet and to implement a high, unified Arab policy notwithstanding the incitement of the Jewish traitors,' argued Ibrahim. 'There is no way we can negotiate with the Jews. Let them take care of their interests and we will ensure our security.'[9]

Things came to a head in mid-January 1948, following the bombing of a Jewish commercial centre in which eight people were killed and scores of others wounded. Carried out by the Mufti's local henchmen, the atrocity brought to an abrupt end the tenuous truce, organized under British pressure in late December, and drove a few hundred (mostly Christian) families to flee the city.[10] At the National Committee's meeting on 18 January, Ibrahim left little doubt as to whom, in his opinion, was culpable for this recent deterioration. 'While we were sailing the ship with your help and maintaining its balance, a sudden storm had rocked us on our way', he told his colleagues, insisting that his words be recorded verbatim, as evidence for future generations. 'And all this has been done by people claiming to be connected to the AHC and to other officials abroad.' In Ibrahim's view, the severity of the situation left the Committee no choice but to seize the bull by its horns: to send a delegation to Cairo in order to ascertain whether the AHC had indeed been behind the latest bombing and to impress upon the Mufti the seriousness of the Haifa situation. Were the Mufti to remain impervious to the city's predicament, he was to be warned that if terrorist activity did not cease the local leadership would leave the country, thus triggering a process that would result in the eventual disappearance of the entire Haifa community.[11]

The delegates' pleas were unavailing. Though evidently shaken by the stark picture they painted, the Mufti rejected their request for an armistice as this would be tantamount to surrender and would have far-reaching adverse implications on the Palestinian struggle. This mortal struggle, he argued, might result in the destruction of half of Palestine's Arab population and it was therefore advisable to move women and children from danger zones so as to reduce casualties. At the same time, the Haifa National Committee had to do its utmost to shore up the town's defence, to stop the mass flight and to call on those who had fled to return. As an enticement the Mufti denied any connection with the January bombing and endorsed the Committee as the supreme political and military body in Haifa, promising to place under its command a soon-to-be-formed 500-strong force.[12]

This failed to impress the Haifa population. Notwithstanding the arrival of fresh arms shipments from Syria, Lebanon and Egypt, as well as military reinforcements, a general sense of nervousness engulfed the city, especially the Christian community. The Mufti's failure to acquiesce in the delegation's plea for emergency food supplies, coupled with the growing lawlessness in the Arab streets, drove many merchants to prepare themselves for leaving Haifa. Moreover, his soft words notwithstanding, Hajj Amin neither changed his attitude towards the Committee nor pressured his Haifa loyalists to cease hostilities.

This, in turn, led to further waves of flight.[13] Thus, for example, following the destruction of several houses in the Wadi Nisnas neighbourhood by the Hagana in early February, the residents complained to the city's commander of the shortage of guards in their neighbourhood, only to be bluntly told that he had no intention of assigning guards to buildings whose owners had fled the country. As the residents saw no point in taking punishment for the actions of their absentee landlords, flight from the neighbourhood ensued. They were shortly followed by the residents of Wadi Rushmiya, Wadi Salib and Halisa fleeing their neighbourhoods in fear of Jewish attacks.[14]

Violence escalated sharply following an abortive attempt by the Hagana on the life of the local religious militant, Muhammad Nimr al-Khatib, on 19 February, as Arab revenge attacks and Jewish reprisals immersed the city in the all-too-familiar cycle of tit-for-tat action, further widening the divisions within the Arab community. Rumours were rife that the Mufti was behind the assassination attempt, having recently fallen out with al-Khatib, who was allegedly considering shifting his loyalty to King Abdallah of Transjordan.[15] In a revealing incident, Christian residents beat up a group of Arab fighters seeking to use their street for the shelling of Jewish targets. Lawlessness spiralled to new heights, with the foreign irregulars stationed in the town unabashedly exploiting their position to abuse those very people they had been brought in to defend. The alarmed Mufti instructed the National Committee to stamp out the burgeoning lawlessness;[16] yet the latter's attempt to enforce tighter discipline by prohibiting individual use of weapons and authorizing the National Guard to arrest persons bearing arms in public places, as well as to open fire on undisciplined crowds, backfired. The National Guard was held in low esteem by the Haifa population both because of its repeated failures to match the Hagana's military successes, and, moreover, because of its implication in numerous acts of lawlessness, notably the plundering of deserted properties. Panic thus spread across the city, with many searching in vain for the odd removal van; those who were fortunate enough to find a vehicle had to pay an exorbitant price for a delivery to Nazareth; others, seeking to flee to Nablus were informed that the town was already swarming with refugees from Jerusalem, Jaffa and Haifa.[17]

III

Against this backdrop, the National Committee had apparently given up hope of stemming further flight. Shortly after the return of the delegation from Cairo, a proposal was passed urging improvements in the condition of Palestinian refugees in the states where they now found themselves, and requesting help in settling them there.[18] This was momentous indeed: the official leadership of the second largest Arab community in Mandate Palestine was not only condoning mass flight but suggesting that Arab refugee status be, however temporarily, institutionalized.

As the months passed and Britain's departure from Palestine neared, such views gained further currency. Even the Mufti, who had warned that 'the flight of ... families abroad will weaken the morale of our noble, struggling nation',[19] was not averse to the evacuation of the non-fighting populace. In March 1948, the AHC evidently ordered the removal of women and children from Haifa; a special committee was established in Syria and Lebanon to oversee the operation, and preparations began in earnest with the chartering of a ship from an Egyptian company.[20]

By early April 1948, according to Rashid Hajj Ibrahim, the city's Arab populace had dwindled to some 35,000–40,000, nearly two-thirds its size four months earlier. A week later a meeting of Haifa's trade, security and political leaders estimated the remaining population at half its original size (or about 31,000–33,000). And 'an Arab source', quoted by the Hebrew daily *Ha-aretz* on 14 April, set the number of Arab escapees at 30,000, leaving in the city some 32,000–36,000 souls.[21]

By now the National Committee had lost whatever vestiges of respect it had commanded. Most of its members fled the town in late March or early April, with its final session on 13 April attended by only four of its original 15 members.[22] In a strongly-worded letter to some of the absentees, Ibrahim threatened that unless they immediately returned to Haifa, the Committee would have to discuss their future;[23] yet he himself left for Egypt shortly after participating in the Committee's meeting of 1 April, never to return to the city in whose public life he had been actively involved for decades.

The Committee's unceremonious demise epitomized the wider disintegration of the Haifa Arab institutions. Arab municipal officialdom had practically withered away at a time when power was being devolved from the Mandatory Government to the local authorities; its absence being further underscored by Mayor Levy's plea to his Arab colleagues to return, widely interpreted in the Arab streets as indicating his greater concern for Arab interests than that of his Arab peers. The hundreds of foreign irregulars (Syrians, Iraqis, Transjordanians) arriving in late March proved to be more of a liability than an asset, spreading mayhem and lawlessness throughout the city. Relations were particularly acrimonious between the local population and the Iraqis – who gained notoriety as plunderers, womanizers and drunkards, and their officers – as seeking nothing more than the satisfaction of their hedonistic desires. In mid-April, about 100 National Guard troops deserted the city, with their weapons, having failed to receive their remuneration.[24]

By way of establishing his military credentials and arresting the Arab community's rapid fragmentation, Amin Izz al-Din, a former captain at Transjordan Frontier Force who assumed command over the city's defence in early April, moved onto the offensive.[25] In the afternoon hours of 15 April, a truck-load of explosives went off near the Haifa Flour Mills, killing one person and causing material damage; it was only Jewish suspicions of the truck driver that averted a greater loss of human life. Jewish vigilance proved more successful the following day, when yet another car bomb, seeking to infiltrate the residential area of Hadar Ha-carmel was stopped and disarmed. These bombing attempts were accompanied by a substantial intensification in fighting, so much so that in the afternoon hours of 16 April, the British Sixth Airborne Division, in charge of northern Palestine, recorded that 'firing in Haifa in general and Sit[uation] appears out of control. Where mil[itary] take action there is temporary quiet but firing soon starts again.'[26] Also, a battalion of the Hagana's Carmeli Brigade, deployed in northern Palestine, reported on the same day that 'in Haifa there is a general reinvigoration of enemy activities, manifested in numerous exchanges of fire in downtown Haifa and Hadar, and in a mortar attack. Four Jews were killed and another five wounded.'[27]

Two days later one of the Sixth Airborne Division's battalions in Haifa reported that 'considerable automatic and mortar fire went on till midnight from both sides with the Arabs mainly on the offensive'. In the early morning hours of 20 April, an Arab attack supported by mortar and machine-gun fire managed to penetrate the garden of the police station in Hadar Ha-carmel, the foremost Jewish neighbourhood in Haifa.[28]

IV

It was not long, however, before the Arab offensive backfired in grand style. For quite some time Major-General Hugh Stockwell, Commander of the Sixth Airborne Division had been deeply concerned about the ability of his forces to carry out their mission of securing the evacuation of British forces from Palestine, in which the port of Haifa figured prominently. Already on 1 March 1948 he had informed Lieutenant-General G.H.A. MacMillan, General Officer Commanding (GOC) the British forces in Palestine, of the inadequacy of the existing Haifa deployment and the required reinforcements 'to enable the final evacuation to be completed without hindrance, and to uphold the British prestige'.[29]

Now that the Arab offensive was seen as aimed at nothing short of penetrating Hadar Ha-carmel, Stockwell feared that a general conflagration was in the offing and decided to redeploy his forces in Haifa in fewer but better protected strategic points. He recognized that the vacation of certain areas entailed the obvious danger of an Arab–Jewish clash, yet considered such a move the least of all evils as the costs of the only viable alternative to prevent a major Arab–Jewish clash, namely the transfer of the British forces in the eastern Galilee to Haifa, exceeded by far its potential gains. For one thing, it was bound to force the Sixth Division:

> ...to fight both Jews and Arabs to quell their attacks; this would estrange very considerably my relations with the two contestants and might lead to determined attacks on all my troops by the Jewish dissident groups who at the moment are held in a measure of control by the Hagana.

For another thing, reasoned Stockwell, 'the Jewish offensive may be launched before I am concentrated in strength and I would then find it difficult to either reinforce the town or to withdraw from it without serious casualties'. Conversely, the redeployment of the Sixth Division in Haifa would secure certain routes and areas vital to the British withdrawal from Palestine, while at the same time safeguarding his troops as far as possible. This was primarily because:

> it would seem from intelligence reports that the Jews may well win this battle and gain control of Haifa in a short space of time. If this were to happen then the security of my forces and my evacuation would probably be considerably improved.[30]

Having received MacMillan's approval for his plan, Stockwell ordered his forces to redeploy to their new positions by first light of 21 April, taking care to ensure the use of the RAF 'if necessary to prevent any Jew or Arab aeroplane flying over this area and prevent either side [from] using long-range artillery in Haifa'. This was completed by 6 a.m., and four hours later Stockwell informed a Jewish delegation of this move and its operational ramifications. At 11a.m. he reiterated the same message to an Arab delegation. Urging the two delegations to stop the ongoing clashes 'if peace and order is to be maintained in Haifa', Stockwell stated his determination not 'to become involved in any way in these Arab–Jewish clashes'. He underscored the vital importance of the redeployment for the completion of the British evacuation of Palestine, as well as his resolve to 'take such measures as I may deem necessary at any time' to prevent interference by either community with his dispositions or with any of the municipal services in Haifa. On a more conciliatory note, Stockwell expressed his readiness:

> ...at all times to assist either community in any way they may desire for the maintenance of peace and order...It is my wish that the withdrawal of the British from Haifa shall be carried out smoothly and rapidly and that our good relations may continue in the future and that we may carry away the respect and comradeship of both Communities

he told his interlocutors as they were taking their leave.[31] This is not what happened. Hardly had the two delegations left Stockwell's office when the battle for the town was joined, as Arabs and Jews rushed to fill the vacuum left by the British departure.

V

For quite some time the two communities had been gearing up for the final battle over the city. In late March, at the height of Arab attacks on Haifa's Jewish community, the Hagana's Carmeli Brigade drew up a plan (code named Operation Scissors) envisaging a series of strikes against enemy bases, forces and arms depots. However, the brigade's involvement in combat operations elsewhere in north Palestine delayed the implementation of the plan, which was eventually set for 22 April regardless of the British military presence throughout the town. Once news of the British redeployment broke, Operation Scissors was immediately cancelled and an alternative plan was quickly implemented, aimed at opening up transportation routes to downtown Haifa by capturing Wadi Rushmiya, so as to secure the communication link between Haifa and the north of the country.[32]

These plans were countered by similarly elaborate planning on the Arab side. On 24 March, the Haifa National Committee was instructed by the Arab Higher Committee to draw up a list of personalities who would administer the town after the completion of the British withdrawal from Palestine. Four days later, the Arab League's Military Committee, in charge of Palestine operations, made the district of Haifa an independent operational unit answerable to the supreme command and assigned to it a detailed war plan. This envisaged the disruption of Jewish transportation throughout the district, attacks on Jewish urban and rural neighbourhoods, and initiated war operations against the Hagana forces, preferably through guerrilla warfare in mountainous areas.[33]

This plan had probably formed the basis of Izz al-Din's offensive of early and mid-April. However, when the moment of truth arrived, the commander of Arab Haifa failed to rise to the challenge. Shortly after his meeting with Stockwell on 21 April, Izz al-Din sailed out of Haifa, ostensibly to gather reinforcements. He was quickly followed by one of his deputies, Amin al-Nabhani, whereas the second deputy, Yunas Nafa, left the next day. 'Nafa's considerable [body] weight did not appear to have materially impeded his rate of progress', an Arab informant of the British ruefully commented.[34]

Whether these desertions stemmed from cowardice, as claimed at the time by embittered Arab fighters and refugees fleeing Haifa,[35] or from 'miscalculation' as suggested several years later by a Palestinian apologist for the exodus,[36] they had a devastating impact on Arab morale. News of the flight quickly spread across the city, fanned by the Arabic-language broadcasts of the Hagana, which provided its numerous Arab listeners with real-time information of these desertions, mainly obtained through the interception of phone conversations.

Knowledge of the desertion of the Haifa Arabs by their military commanders was not limited to the Hagana and the Arab community. The British also had real-time information of this development,[37] as did the American Haifa consulate,[38] and both deemed it the foremost cause of Arab collapse in Haifa. 'There was little unity of command in Haifa and as it transpired, the actual leaders left at the crucial stage,' wrote Stockwell on 24 April, in his report on the events leading to the Jewish occupation of Haifa.[39] Also, the American vice consul in Haifa, Aubrey Lippincott, who had spent the night before the crucial fight with the Arab fighters, reported on 23 April that:

> They were much too remote from their higher command…some fairly reliable sources state that the Arab higher command all left Haifa some hours before the battle took place…those Arabs who escaped and with whom this officer has talked all feel that they have been let down by their leaders. The blow to Arab confidence is tremendous.[40]

This point was well taken. The desertion of military commanders at the most critical moment can wreak havoc even on the best of armies; its impact on a weakened and disorientated society can be nothing short of catastrophic. Debilitated by months of fighting, deeply divided along religious, political and socio-economic lines, and lacking a coherent and accepted leadership, the depleted Arab community remaining in Haifa up to the final battle was simply too demoralized and disorientated to mount the final collective effort in its national defence, especially after the desertion of those charged with its defence. Describing this phenomenon in typical English understatement, Stockwell reported that 'I think local Arab opinion felt that the Jews would gain control if in fact they launched their offensive';[41] while a fortnightly intelligence report by the headquarters of the British forces in Palestine scathingly observed that 'the desertion of their leaders and the sight of so much cowardice in high places completely unnerved the inhabitants'.[42] And Lippincott put it in far harsher terms:

> The local Arabs are not 100 per cent behind the present effort. Those who are fighting are in small minority…It may be that the Haifa Arab, particularly the Christian Arab, is an exception, but generally speaking he is a coward and he is not the least bit interested in going out to fight his country's battles. He is definitely

counting on the interference of outside Arab elements to come in and settle this whole question for him.[43]

It was only a question of time, therefore, before this defeatist mood was translated into the all-too-familiar pattern of mass flight. Disorientated by the desertion of their leaders and petrified by wildly exaggerated accounts of an alleged Zionist atrocity at the village of Deir Yasin near Jerusalem (9 April),[44] the Haifa Arabs took to the road. In the early morning of 22 April, as Hagana forces battled their way to the downtown market area, thousands streamed into the port, still held by the British Army. Within hours, many of these had fled by trains and buses, while the rest awaited evacuation by sea.[45]

What was left of the local Arab leadership now asked the British military to stop the fighting. When this failed, a delegation requested a meeting with Stockwell 'with a view to obtaining a truce with the Jews'.[46] Having learned from Stockwell the Hagana's terms for such a truce, the delegates then left to consult with their peers, and pre-eminently with the Syrian consul in Haifa. In no time, the British ambassador in Damascus, P.M. Broadmead, was summoned to a meeting with Shukri al-Quwaitly, the President of Syria. 'An Arab delegation had seen the British Commander of the troops and had asked for intervention in order to stop [the] violent attack of the Jews against the Arabs,' said Quwaitly:

> The Commander had refused to intervene, to allow Arab help to enter the town or to takes measures to stop the killing of Arab women and children unless Arabs conclude a truce with [the] Hagana on conditions explained by the Commander, chief of which was the delivery of all arms to the Jews. Immediate instructions were asked for in view of the meeting between the Arab Delegation, [the] British Commander and the Jewish representatives at 4 p.m.

Quwaitly then expressed his bewilderment at the Jewish demand for the surrender of Arab weapons. Nor could he see what instructions he could send. What did the ambassador suggest?

Reminding the president that neither of them was familiar with the real situation on the ground, Broadmead begged Quwaitly 'to urge moderation and to take no action which would bring this local Haifa issue on to a wider plane'. To this, Quwaitly responded that he 'was very nervous concerning public opinion', yet refrained from any threat of military intervention.[47] Thus, no instructions from Damascus seem to have reached the Haifa truce delegation by four in the afternoon, when it met its Jewish counterpart at City Hall at 16.00.

There, after an impassioned plea for peace and reconciliation by the town's Jewish mayor, Shabtai Levy,[48] the assembled delegates went through the truce terms point by point, modifying a number of them to meet Arab objections. These included the retention (rather than the surrender, as demanded by the Hagana) of licensed arms by their Arab owners, as well as the extension of the deadline for the surrender of all other weapons from the three hours demanded by the Hagana to 19 hours – with a possible further extension to 24 hours at Stockwell's discretion. Most importantly, in view of the adamant Arab refusal to surrender their weapons to the Hagana, as demanded by the latter, it was agreed that the confiscated weapons would be 'held by the military in trust of the Hagana and will be handed to them at the discretion of the GOC North Sector not later than midnight 15/16 May 1948'. As for the Arabs' future status, they were to 'carry on their work as equal and free citizens of Haifa'.[49]

At this stage the Arabs requested a 24-hour recess 'to give them the opportunity to contact their brothers in the Arab states'.[50] Although this was deemed unacceptable, a briefer break was agreed and the meeting adjourned at 5.20.

When the Arabs returned that evening at 7.15, they had a surprise in store: as Stockwell would later put it in his official report, they stated:

> ...that they were not in a position to sign the truce, as they had no control over the Arab military elements in the town and that, in all sincerity, they could not fulfil the terms of the truce, even if they were to sign.

Then they offered, 'as an alternative, that the Arab population wished to evacuate Haifa and that they would be grateful for military assistance'.[51]

This came as a bombshell. With tears in his eyes, the elderly Levy pleaded with the Arabs, most of whom were his personal acquaintances, to reconsider, saying that they were committing 'a cruel crime against their own people'. Yaacov Salomon, a prominent Haifa lawyer and the Hagana's chief liaison officer in the city, followed suit, assuring the Arab delegates that he 'had the instructions of the commander of the zone... that if they stayed on they would enjoy equality and peace, and that we, the Jews, were interested in their staying on and the maintenance of harmonious relations'. Even the stoic Stockwell was shaken. 'You have made a foolish decision', he thundered at the Arabs:

> Think it over, as you'll regret it afterward. You must accept the
> conditions of the Jews. They are fair enough. Don't permit life to
> be destroyed senselessly. After all, it was you who began the fight-
> ing, and the Jews have won.[52]

However, the Arabs were unmoved. The next morning, they met with
Stockwell and his advisers to discuss the practicalities of the evacuation.
Of the 30,000-plus Arabs still in Haifa, only a handful, they said, wished
to stay. Perhaps the British could provide 80 trucks a day, and in the
meantime ensure an orderly supply of foodstuffs in the city and its envi-
rons? At this, an aide to Stockwell erupted, 'If you sign your truce you
would automatically get all your food worries over. You are merely starv-
ing your own people.' 'We will not sign,' the Arabs retorted. 'All is
already lost, and it does not matter if everyone is killed so long as we do
not sign the document.'[53]

Within a matter of days, only about 3,000 of Haifa's Arab residents
remained in the city.

VI

What had produced the seemingly instantaneous sea change from
explicit interest in a truce to its rejection only a few hours later? In an
address to the UN Security Council on 23 April, Jamal al-Husseini of
the AHC contended that the Arabs in Haifa had been 'presented with
humiliating conditions and preferred to abandon all their possessions
and leave'.[54] However, this was not so: not only had the Arab leadership
in Haifa and elsewhere been apprised of the Hagana's terms several
hours before the meeting on 22 April, but, as we have seen, the Arab delegates to the meeting had proceeded to negotiate on the basis of those
terms and had succeeded in modifying several key elements.

Later writers have spoken of 'a Jewish propaganda blitz' aimed at
frightening the Arabs into fleeing. Yet the only evidence offered for this
'blitz' is a single sentence from a book by the Jewish writer Arthur
Koestler, who was not even in Palestine at the time of the battle for
Haifa but (in his own words) 'pieced together the improbable story of
the conquest by the Jews of this key harbour' about a week after his
arrival on 4 June – that is, nearly two months after the event.[55] As against
this isolated second-hand account, there is an overwhelming body of
evidence from contemporary Arab, Jewish, British and American
sources to prove that, far from seeking to drive the Arabs out of Haifa,

the Jewish authorities went to considerable lengths to convince them to stay.

This effort was hardly confined to Levy and Salomon's impassioned pleas at the City Hall. The Hagana's armistice terms stipulated that Arabs were expected to 'carry on their work as equal and free citizens of Haifa'.[56] In its Arabic-language broadcasts and communications, the Hagana consistently articulated the same message. On 22 April, at the height of the fighting, it distributed an Arabic-language circular noting its ongoing campaign to clear the town of all 'criminal foreign bands' so as to allow the restoration of 'peace and security and good neighbourly relations among all of the town's inhabitants'. 'We implore you again to keep your women, children, and the elderly from dangerous places', read the circular, 'and to keep yourselves away from the centres of the bands which are still subjected to our retaliatory action. We do not wish to shed the innocent blood of the town's peace-loving inhabitants'.[57]

The following day, a Hagana broadcast asserted that 'the Jews did, and do still, believe that it is in the real interests of Haifa for its citizens to go on with their work and to ensure that normal conditions are restored to the city'. On 24 April a Hagana radio broadcast declared:

> Arabs, we do not wish to harm you. Like you, we only want to live in peace. Like you, we want to expel all imperialists from our country. If the Jews and [the] Arabs co-operate, no Power in the world will ever attack our country or ignore our rights.

Two days later, informing its Arab listeners that 'Haifa has returned to normal[cy]', the Hagana reported that 'between 15,000 and 20,000 Arabs had expressed their willingness to remain in the city', that 'Arab employees had been appointed to key posts such as that looking after Arab property, religious matters and other work', and that Arabs had been given 'part of the corn, flour and rice intended for the Jews in Haifa'. Also on 27 April, the Hagana distributed an Arabic-language leaflet urging the fleeing Arab population to return to their homes: 'Peace and order reign supreme across the town and every resident can return to his free life and to resume his regular work in peace and security.'[58]

That these were no hollow words was evidenced, *inter alia*, by the special dispensation given to Jewish bakers by the Haifa rabbinate to bake bread during the Passover holiday for distribution among the Arabs, and by the 23 April decision of the joint Jewish–Arab Committee for the Restoration of Life to Normalcy to dispatch two of its members to inform women, children and the elderly that they could return home.[59] In a 6 May fact-finding report to the Jewish Agency Executive (the effective government of Jewish Palestine), Golda Meir, Acting Head of the Jewish Agency's Political Department, told her colleagues that while:

> ...we will not go to Acre or Nazareth to return the Arabs [to Haifa]...our behaviour should be such that if it were to encourage them to return – they would be welcome; we should not mistreat the Arabs so as to deter them from returning.[60]

The sincerity of the Jewish position is also attested by reports from the US consulate in Haifa. Thus, on 25 April, after the fighting was over, Vice-Consul Lippincott cabled Washington that the 'Jews hope poverty will cause labourers [to] return [to] Haifa as many are already doing despite Arab attempts [to] persuade them [to] keep out'. And the following day: '[The] Jews want them [to] remain for political reasons to show democratic treatment they will get [and] also need them for labour although [the] Jews claim latter not essential.' On 29 April, according to Lippincott, even Farid Saad of the Arab National Committee was saying that the Jewish leaders 'have organized a large propaganda campaign to persuade [the] Arabs to return'.[61]

Similarly, on 25 April, a British report asserted that:

> At this sub-committee [that is, the joint Jewish–Arab Committee for the Restoration of Life to Normalcy] [the] Jews, fearing for the economic future of the town, pressed [the] Arabs to reconsider their decision of complete evacuation; and [the] matter is still under discussion.[62]

The following day, the British district Superintendent of Police reported that:

> Every effort is being made by the Jews to persuade the Arab populace to stay and carry on with their normal lives, to get their shops and businesses open and to be assured that their lives and interests will be safe.

On 28 April he reported that 'the Jews are still making every effort to persuade the Arab populace to remain and settle back into their normal lives in the town'. For its part, the Sixth Airborne Division recorded in its logbook on 1 May 1948, that the 'Jews in Haifa [are] now trying to get better relations with [the] Arabs and are encouraging them to return to the town'. A field security weekly report from the same day noted that:

> The Jews have been making strenuous efforts to check the stream

of refugees, in several cases resorting to actual intervention by [the] Hagana. Appeals have been made on the radio and in the press, urging Arabs to remain in the town. [The] Hagana issued a pamphlet along these lines, and the Histadruth in a similar publication appealed to those Arabs previously members of their organization to return. On the whole, [the] Arabs remain indifferent to this propaganda and their attitude to the present situation is one of apathetic resignation.[63]

Several more reports in the same vein were sent by the British authorities in Palestine to their superiors in London. On 25 April, for example, General Sir Alan Cunningham, the High Commissioner for Palestine, reported that at the Jewish–Arab Committee established following the Arab decision to evacuate Haifa, under the Mayor's chairmanship, the 'Jews fearing for the economic future of the town, pressed [the] Arabs to reconsider their decision of complete evacuation'. A fortnight later, Cyril Marriott, the British Consul-Designate in Haifa, reported that:

> They [that is, the Jews] obviously want the Arab labour to return and are doing their best to instil confidence. Life in [the] town is normal even last night except of course for the absence of Arabs. I see no reason why [the] Palestine Arab residents of Haifa should not return.

And a fortnightly intelligence report by the headquarters of the British forces in Palestine reported that:

> If it had not been for [the] conference held under the auspices of the British authorities (which included representatives from both communities), together with great efforts made by the Jews themselves and the voluntary return of a very small number of Arabs who had met with a cold reception in their places of asylum, the position in Haifa would have been a great deal worse than it now is.[64]

In fact, it was a commonplace perception among contemporary observers that the perseverance of the Arabs in Haifa, or their return home, would constitute a Jewish victory whereas their departure would amount to a Jewish setback. As reported by the United Press (UP) correspondent in Haifa, Mano Dierkson:

> The shooting battle was followed by a political campaign between the Arabs and the Jews. The Arab leaders ordered the town's complete evacuation whereas the Jewish leaders felt that such a development would be a tremendous defeat for them...Should the

situation remain calm, there is little doubt that many Arabs will stay despite the evacuation order by the Arab leadership, and one can hear many Arabs expressing their decision to stay. Jewish leaders walked around the Arab quarters today, talking to the Arab leaders who were busy urging their congregation to leave. It would seem today that the Arabs may well lose the political campaign just as they had lost the military campaign last Wednesday.[65]

VII

Meanwhile, however, as the Jews were attempting to keep the Arabs in Haifa, an *ad-hoc* body, the Arab Emergency Committee, was doing its best to get them out. Scaremongering was a major weapon in its arsenal. Some Arab residents received written threats that, unless they left town, they would be branded as traitors deserving of death.[66] Others were told they could expect no mercy from the Jews. Sheikh Abd al-Rahman Murad of the National Committee, who had headed the truce-negotiating team, proved particularly effective at this latter tactic: on 23 April he warned a large group of escapees from the neighbourhood of Wadi Nisnas, who were about to return to their homes, that if they did so they would all be killed, as the Jews spared not even women and children. On the other hand, he continued, the Arab Legion had 200 trucks ready to transfer the Haifa refugees to a safe haven, where they would be given free accommodation, clothes and food.[67]

The importance of these actions cannot be overstated. The Emergency Committee was not a random collection of self-appointed vigilantes, as some Palestinian apologists would later argue. Rather, it was the successor to the Haifa National Committee and comprised two National Committee members: Farid Saad and Sheikh Murad. In other words, *the evacuation of the Haifa Arab community was ordered, and executed, by the Arab Higher Committee's official local representatives.* The only question is whether those representatives did what they did on their own, or under specific instructions from above.

As indicated earlier, the Haifa leaders had been extremely reluctant to accept or reject the Hagana's truce terms on their own recognizance: hence the initial appeal to their peers, and hence the request for a 24-hour recess to seek the advice of the Arab States. When this was not granted, and the Committee had to make do with the brief respite granted to it, its delegates proceeded to telephone the AHC office in Beirut for instructions. They were told explicitly not to sign, but rather to evacuate. Astonished, the Haifa delegates protested, but were assured that 'it is only a matter of days' before Arab retaliatory action would commence, and 'since there will be a lot of casualties following our intended action...you [would] be held responsible for the casualties among the Arab population left in the town'.

This entire conversation was secretly recorded by the Hagana, and its substance was passed on to the Jewish negotiators at City Hall.[68] In retrospect, it helps to explain a defiant comment made at the meeting by the Arab delegates after they announced the intended evacuation – namely, that 'they had lost [the] first round but...there were more to come'.[69] It also sheds light on Golda Meir's assessment of the future of the Haifa Arab community in her report to the JAE on 6 May 1948. Having told her colleagues of her personal distress at the sight of the Arab exodus, she added:

> For my part I think that whether or not the Arabs will remain in Haifa will not depend on our behaviour but rather on the instructions they will receive from their leaders. Until now the Arab leaders have said: 'Leave Haifa, we will bomb it, we will send [our] army there and we do not want you to be hurt.' Should they receive different orders from Damascus and Amman, they will act accordingly.[70]

From Yaacov Salomon, one of the Jewish negotiators, we also learn of certain other emotions experienced by his Arab interlocutors:

> The Arab delegation arrived at the evening meeting under British escort, but when the meeting broke up they asked me to give them a lift and to take them home. I took them in my car.
>
> On the way back they told me that they had instructions not to sign the truce and that they could not sign the truce on any terms, as this would mean certain death at the hands of their own people, particularly the Muslim leaders, guided by the Mufti. While therefore they would remain in town, as they thought that would be best in their own interests, they had to advise the Arabs to leave.[71]

In any case, what the Hagana had learned by covert means became public knowledge within days. Already on 25 April the American consulate in Haifa was reporting that the 'local Mufti-dominated Arab leaders urge all Arabs [to] leave [the] city and large numbers [are] going'. Three days later it was more specific: 'Reportedly [the] Arab Higher Committee [is] ordering all Arabs [to] leave'.[72] Writing on the same day to the colonial secretary in London, Sir Alan Cunningham was equally forthright: 'British authorities in Haifa have formed the impression that [the] total evacuation is being urged on the Haifa Arabs from higher Arab quarters and that the townsfolk themselves are against it.'[73] Finally, a British intelligence report summing up the events of the week judged that, had it not been for the incitement and scaremongering of the Haifa Arab leadership, most Arab residents might well have stayed:

> After the Jews had gained control of the town, and in spite of a subsequent food shortage, many would not have responded to the call for a complete evacuation but for the rumours and propaganda spread by the National Committee members remaining in the town. Most widespread was a rumour that Arabs remaining in Haifa would be taken as hostages by [the] Jews in the event of future attacks on other Jewish areas: and an effective piece of propaganda with its implied threat of retribution when the Arabs recapture the town, is that [those] people remaining in Haifa acknowledged tacitly that they believe in the principle of a Jewish State. It is alleged that Victor Khayyat is responsible for these reports.[74]

VIII

Without a past there can be no future. Today, as the saga of Israel's birth is being turned upside down, with aggressors portrayed as hapless victims and victims as aggressors, it can be only a matter of time before the Jewish State is presented with the bill for its alleged crimes against the Palestinian refugees. Indeed, in May 2000, as part of the commemoration of the fifty-second anniversary of the 1948 War (in Palestinian parlance, *al-Nakba*, the catastrophe), Yasser Arafat's Palestinian Authority attempted to link any final-status settlement with Israel to the return of refugees to their homes in Haifa and Jaffa. Organized tours brought scores of Palestinians to locations in Israel abandoned in 1948, and the Arab-language Jerusalem newspaper *al-Quds* bemoaned 'the uprooting of the Palestinian people in one of the worst crimes of modern history'.

However, were they uprooted; and, if so, by whom? In Haifa, one of the largest and most dramatic locales of the Palestinian exodus, not only had half the Arab community fled the city before the final battle was joined, but another 5,000–15,000 left voluntarily during the fighting while the rest, some 15,000–25,000 souls, were ordered or bullied into leaving against their wishes on the instructions of the Arab Higher Committee. The crime was exclusively of Arab making. There was no

Jewish grand design to force this departure, nor was there a psychological 'blitz'. To the contrary, both the Haifa Jewish leadership and the Hagana went to great lengths to convince the Arabs to stay.

These efforts, indeed, reflected the wider Jewish attitude in Palestine. *All* deliberations of the Jewish leadership regarding the transition to statehood were based on the assumption that, in the Jewish State that would arise with the termination of the British Mandate, Palestine's Arabs would remain as equal citizens.

And just there, no doubt, lay the reason why the Arab leadership preferred the evacuation of Haifa's Arabs to any truce with the Hagana. For, according to the UN Partition Resolution, Haifa was to be one of the foremost towns of the new Jewish State; hence, any agreement by its Arab community to live under Jewish rule would have amounted to acquiescence in Jewish statehood in a part of Palestine. This, to both the Palestinian leadership and the Arab world at large, was anathema.

Shortly after the fall of Haifa to the Hagana, Abd al-Rahman Azzam, the secretary-general of the Arab League, declared: 'The Zionists are seizing the opportunity to establish a Zionist state against the will of the Arabs. The Arab peoples have accepted the challenge and soon they will close their account with them.'[75] At the time, the cost of this fiery determination of the Arab peoples to 'close their account' with the Zionists included the driving of tens of thousands of their hapless fellow-Arabs from their homes. This simple, incontrovertible fact has never been acknowledged in the Arab world. Instead, and in moral collusion with many war-weary Israelis, responsibility for the 1948 Arab aggression and its tragic consequences has been placed squarely on the shoulders of the Zionists themselves.

So the account lies open. Today, Hanan Ashrawi, Fawaz Turki and a host of others are keeping faith with the spirit of Abd al-Rahman Azzam. It only remains to be seen whether the descendants of the Jews who in 1948 pleaded with Haifa's Arabs to stay will keep faith with the truth, and act on it.

NOTES

1. Reprinted from *Commentary* (July–August 2000), and *Middle Eastern Studies* (October 2001), by permission; all rights reserved.
2. British Government for Palestine, *Village Statistics, 1945, Haifa Sub-District* (Jerusalem, 1945); British Government for Palestine, *A Survey of Palestine: Prepared in December 1945 and January 1946 for the Information of the Anglo-American Committee of Inquiry* Vol. 1 (Jerusalem, n.d.), pp. 151, 696.
3. Sixth Airborne Division, 'Weekly Intelligence Summary N. 61, Based on Information

Received up to 23 October 1947', WO 275/60, p. 3. For a similar report issued a fort-night later *see* HQ British Troops in Palestine, 'Fortnightly Intelligence Newsletter No. 54', 8 November 1947, WO 275/64, p. 2.

4. Sixth Airborne Division, Historical Section: GHQ MELF, 'Weekly Intelligence Review', issued on 21 November 1947, WO 275/120, No. 138.

5. David Ben-Gurion, *Yoman Ha-milhama, Tashah-Tashat*, Vol. 1 (Tel Aviv, 1982), entry for 5 January 1948, p. 114. The Hagana's Arab sources put the number of escapees by mid-January 1948 at 25,000; while the Hagana's intelligence officer in Haifa gave the somewhat lower figure of 20,000. In the estimate of a delegation of the Haifa National Committee to the Mufti in late January 1948, some 12,000–15,000 Arabs had fled the town. *See*, 'Tene News: 2, 3 and 4 Jnauary 1948', HA 105/61, p. 158; Ben-Gurion, *Yoman Ha-milhama*, Vol. 1, 22 January 1948, p. 177; 'To Our Comrades – Daily Information Bulletin No. 5', Haifa, 12 December 1947, HA 105/61, p. 45; 'Yishuv Circular No. 18', 6 February 1948, Irgun Archive (hereinafter IA), K4-31/1/12.

6. 'Tene News', 11 and 25 December 1947, 2–5 January 1948, HA, 105/61, pp. 43, 84, 155, 158, 164; 'To Our Comrades: a Daily Information Bulletin, No. 16', Haifa, 26 December 1947, *ibid.*, p. 91; 'Tene News - Daily Brief', 12 January 1948, HA 105/61a, p. 32; Muhammad Nimr al-Khatib, *Min Athar al-Nakba* (Damascus, 1951), pp. 247, 276; Ben-Gurion, *Yoman Ha-milhama*, Vol. 1, 5 January 1948, p. 114; 317 Airborne Field Security Section, 'Report No. 63 for the Week Ending 21 January 48', paragraph 8, WO 275/79.

7. *See*, for example, 'Protocol of the Haifa National Committee's 9th Meeting, Held at the Residence of Hajj Muhammad al-Awwa on 16 December 1947', HA 100/60, p. 15; 'Protocol of the Haifa National Committee's Eleventh Meeting, Held at the Committee's Office on Sunday, 21 December 1947', *ibid.*, p. 18; 'Protocol of the Haifa National Committee's Fourteenth Meeting, Held at the Committee's Office on 26 December 1947', *ibid.*, p. 22; 'Protocol of the Haifa National Committee's 15th Meeting, Held at the Committee's Office on 30 December 1947', *ibid.*, p. 22; 'Protocol of the Haifa National Committee's Twenty-fifth Meeting, Held at the Committee's Office on Tuesday, 27 January 1948', *ibid.*, p. 42; 'Protocol of the Haifa National Committee's Thirty-first Meeting, Held on 9 March 1948', *ibid.*, p. 51; 'Protocol of the Haifa National Committee's Thirty-second Meeting, Held at the Committee's Office on Tuesday, 16 March 1948', *ibid.*, p. 55; 'Protocol of the Haifa National Committee's Thirty-seventh Meeting, Held at the Committee's Office on Tuesday, 13 April 1948', *ibid.*, p. 59.

8. 317 Airborne Field Security Section, 'Report No. 63 for the Week Ending 21 January 48', paragraph 8d, WO 275/79. See also *Mudhakkirat Taha al-Hashimi. Al-Juz' al-Thani: 1946–1955 – al-Iraq, Surya, al-Qadiyya al-Filastiniyya* (Beirut, 1978), p. 173.

9. 'Protocol of the Haifa National Committee's Sixth Meeting, Held at the Islamic Committee Centre on Friday, 12 December 1947', HA 100/60, p. 10; 'Protocol of the Haifa National Committee's Seventh Meeting, Held at the Islamic Committee Centre on Saturday, 13 December 1947', *ibid.*, p. 11. *See also* al-Khatib, *Min Athar al-Nakba*, p. 150–1; Bayan Nuwayhad al-Hut, *al-Qiyadat wa-l-Mu'asasat al-Syasiya fi Filastin. 1917–1948* (Beirut, 1986), p. 628.

10. 'To Tene from Hiram', 18 January 1948, HA 105/32a, p. 18; 'Report on the Haifa Situation on Friday, 16 January 1948', *ibid.*, p. 23; 'Hiram, 19 January 1948', *ibid.*, p. 25; 'Report on Developments Among the Haifa Arabs during January 1948', 1 February 1948, HA 105/69, pp. 272–3; HA 105/61a, p. 112; 317 Airborne Field Security Section,

'Report No. 62 for the Week Ending 14 January 1948', paragraph 8e and 'Report No. 63 for the Week Ending 21 January 1948, pp. 1, 3–5, both in WO 275/79.

11. 'Protocol of the Haifa National Committee's Twenty-second Meeting', HA 100/60, pp. 36–7; 'Tene News – Daily Brief', 20 January 1948, HA 105/61a, pp. 98, 105; 'Developments Among the Arabs', 22 January 1948, HA 105/54, p. 108; 'A Report on Developments in Haifa on the 20.1', HA, 105/72, p. 62; Hadad to Adina, 'Details of Notes Taken Yesterday and Today of Various Conversations with Arabs Held in Haifa during the Last Couple of Days', entry for 19 January 1948, pp. 4–5, Central Zionist Archives (hereinafter CZA), S25/7721.

12. 'Protocol of the Haifa National Committee's Twenty-fifth meeting, Held at the Committee's Headquarters on Tuesday, 27 January 1948', HA 100/60, pp. 40–1; Hiram-Nagid, 'The Mufti and Haifa', HA 105/54a, p. 24; 'Yishuv Circular No. 18, 6 February 1948', IA, K4-31/1/12; Hadad to Adina, 'On the Haifa Situation: the Delegation to Egypt', 31 January 1948, CZA, S25/7721; 'Fortnightly Intelligence Newsletter No. 61, issued by HQ British Troops in Palestine, for the period 23.59 hours 28 January – 23.59 hours 11 February 1948', 13 February 1948, WO 275/64, p. 3.

13. 317 Airborne Field Security Section, 'Report No. 65 for the Week Ending 4 February 1948', paragraph 8c and 'Report No. 66 for the Week Ending 11 February 1948', paragraph 8b, both in WO 275/79; 'Protocol of the Haifa National Committee's Twenty-fifth Meeting, pp. 41–2; 'Tene News: Daily Brief', 2 February 1948, 105/61a, p. 152; 'Report on Developments Among the Haifa Arabs during January 1948', 1 February 1948, HA 105/69, pp. 273–4; 'Tene News', 12 and 23 February 1948, HA 105/98, pp. 15, 25.

14. Hiram to Tene, 'Report on the Haifa Situation', 10 and 13 February 1948, HA 105/32a, pp. 65, 71; Hiram to Tene, 15 February 1948, *ibid.*, p. 73; Hiram to Tene, 'Various News Items', 18 February 1948, *ibid.*, p. 83; 'Tene News', 18 and 22 February 1948, HA 105/98, pp. 21, 24.

15. 317 Airborne Field Security Section, 'Report No. 68 for the Week Ending 25 February 1948', paragraph 8, WO 275/79.

16. Hajj Amin al-Husseini to the Haifa National Committee, 12 February 1948, No. 608, IDFA, 20/1/57 (captured Arab documents).

17. *See*, for example, Hiram to Tene, 'Summary of Ahitofel-Nitzoz News from 20 February 1948', HA 105/32a, p. 87; Hiram to Tene, 'Report on the Haifa Situation on Friday, 20 February', *ibid.*, p. 90; Hiram to Tene, 'Report on the Haifa Situation on Saturday, 21 February', *ibid.*, p. 89; Hiram, 23, 24, 25 February 1948, *ibid.*, pp. 98–9; Hiram to Tene, 'Report on the Haifa Situation on Friday, 27 February', *ibid.*, p. 102; 'Tene News', 25 February 1948, HA 105/98, p. 29; report by Hiram, 7 March 1948, HA 105/257, p. 55.

18. 'Protocol of the Haifa National Committee's Twenty-fifth Meeting, Held at the Committee's Headquarters on Tuesday, 27 January 1948', HA 100/60, p. 42.

19. Hajj Amin al-Husseini to Rashid Hajj Ibrahim, 13 March 1948, IDFA, 20/1/57 (captured Arab documents).

20. *See*, for example, Hiram to Tene, 'Vacation of Women and Children from Haifa', 8 March 1948; HA 105/257 p. 1; Hiram, 'Vacation of Women', 10 March 1948 and Dr Yatsliah, 'Haifa', 10 March 1948, *ibid.*, p. 112; Hiram, untitled report on AHC instructions to vacate women, children and the elderly, 17 March 1948 and 'Transfer of Children to Beirut', 14 March 1948, *ibid.*, p. 108; Hiram, untitled report on the evacuation, *ibid.*; 'Tene News', 21 March 1948, HA 105/98, p. 53; 'Precis of Hiram News', 25 March 1948, HA, 105/143, p. 121.

21. Hiram to Tene, 'The Food [Situation] in the Town', 6 April 1948, HA 105/257, p. 53; Haifa National Committee, 'Protocol of a Meeting at the Arab Bank, 12 April 1948', HA 105/400, p. 45; *Ha-aretz*, 14 April 1948, p. 4.
22. *See*, 'Protocol of the Haifa National Committee's Thirty-sixth meeting, Held at the Committee's Headquarters on Tuesday, 13 April 1948', 100/60, p. 59.
23. Hiram to Tene, 'Various Messages from Abu Zaidan', 5 April 1948, HA 105/257, p. 52.
24. Hiram, 2 April 1948, HA 105/257, p. 23; Hiram-Kafri, untitled report, 20 April 1948, *ibid.*, p. 57; Hiram-Farid, untitled report, 8 April 1948, *ibid.*; 'Tene News', 25 and 26 March 1948, HA 105/98, pp. 59–60.
25. '257 and 317 FS Section Weekly Report No. 2 for Week Ending 21 April 1948', pp. 1–2, WO 275/79.
26. Logbook of the Sixth Airborne Division, 15 April 1948, Sheet 65, Serials 283 and 284; 16 April 1948, Sheet 69, Serial 306 (see also serials 307, 314, 316, 323, 350, 352, 366, 380, 385, 386, 387 and 399 of 16 20 April 1948), Liddell Hart Centre for Military Archives, King's College London, Stockwell Collection, 6/17; *Davar* and *Ha-aretz*, 14, 16 and 18 April 1948.
27. Carmeli Brigade, 'Summary of Events', 16 April 1948, 09.00, David Ben-Gurion Archive, Sde Boqer (hereinafter BGA).
28. First Battalion Coldstream Guards, 'Battalion Sitrep, No. 13, 19 April 1948, 16.30 hours', WO 261/297; Logbook of the Sixth Airborne Division, 20 April 1948, Sheet 90, Serial 399. For descriptions of the clashes see also *Falastin*, 10, 11 and 14 April 1948; *al-Difa'a*, 14, 15 and 19 April 1948; *Ha-aretz*, 11, 12, 15, 18 and 19 April 1948.
29. Stockwell to HQ, Palestine, 'Withdrawal from Palestine', 1 March 1948, annex in Lieutenant-General G.H.A. MacMillan, 'Palestine: Narrative of Events from February 1947 until Withdrawal of all British Troops', Stockwell Collection 6/25/2, Liddell Hart Centre for Military Archives, King's College London.
30. 'Appreciation of the situation by Major General H.C. Stockwell CB, CBE, DSO, at 09.00 hours 20 April 1948 at Haifa', Stockwell Collection, 6/13, pp. 1–3.
31. For the text of Stockwell's message see his: 'To:- The Arab and Jewish Executives in Haifa', 21 April 1948, Stockwell Collection, 6/13.
32. Second Brigade (Carmeli), Battalion 22, 'War Diary', entries for 20 and 21 April 1948, IDFA 389/721/72.
33. From Hiram, 'Report on Events in Haifa on Wednesday, 24 March 1948', 28 March 1948, IDFA 152/7249/49; General Headquarters of the Palestine Forces, 'Operational Orders: Specifically for the Commander of the Haifa District', 28 March 1948, and 'Operational Order No. 1 Regarding the Establishment of an Independent Headquarters in the Haifa District', 28 March 1948, IDFA, 64/100001/57 (captured Arab documents).
34. al-Khatib, *Min Athar al-Nakba*, p. 265; Stockwell Report, p. 4, paragraph 14; Hiram to Tene, 'News Bulletin', 21 April 1948, HA 105/143, p. 282; '257 and 317 FS Section Weekly Report No. 3 for Week Ending 28 April 1948', paragraph 4, WO 275/79.
35. *See*, for example, Hiram to Tene, 'News Bulletin', 23 April 1948, HA 105/149, p. 287; Hiram to Tene, 'General Moods', 25 April 1948, HA 105/257, p. 355; Lippincott (American Consulate, Haifa) to the Secretary of State, Airgram A-5, 23 April 1948, p. 3, NA Record Group 84, Haifa Consulate, 800 – Political Affairs.
36. Walid Khalidi, 'Why did the Palestinians Leave? An Examination of the Zionist Version of the Exodus of 1948', Information Paper No. 3 (London, n.d.), p. 22.
37. *See*, for example, NorthSec to Troopers, 23 April 1948, 0030, Stockwell Collection,

6/13.

38. *See*, for example, Lippincott (American Consulate, Haifa) to Secretary of State, Airgram A-5, 23 April 1948, pp. 2–3, NA Record Group 84, Haifa Consulate, 800 – Political Affairs; and his telegram 33 of the same day (13.00 hours), *ibid.*

39. Stockwell Report, p. 5, paragraph 14e.

40. Lippincott, airgram A-5 of 23 April 1948.

41. Stockwell Report, p. 5, paragraph 14d.

42. 'Fortnightly Intelligence Newsletter No. 67, issued by HQ British Troops in Palestine, for the period 23.59 hrs 19 April – 23.59 hours 3 May 48', WO 275/64, p. 1.

43. Lippincott's airgram A-5 of 23 April 1948.

44. *See*, for example, *Falastin*, 13, 14 and 16 April 1948; *al-Difa'a*, 11, 12, 13, 14, 15 and 16 April 1948. *See also* Radio Jerusalem in Arabic to the Middle East, 13 April 1948 and Radio Damascus, 14 April 1948, in FBIS, *European Section: Near and Middle East – North African Transmitters*, 15 April 1948, pp. II4; *al-Sharq al-Adna* (Jerusalem), 15 April 1948, *ibid.*, 16 April 1948, p. II5 (hereinafter FBIS). *See also* Hiram to Karmeli, 'News Bulletin, 23 April 1948' noting the impact of Deir Yasin as a cause of the mass flight (HA 105/149, p. 286).

     In a BBC documentary on the fiftieth anniversary of the State of Israel, Hazem Nusseiba, in 1948 a broadcaster of the Palestine-Arab radio, lamented the broadcasting of wildly exaggerated descriptions of the Deir Yasin tragedy, notably the alleged raping of women, which had never taken place. In his account it was the Secretary of the Arab Higher Command, Dr Hussein Khalidi, who personally drafted these announcements, despite his keen awareness of their falsehood, so as to maximize Arab political gain of this tragic episode. This scare mongering, in Nusseiba's opinion, backfired in grand style by generating mass flight from Arab villages across the country. See BBC 2, *The Fifty Years War: Israel and the Arabs*, programme 1, broadcast on 15 March 1998.

45. Logbook of the Sixth Airborne Division, 22 April 1948, Sheet 101, Serials 444 and 446; Sheet 102, Serial 450; 'Intelligence Diary: the Occupation of Haifa', entry for 22 April 1948, 0805, IDFA 1/815/49.

46. Stockwell Report, p. 5, paragraph 15. *See also* Northsec to Troopers, 23 April 1948, Stockwell Collection, 6/13; report by the superintendent of the District Police, 'General situation – Haifa District', 23 April 1948.

47. Broadmead (Damascus) to Foreign Office, telegram 203, 22 April 1948, 11.58 a.m., FO 371/68544/E5019; Broadmead (Damascus) to Foreign Office, telegram 204, 22 April 1948, 3.14 p.m., FO 371/68544/E5028.

48. 'Précis of a Meeting Held in the Town Hall Haifa between the Representatives of the Arab and Jewish Communities under the Chairmanship of the GOC North Sector on 22 April', Appendix 'A' to HQ North Sector letter 383/G (Ops), dated 24 March 1948, Stockwell Collection, 6/15, p. 1.

49. For the original terms of the truce and the amended version see: 'Terms of the Hagana Command for a Truce in Haifa', Haifa 22 April 48, Annexure I: to HQ North Sector letter 383/G (Ops) dated 24 March 1948, Stockwell Collection, 6/15; 'Terms of the Hagana Command for a Truce in and Applicable to Haifa, between Jews and Arabs, Haifa, 22 April 48', Annexure II: to HQ North Sector letter 383/G (Ops) dated 24 March 1948, Stockwell Collection, 6/15.

50. Arab Emergency Committee, 'Mudhakkira Hawla Hujum al-Yahud', p. 8.

51. Stockwell Report, p. 6, paragraph 24; Beilin, 'Operation Haifa', p. 2. In reporting on the City Hall negotiations, the Arabic daily *Falastin* noted laconically that the Arab del-

egates 'did not sign on any of these [that is, the Hagana's] terms and only agreed on evacuation [of the city]'. *Falastin*, 24 April 1948, p. 1.

52. Salomon's report to the Political Department, Israel's Foreign Office, 1 April 1949, ISA, FM 2401/11; Beilin, 'Operation Haifa', pp. 2–3; recollection of Abraham Kalfon (participant in the truce negotiations), 24 February 1972, HA, File 284 (David Nativ's personal archive), p. 27; Dan Kurzman, *Genesis 1948: The First Arab–Israeli War* (New York, 1972), pp. 191–2; Moshe Carmel, *Maarachot Tsafon* (Tel Aviv, 1949), p. 107.

53. Marriott Report, paragraphs 18–21; undated précis of a meeting between Stockwell and his advisers with the Arab delegation (held on 23 April), Stockwell Collection, 6/13; Elias Koussa's (a member of the Arab delegation) conversation with a correspondent of the *Jewish Observer and Middle East Review*, 18 September 1959.

54. From Secretary of State for the Colonies to High Commissioner for Palestine, 24 April 1948, Cunningham Collection, III/4/23. Bayan Nuwayhad al-Hut has similarly claimed (*al Qiyadat*, p. 630) that the Jews refused to make the slightest amendment to the truce terms, thereby making them unacceptable to the Arab delegation.

55. Khalidi, *Why did the Palestinians Leave?*, p. 8; Erskine Childers, 'The Other Exodus', *Spectator*, 12 May 1961, p. 673; Arthur Koestler, *Promise and Fulfilment: Palestine 1917–1949* (New York, 1949), pp. 187, 207.

56. *See* 'Terms of the Hagana Command for a Truce in Haifa', Haifa, 22 April 1948, Annexure I: to HQ North Sector letter 383/G (Ops) dated 24 April 1948, Stockwell Collection, 6/15.

57. Hagana Haifa Command, 'Announcement No. 2 to the Haifa Arab Residents', 22 April 1948, 12.00, HA 15/14.

58. Hagana Arabic broadcasts, 23, 24 and 26 April 1948, in BBC, *Summary of World Broadcasts: Western Europe, Middle East, Far East and Americas*, Part 3, No. 48, 29 April 1948, p. 61; Part 3, No. 49, 6 May 1948, p. 70; *Ha-aretz and Palestine Post*, 27 April 1948.

59. ISA, Protocol of the joint committee meeting, 23 April 1948, 69-4/941/440a.

60. CZA, Protocol of the Jewish Agency Executive Meeting, 6 May 1948, p. 125,867.

61. Lippincott to the Secretary of State, No. 40, 25 April 1948; No. 44, 26 April 1948; Airgram A-6, 29 April 1948; all in NA Record Group 84, Haifa Consulate, 800 – Political Affairs.

62. Cunningham to Creech-Jones, 25 April 1948, No. 1,127, Cunningham Collection, III/4/52.

63. '257 and 317 FS Section Weekly Report No. 4 for Week Ending 5 May 1948', paragraph 4, WO 275/79.

64. Cunningham to Secretary of State, 25 April 1948, St Antony's Centre, Cunningham Collection, III/4/52; Marriott to Foreign Office, 15 May 1948, FO 371/68553/E6322; Superintendent of Police (CID), 'Subject: General Situation – Haifa District', 26 and 28 April 1948, HA 8/15, pp. 158, 161; Logbook of the Sixth Airborne Division, 1 May 1948, Sheet 135, Serial 602.'Fortnightly Intelligence Newsletter No. 67, issued by HQ British Troops in Palestine, for the period 23.59 hours 19 April–23.59 hours 3 May 1948', WO 275/64, p. 2.

65. UP Haifa report of 24 April 1948, as quoted by Ha-aretz, 25 April 1948. *See also Davar*, 25 April 1948.

66. Hiram to Tene, 'The Returning Arabs to Haifa', 28 April 1948, HA 105/257, p. 365; report by Kafri, 'Occurrences in Haifa on Sunday, 9 May 1948', 11 May 1948, IDFA, 152/7249/49; Hiram, 'Tour of the Christian Neighbourhoods in Haifa', 9 May 1948, IDFA, 152/7249/49.

67. Hiram to Tene, 'The Situation of the Arabs in Abbas Street', 25 April 1948, HA 105/257, p. 354.
68. Testimony of Ephraim Elroi (who carried out the tapping operation), 24 December 1972, p. 10, HA, File 284 (David Nativ's personal archive); testimony of Aharon Kari (Kramer) who recorded the conversation, 17 January 1973, pp. 6–7, HA, File 284 (David Nativ's personal archive); testimony of Naftali Lifschitz (participant in the truce negotiations), 19 September 1978, p. 1, HA, File 284 (David Nativ's personal archive); testimony of Yaacov Solomon, (participant in the truce negotiations), 10 March 1971, p. 8, HA, File 284 (David Nativ's personal archive); interview with Naftali Lifschitz by Tamir Goren, 13 April 1994, 'Why did the Arab Residents Leave Haifa? Examination of a Disputed Issue', *Katedra*, No. 80 (1996), p. 189, fn. 92.
69. Telegram from Marriott to Foreign Office, sent by Northsec via Mideast, 25 April 1948, Stockwell Collection, 6/13.
70. CZA, Protocol of the Jewish Agency Executive Meeting of 6 May 1948, p. 12,586.
71. Salomon's report to the Political Department, Israel's Foreign Office, 1 April 1949, ISA, FM 2401/11.
72. Lippincott (American Consulate, Haifa) to Department, No. 40, 25 April 1948 and No. 44, 26 April 1948, NA Record Group 84, Haifa Consulate, 800 – Political Affairs.
73. Cunningham to Secretary of State, telegram 1,127, 25 April 1948, Cunningham Collection, III/4/52, Middle East Centre, St Antony's College, Oxford University.
74. '257 and 317 FS Section Weekly Report No. 3 for Week Ending 28 April 1948', paragraph 4, WO 275/79.
75. Cairo Radio, 26 April 1948, 20.00, in BBC, *Summary of World Broadcasts: Western Europe, Middle East, Far East and Americas*, Part 3, No. 48, 29 April 1948, p. 57.

9

The Palestinians and the
Right of Return[1]

1

By the early 1990s, most Israelis, on both sides of the political spectrum, had come to embrace a two-state solution to their decades-long conflict with the Palestinian Arabs, a solution based on the idea of trading 'land for peace'. For these Israelis, and especially for the doves among them, the twilight hours of Ehud Barak's short-lived government came as a terrible shock.

During a span of six months, from the Camp David summit of July 2000 to the Taba talks a few days before his crushing electoral defeat in February 2001, Barak crossed every single territorial 'red line' upheld by previous Israeli governments in his frenzied quest for an agreement with the Palestinians based on the formula of land for peace. Unquestioningly accepting the Arab side's interpretation of UN Security Council Resolution 242, passed in the aftermath of the Six Day War of 1967, Barak's government offered to cede virtually the entire West Bank and Gaza Strip to the nascent Palestinian State and made breathtaking concessions over Israel's capital city of Jerusalem. However, to its amazement, rather than reciprocating this sweepingly comprehensive offer of land with a similarly generous offer of peace, the Palestinians responded with wholesale violence.

At Taba, the Palestinians also insisted, with renewed adamancy, on another non-negotiable condition that had been lying somewhat dormant in the background of the Oslo negotiations begun in 1993. No peace would be possible, they declared, unless Israel guaranteed the right of the Arab refugees of the 1948–49 War, and their descendants, to return to territory that is now part of the State of Israel, and to be compensated financially for lost property and for decades of privation and suffering.

The reintroduction of this issue, at a moment when Israel had effectively agreed to withdraw to its pre-1967 lines, shook the Israeli peace camp to the core. All of a sudden, it seemed that the Arab States and the

Palestinians really meant what they had been saying for so long – namely, that peace was not a matter of adjusting borders and territory but was rather a euphemism for eliminating the Jewish State altogether, in this case through demographic subversion. 'Implementing the "right of return" means eradicating Israel', lamented Amos Oz, the renowned author and peace advocate. 'It will make the Jewish people a minor ethnic group at the mercy of Muslims, a "protected minority", just as fundamentalist Islam would have it.'

Oz's plaintive cry struck no responsive chord with his Palestinian counterparts, however. 'We as Palestinians do not view our job to safeguard Zionism. It is our job to safeguard our rights,' stated the prominent politician Hanan Ashrawi, vowing to uphold the 'right of return' even at the cost of undermining Israel's demographic balance. 'The refugee problem', she continued, 'has to be solved in total as a central issue of solving the Palestinian question based on the implementation of international law'; for not only has this right of return 'never been relinquished or in any way modified', it 'has been affirmed annually by the UN member states'.

As it happens, Hanan Ashrawi is very much mistaken; and so, in his own way, is Amos Oz. There is no such collective 'right of return' to be 'implemented'. However, to grasp what is at issue here requires a deeper look into history, demography, international law and politics.

II

Whatever the strengths and weaknesses of the Palestinians' legal case, their foremost argument for a 'right of return' has always rested on a claim of unprovoked victimhood. In the Palestinians' account, they were and remain the hapless targets of a Zionist grand design to dispossess them from their land, a historical wrong for which they are entitled to demand redress. In the words of Mahmoud Abbas (aka Abu Mazen), Yasser Arafat's second-in-command and a chief architect of the 1993 Oslo Accords: 'When we talk about the right of return, we talk about the return of refugees to Israel, because Israel was the one who deported them.' The political activist Salman Abu Sitta has put it in even more implacable terms:

> There is nothing like it in modern history. A foreign minority attacking the national majority in its own homeland, expelling virtually all of its population, obliterating its physical and cultural

landmarks, planning and supporting this unholy enterprise from abroad, and claiming that this hideous crime is a divine intervention and victory for civilization. This is the largest ethnic cleansing operation in modern history.

One may be forgiven for pausing a moment at the last sentence. To identify the Palestinian exodus – some 600,000 persons at most – as 'the largest ethnic cleansing operation in modern history' requires at the very least a drastic downgrading of other rather well-documented incidents: the 18–20 million Germans forced out of their homes in Poland and Czechoslovakia after the Second World War; the millions of Muslims and Hindus fleeing the newly established states of India and Pakistan during the partition of the Indian subcontinent in 1948; the millions of Armenians, Greeks, Turks, Finns, Bulgarians and Kurds, among others, driven from their lands and resettled elsewhere during the twentieth century; and so forth and so on.

However, put aside the hyperbole. The claim of premeditated dispossession is itself not only baseless, but the inverse of the truth. Far from being the hapless victims of a predatory Zionist assault, the Palestinians were themselves the aggressors in the 1948–49 War, and it was they who attempted, albeit unsuccessfully, to 'cleanse' a neighbouring ethnic community. Had the Palestinians and the Arab world accepted the United Nations resolution of 29 November 1947, calling for the establishment of two states in Palestine, and not sought to subvert it by force of arms, there would have been no refugee problem in the first place.

It is no coincidence that neither Arab propagandists nor Israeli 'new historians' have ever produced any evidence of a Zionist master plan to expel the Palestinians during the 1948–49 War. For such a plan never existed. In accepting the UN Partition Resolution, the Jewish leadership in Palestine acquiesced in the principle of a two-state solution, and all subsequent deliberations were based on the assumption that Palestine's Arabs would remain as equal citizens in the Jewish State that would arise with the termination of the British mandate. As David Ben-Gurion, soon to become Israel's first prime minister, told the leadership of his Labour (Mapai) party on 3 December 1947: 'In our state there will be non-Jews as well – and all of them will be equal citizens; equal in everything without any exception; that is: the State will be their state as well.'[2]

In line with this conception, committees laying the groundwork for the nascent Jewish State discussed in detail the establishment of an Arabic-language press, the improvement of health in the Arab sector, the incorporation of Arab officials into the government, the integration of Arabs within the police and the ministry of education, and Arab–Jewish cultural and intellectual interaction. No less importantly, the military plan of the Hagana (the foremost Jewish underground organization in Mandatory Palestine) for rebuffing an anticipated pan-Arab invasion was itself predicated, in the explicit instructions of Israel Galili, the Hagana's commander-in-chief, on the 'acknowledgement of the full rights, needs, and freedom of the Arabs in the Hebrew State without any discrimination, and a desire for coexistence on the basis of mutual freedom and dignity'.[3]

The Arabs, however, remained unimpressed by Jewish protestations of peace and comity. A few days before the passing of the UN Partition Resolution, Hajj Amin al-Husseini, the former Mufti of Jerusalem and then head of the Arab Higher Committee (AHC), told an Egyptian newspaper that 'we would rather die than accept minority rights' in a prospective Jewish State. The Secretary-General of the Arab League, Abd al-Rahman Azzam, promised to 'defend Palestine no matter how strong the opposition'. 'You will achieve nothing with talk of compromise or peace', he told a secret delegation of peace-seeking Zionists in September 1947:

> For us there is only one test, the test of strength…We will try to rout you. I am not sure we will succeed, but we will try. We succeeded in expelling the Crusaders, but lost Spain and Persia, and may lose Palestine. But it is too late for a peaceable solution.[4]

In the event, the threats to abort the birth of Israel by violence heralded the Palestinians' collective undoing. Even before the outbreak of hostilities, many of them had already fled their homes. Still larger numbers left before war reached their doorstep. By April 1948, a month before Israel's declaration of independence, and at a time when the Arabs appeared to be winning the war, some 100,000 Palestinians, mostly from the main urban centres of Jaffa, Haifa and Jerusalem, and from villages in the coastal plain, had gone. Within another month those numbers had nearly doubled; and by early June, according to an internal Hagana report, some 390,000 Palestinians had left. By the time the war was over in 1949, the number of refugees had risen to between 550,000 and 600,000.[5]

Why did such vast numbers of Palestinians take to the road? There were the obvious reasons commonly associated with war: fear, disorientation, economic privation. But to these must be added the local Palestinians' disillusionment with their own leadership, the role taken by that leadership in *forcing* widespread evacuations, and, perhaps above all, a lack of communal cohesion or of a willingness, especially at the highest levels, to subordinate personal interest to the general good.

On this last point, a number of Palestinians have themselves spoken eloquently. 'There was a Belgian ship', recalls the academic Ibrahim Abu Lughod, who fled Jaffa in 1948:

> ...and one of the sailors, a young man, looked at us – and the ship was full of people from Jaffa, some of us were young adults – and he said: 'Why don't you stay and fight?' I have never forgotten his face and I have never had one good answer for him.

Another former resident of Jaffa was the renowned Palestinian intellectual Hisham Sharabi, who in December 1947 left for the United States. Three decades later he asked himself, 'How we could leave our country when a war was raging and the Jews were gearing themselves to devour Palestine'. His answer:

> There were others to fight on my behalf; those who had fought in the 1936 revolt and who would do the fighting in the future. They were peasants...[whose] natural place was here, on this land. As for us – the educated ones – we were on a different plane. We were struggling on the intellectual front.

In fact, the Palestinian peasants proved no more attached to the land than the educated classes. Rather than stay behind and fight, they followed in the footsteps of their urban brothers and took to the road from the first moments of the hostilities. Still, the lion's share of culpability for the Palestinian collapse and dispersion does undoubtedly lie with the 'educated ones', whose lack of national sentiments, so starkly portrayed by Sharabi and Abu Lughod, set in train the entire Palestinian exodus.

In 1948, both the Jewish and the Arab communities in Palestine were thrown into a whirlpool of hardship, dislocation and all-out war – conditions that no society can survive without the absolute commitment of its most vital élites. Yet, while the Jewish community (or Yishuv), a cohesive national movement, managed to weather the storm by extreme effort, and at a comparatively far higher human cost than any of its Arab adversaries, the atomized Palestinian community, lacking an equivalent sense of corporate identity, fragmented into small pieces. The moment its leading members chose to place their own safety ahead of all other considerations, the exodus became a foregone conclusion.

The British High Commissioner for Palestine, General Sir Alan Cunningham, summarized what was happening with quintessential British understatement:

The collapsing Arab morale in Palestine is in some measure due to the increasing tendency of those who should be leading them to leave the country...In all parts of the country the effendi class has been evacuating in large numbers over a considerable period and the tempo is increasing.

Hussein Khalidi, Secretary of the Arab Higher Committee, was more forthright. 'In 1936 there were 60,000 [British] troops and [the Arabs] did not fear', he complained to the Mufti on 2 January 1948. 'Now we deal with 30,000 Jews and [the Arabs] are trembling in fear.' Ten days later, he was even more scathing. 'Forty days after the declaration of *jihad*, and I am shattered', he complained to a fellow Palestinian:

Everyone has left me. Six [AHC members] are in Cairo, two are in Damascus – I won't be able to hold on much longer...Everyone is leaving. Everyone who has a check or some money – off he goes to Egypt, to Lebanon, to Damascus.

The desertion of the élites had a domino effect on the middle classes and the peasantry. However, huge numbers of Palestinians were also *driven* out of their homes by their own leaders and/or by Arab military forces, whether out of military considerations or, more actively, to prevent them from becoming citizens of the Jewish State. In the largest and best-known example of such a forced exodus, tens of thousands of Arabs were ordered or bullied into leaving the city of Haifa against their wishes on the instructions of the Arab Higher Committee, despite sustained Jewish efforts to convince them to stay. Only days earlier, thousands of Arabs in Tiberias had been similarly forced out by their own leaders. In Jaffa, the largest Arab community of Mandatory Palestine, the municipality organized the transfer of thousands of residents by land and sea, while in the town of Beisan, in the Jordan valley, the women and children were ordered out as the Arab Legion dug in. Then there were also the tens of thousands of rural villagers who were likewise forced out of their homes by order of the AHC, local Arab militias, or the armies of the Arab states.[6]

None of this is to deny that Israeli forces did on occasion expel Palestinians. However, this occurred not within the framework of a premeditated plan but in the heat of battle, and was dictated predominantly by *ad-hoc* military considerations (notably the need to deny strategic sites to the enemy if there were no available Jewish forces to hold them). Even the largest of these expulsions – during the battle for the town of Lydda in July 1948 – emanated from a string of unexpected developments on the ground and was in no way foreseen in military plans for the capture of the town or reflected in the initial phase of its occupation. It was only when the occupying forces encountered stiffer resistance than expected that they decided to 'encourage' the population's departure to Arab-controlled areas, a few miles to the east, so as not to leave a hostile armed base at the rear of the Israeli advance and to clog the main roads in order to forestall a possible counter-attack by the Arab Legion. Finally, whatever the extent of the Israeli expulsions, they accounted for only a small fraction of the total exodus.

It is true that neither the Arab Higher Committee nor the Arab States envisaged a Palestinian dispersion of anything like the one that took place, and that both sought to contain it once it began snowballing. However, it is no less true that they acted in a way that condemned hundreds of thousands of Palestinians to exile.

As early as September 1947, more than two months before the passing of the UN Partition Resolution, an Arab League summit in the Lebanese town of Sofar urged the Arab States to 'open their doors to Palestinian children, women, and the elderly and to fend for them, should the developments in Palestine so require'.[7] This recommendation was endorsed the following month by a gathering of Haifa's Arab leadership, and reiterated by the Mufti in person in January 1948. For his part, Transjordan's King Abdallah reportedly promised that 'if any Palestine Arabs should become refugees as a result of the Husseini faction's activities, the gates of Transjordan would always be open to them'.[8]

The logic behind this policy was apparently that 'the absence of the women and children from Palestine would free the men for fighting', as the Secretary-General of the Arab League, Abd al-Rahman Azzam put it.[9] This thinking, nevertheless, proved disastrously misconceived. Far from boosting morale and freeing the men for fighting, the mass departure of women and children led to the total depopulation of towns and villages as the men preferred to join their families rather than to stay behind and fight.

In recognition of its mistake, in early March 1948, the AHC issued a circular castigating the flight out of the country as a blemish on both 'the *jihad* movement and the reputation of the Palestinians', and stating that 'in places of great danger, women, children, and the elderly should be moved to safer areas' within Palestine. But, only a week later, the AHC itself was evidently allowing those same categories of persons to leave Jerusalem for Lebanon, and also ordering the removal of women and children from Haifa. By late April nothing remained of the AHC's stillborn instruction as Transjordan threw its doors open to the mass arrival of Palestinian women and children and the Arab Legion was given a free hand to carry out population transfers at its discretion.[10]

Muhammad Nimr al-Khatib, a prominent Palestinian leader during the 1948 War, summed up his nation's dispersion in these words: 'The Palestinians had neighbouring Arab states which opened their borders and doors to the refugees, while the Jews had no alternative but to triumph or to die.'

That is true as far as it goes – yet it severely underplays the extent of mutual recrimination between the Palestinians and their supposed saviours. From the moment of their arrival in the 'neighbouring Arab states which opened their borders and doors', tension between the refugees and the host societies ran high. The former considered these states derelict for having issued wild promises of military support on which they never made good. The latter regarded the Palestinians as a cowardly lot who had shamefully deserted their homeland while expecting others to fight for them.[11]

This mutual animosity was also manifest within Palestine itself, where the pan-Arab volunteer force that entered the country in early 1948 found itself at loggerheads with the community it was supposed to defend. Denunciations and violent clashes were common, with the local population often refusing to provide the Arab Liberation Army with the basic necessities for daily upkeep and military operations, and with army personnel abusing their Palestinian hosts, of whom they were openly contemptuous. When an Iraqi officer in Jerusalem was asked to explain his persistent refusal to greet the local populace, he angrily retorted that 'one doesn't greet these dodging dogs, whose cowardice causes poor Iraqis to die'.[12]

The Palestinians did not hesitate to reply in kind. In a letter to the Syrian representative at the UN, Jamal al-Husseini, vice president of the Arab Higher Committee, argued that 'the regular [Arab] armies did not enable the inhabitants of the country to defend themselves, but merely facilitated their escape from Palestine'. The prominent Palestinian leader, Emile Ghoury, was even more forthright. In an interview with the London *Telegraph* in August 1948, he blamed the Arab States for the creation of the refugee problem; so did the organizers of protest demonstrations that took place in many West Bank towns on the first anniversary of Israel's establishment.[13] During a fact-finding mission to Gaza in June 1949, Sir John Troutbeck, head of the British Middle East office in Cairo, and no friend to Israel or the Jews, was surprised to discover that while the refugees:

> ...express no bitterness against the Jews (or for that matter against the Americans or ourselves) they speak with the utmost bitterness

of the Egyptians and other Arab states. 'We know who our enemies are', they will say, and they are referring to their Arab brothers who, they declare, persuaded them unnecessarily to leave their homes...I even heard it said that many of the refugees would give a welcome to the Israelis if they were to come in and take the district over.[14]

The prevailing conviction among Palestinians that they had been, and remained, the victims of their fellow Arabs rather than of Israeli aggression was grounded not only in experience but in the larger facts of inter-Arab politics. Indeed, had the Jewish State lost the war, its territory would not have been handed over to the Palestinians but rather divided among the invading forces, for the simple reason that none of the Arab regimes viewed the Palestinians as a distinct nation. As the American academic, Philip Hitti, put the Arab view to a joint British and American committee of inquiry in 1946: 'There is no such thing as Palestine in history, absolutely not.'[15]

This fact was keenly recognized by the British authorities as they were departing from Palestine. In mid–December 1947 they estimated that:

> As events are at the moment it does not appear that Arab Palestine will be an entity, but rather that the Arab countries will each claim a portion in return for their assistance, unless King Abdallah takes rapid and firm action as soon as the British withdrawal is completed.

A couple of months later, High Commissioner Cunningham informed the Colonial Secretary, Arthur Creech Jones, that: 'the most likely arrangement seems to be Eastern Galilee to Syria, Samaria and Hebron to Abdallah, and the South to Egypt, and it might well end in annexation of this pattern, the centre remain uncertain.'[16]

Perhaps the best proof of this was that neither Egypt nor Jordan ever allowed Palestinian self-determination in the parts of Palestine they conquered during the 1948 War: respectively, Gaza and the West Bank. As the Egyptian representative to the 1949 armistice talks with Israel told a British journalist: 'We don't care if all the refugees will die. There are enough Arabs around.'[17]

So much for 'the largest ethnic-cleansing operation in modern history'.

III

However, the appeal to history – to what did or did not happen in 1948–49 – is only one arrow in the Palestinian quiver. Another is the appeal to international law, and in particular to the United Nations resolution that, as Hanan Ashrawi sternly reminds us, 'has been affirmed annually by the UN member states'.

The resolution in question, number 194, was passed by the UN General Assembly on 11 December 1948, in the midst of the Arab–Israeli War. The first thing to be noted about it is that, like all General Assembly resolutions (and unlike Security Council resolutions), it is an expression of sentiment and carries no binding force whatsoever. The second thing to be noted is that its primary purpose was not to address the refugee problem but rather to create a 'conciliation commission' aimed at facilitating a comprehensive peace between Israel and its Arab neighbours. Only one of its 15 paragraphs alludes to refugees in general – *not* 'Arab refugees' – in language that could as readily apply to the hundreds of thousands of Jews who were then being driven from the Arab States in revenge for the situation in Palestine.

This interpretation is not merely fanciful. The resolution expressly stipulates that compensation for the property of those refugees choosing *not* to return 'should be made good by the governments or the authorities responsible'. Had the provision applied only to Palestinians, Israel would surely have been singled out as the compensating party; instead, the wording clearly indicates that Arab States were likewise seen as potential compensators of refugees created by them.

Most importantly, far from recommending the return of the Palestinian refugees as the only viable solution, Resolution 194 put this particular option on a par with resettlement elsewhere. It advocated, in its own words, that 'the refugees wishing to return to their homes and live at peace with their neighbours should be permitted to do so at the earliest practicable date', but also that efforts should be made to facilitate the 'resettlement and economic and social rehabilitation of the refugees'.

It was, indeed, just these clauses in Resolution 194 that, at the time, made it anathema to the Arabs, who opposed it vehemently and voted unanimously *against* it. Equating return and resettlement as possible solutions to the refugee problem; linking resolution of this issue to the achievement of a comprehensive Arab–Israeli peace; placing on the Arab States some of the burden for resolving it; and, above all, establishing no absolute 'right of return', the measure was seen, correctly, as rather less than useful to Arab purposes.

Only in the late 1960s, and with the connivance of their Soviet and Third World supporters, did the Arabs begin to transform Resolution 194 into the cornerstone of an utterly spurious legal claim to a 'right of return'. Today, after decades of fervent Palestinian rejection of the very idea of living 'at peace with their neighbours', the most that can be said of those who appeal to its language is that they are being disingenuous – though stronger and more accurate words also come to mind.

IV

What about the refugees themselves? As is well known, they were kept in squalid camps for decades as a means of derogating Israel in the eyes of the West and arousing pan-Arab sentiments. There they have largely remained, with the sole exception of those allowed to settle and take citizenship in Jordan.

At the end of the 1948–49 War, the Israeli Government set the number of Palestinian refugees at 550,000–600,000; the British Foreign Office leaned towards the higher end of this estimate. However, within a year, as large masses of people sought to benefit from the unprecedented influx of international funds to the area, some 914,000 alleged refugees had been registered with the UN Relief and Works Agency (UNRWA).

More than half a century later, these exaggerated initial numbers have swollen still further: as of June 2000, according to UNRWA, the total had climbed close to three and three-quarter million. Of course, UNRWA itself admits that the statistics are inflated, since they 'are based on information voluntarily supplied by refugees primarily for the purpose of obtaining access to Agency services'. However, the PLO, for its part, has set a still higher figure, of five million refugees, claiming that many have never registered with UNRWA.

Aside from demanding an unconditional right of return for these individuals, Palestinian spokesmen have calculated that justice will also require monetary 'reparations' to the amount of roughly $500 billion – half for alleged material losses, and the rest for lost income, psychological trauma, and non-material losses. To this figure would also be added the hundreds of billions to be claimed by the refugees' host countries (notably Lebanon, Syria and Jordan) for services rendered, bringing the total to about $1 trillion.

Needless to say, Israel has challenged UNRWA's figures, not to speak of the PLO's; it has unofficially estimated the current number of refugees and their families at closer to two million. However, even if the more restrictive Israeli figures were to be accepted, it is certainly true, just as Amos Oz darkly predicts, that the influx of these refugees into the Jewish State would irrevocably transform its demographic composition. At the moment, Jews constitute about 79 per cent of Israel's six-million-plus population, a figure that would rapidly dwindle to under 60 per cent. Given the Palestinians' far higher birth rate, the implementation of a 'right of return', even by the most conservative estimates, would be tantamount to Israel's transformation into an 'ordinary' Arab state.

Not that this stark scenario should surprise anyone. As early as October 1949, the Egyptian politician Muhammad Salah al-Din, soon to become his country's foreign minister, wrote in the influential Egyptian daily *al-Misri* that 'in demanding the restoration of the refugees to Palestine, the Arabs intend that they shall return as the masters of the homeland and not as slaves. More specifically, they intend to annihilate the State of Israel.'

In subsequent years, this understanding of the 'right of return' was to be reiterated by all Arab leaders, from Gamal Abdel Nasser, to Hafez al-Asad, to Yasser Arafat. Only during the 1990s did the PLO temporarily elide the issue as it concentrated on gaining control of the territories vacated by Israel as part of the Oslo peace process. Its Israeli interlocutors, for their part, chose to think of the 'right of return' as a PLO bargaining chip, to be reserved for talks on a final-status settlement and then somehow disposed of symbolically or through some token gesture of good will.

Throughout the 1990s, successive academic study groups, made up of the most earnestly forthcoming Israelis and the most grudgingly tractable Palestinians, devoted themselves to formulating a compromise proposal on this issue. They all failed – a fact that should have raised a large warning flag, but did not.

The reason for the failure is plain enough, however. The 'right of return' is not, for the Palestinians, a bargaining chip; it is the heart of the matter. That is why, over the decades, perfectly commendable Israeli gestures towards dealing with the plight of the refugees have consistently met with indifference or rebuff.

In 1949, Israel offered to take back 100,000 Palestinian refugees; the Arab States refused. Nevertheless, some 50,000 refugees *have* returned over the decades under the terms of Israel's family-reunification programme, and another 75,000 who were displaced from the West Bank and Gaza in the 1967 War have also returned to those territories. As Alexander Safian of Committee for Accuracy in Middle East Reporting in America (CAMERA) has documented, 90,000 Palestinians have also been allowed to gain residence in territory controlled by the Palestinian Authority since the beginning of the Oslo process. Safian similarly points out that millions have been paid by Israel in settlement of individual claims of lost property, 'despite the fact that not a single penny of compensation has ever been paid to any of the more than 500,000 Jewish refugees from Arab countries'.

However, in the end none of this matters. What is at issue in the dispute over the 'right of return' is not practicality, not demography, not legality, and certainly not history. What is at issue is not even the refugees themselves, shamefully left to homelessness and destitution and nourished on hatred and false hope while all over the world tens of millions of individuals in similar or much worse straits have been resettled and have rebuilt their lives. What is at issue is quite simply the existence of Israel – or rather, to put it in the more honest terms of Muhammad Salah al-Din – the still vibrant hope among many Arabs and Palestinians of annihilating that existence, if not by one means then by another.

Tactically, 'we may win or lose', declared Faisal al-Husseini, the 'moderate' Minister for Jerusalem Affairs in Yasser Arafat's Palestinian Authority, in late March 2001, 'but our eyes will continue to aspire to the strategic goal, namely, to Palestine from the [Jordan] River to the [Mediterranean] Sea – that is, to a Palestine in place of an Israel'. 'Whatever we get now', he continued, 'cannot make us forget this supreme truth.' Until this 'supreme truth' is buried once and for all, no amount of good will, of partial compensation, or of symbolic acceptance of responsibility can hope to create anything but an appetite for more.

NOTES

1. Reprinted from *Commentary* (May 2001), by permission; all rights reserved.
2. David Ben-Gurion, *Ba-ma'araha*, Vol. 4, Pt 2 (Tel Aviv, 1949), p. 260.
3. Rama to brigade commanders, 'Arabs Residing in the Enclaves', 24 March 1948, Hagana Archives (HA) 46/109/5.
4. HA, 105/105a, p. 47; Aharon Cohen, *Israel and the Arab World* (London, 1970), p. 381.
5 *See*, for example, Moshe Sasson, 'The emigration of the Eretz Israel Arabs in the period 1 December 1947–1 June 1948', 30 June 1948, IDF Archive, Intelligence-Golani, pp. 2-3; estimate by Sir Raphael Cilento, Director of the UN Disaster Relief Operation, October 1948, HA, 105/88; Yossef Weitz, Ezra Danin and Elias Sasson , 'Memorandum on the Settlement of the Arab Refugees', submitted to Prime Minister David Ben-Gurion in November 1948, HA 105/88; Report by the Research Department of the British Foreign Office, FO 371/75437/51809.
6. *See*, for example, HA, 105/22, p. 149; HA 105/61, p. 172; HA, 105/134, 'Village Files', p. 198; HA 105/143, pp. 171, 185; HA 105/215, pp. 14, 20, 24, 44, 55, 78, 82; 105/215a,

p. 83; Sasson, 'The Emigration', pp. 4, 5, 7, 9, 15, 24; HA 105/257, pp. 8, 113, 290, 325.

7. *Behind the Scenes: a Report by an Iraqi Parliamentary Committee on the Palestine War* (trans. S. Sabag) (Tel-Aviv, 1954), p. 50, Article 4.

8. *See*, for example, Muhammad Nimr al-Khatib, *Min Athar al-Nakba* (Damascus, 1951), pp. 197, 266; Arif al-Arif, *al-Nakba: Nakbat Bait al-Maqdas wa-l-Firdaws al-Mafqud, 1948–1955*, Vol.1 (Sidon/Beirut, 1956), pp. 206–7; Hajj Amin al-Husseini to Rashid Hajj Ibrahim, 13 March 1948, IDFA, 20/1/57 (captured Arab documents); Sixth Airborne Division, 'Weekly Intelligence Summary No. 61, Based on Information Received up to 23 October 1947', WO 275/60, pp. 3–4; 'Fortnightly Intelligence Newletter No. 56', issued by HQ British Troops in Palestine for the period 22 November–5 December 1947, WO 275/64, p. 3.

9. Ireland to Department of State, 28 April 1948, RG 84 – Jerusalem Consulate, 800 – Refugees.

10. *See*, for example, David Ben-Gurion, *Yoman Ha-milhama, Tashah-Tashat*, Vol. 1 (Tel Aviv, 1982), p. 369; HA 105/215, p. 41; HA 105/257, p. 1; Hiram to Tene, 'Vacation of Women and Children from Haifa', 8 March 1948; HA 105/257 p. 1; Hiram, 'Vacation of Women', 10 March 1948 and Dr. Yatsliah, 'Haifa', 10 March 1948, *ibid.*, p. 112; Hiram, untitled report on AHC instructions to vacate women, children and the elderly, 17 March 1948, and 'Transfer of Children to Beirut', 14 March 1948, *ibid.*, p. 108; Hiram, untitled report on the vacation, *ibid.*; 'Tene News', 21 March 1948, HA 105/98, p. 53; 'Précis of Hiram News', 25 March 1948, HA, 105/143, p. 121.

11. *See*, for example, HA 105/215, pp. 19, 25, 51, 101; HA 105/143, p. 174; American Consulate (Port Said) to Department of State, 29 April 1948, RG 84, 800 – Refugees.

12. HA 105/257.

13. HA 105/114, p. 24; HA 105/215, pp. 19, 25, 51, 101; HA 105/143, p. 174; American Consulate (Port Said) to Department of State, April 29, 1948, RG 84, 800 – Refugees.

14. Sir J. Troutbeck, 'Summary of General Impressions Gathered During Week-end Visit to the Gaza District', 16 June 1949, FO 371/75342/E7816, p. 123.

15. Hearing before the Anglo-American Committee of Inquiry, Washington, DC, State Department, 11 January 1946, Central Zionist Archives (Jerusalem), V/9960/g, p. 6.

16. 'Fortnightly Intelligence Newletter No. 57', issued by HQ British Troops in Palestine for the period 6 December–18 December 1947, WO 275/64, p. 2.

17. David Ben-Gurion's Diary, Sde Boker, 2, 5, 6 June 1949. *See also* 'The Gaza Strip and Refugees', 4 July 1949, FO 371/75432/E8543; Sir R. Campbell, 'Comments on British and United States Representations to the Egyptian Government Regarding its Attitude to the Arab Refugee Problem', 4–5 July 1949, FO 371/75431/E8161.

10

Rewriting
Israel's History[1]

As Israel edged towards peace with the Palestinians in the late 1990s, old, highly controversial, and seemingly defunct issues were back on the table, such as the future status of Jerusalem and the question of the Palestinian refugees. The latter issue inspires two very different approaches. The Israeli view, based on an assessment of the 1947–49 period that ascribes primary responsibility for the Palestinian tragedy to an extremist and short-sighted Arab leadership, sees Palestinian wounds as primarily self-inflicted and so not in need of compensation. In contrast, Palestinian spokesmen justify their 'right of return' to the territory that is now part of the State of Israel (or for alternative compensation) by presenting themselves as victims of Jewish aggression in the late 1940s.

Ironically, it is a group of Israelis who have given the Palestinian argument its intellectual firepower. Since the mid-1980s, an array of self-styled 'new historians' has sought to debunk what it claims to be a distorted 'Zionist narrative'. How valid is this sustained assault on the received version of Israel's early history? This question has direct political importance, for the answer is bound to affect the course of Israeli–Palestinian efforts at making peace.

The New Historians and Their Critics

Simha Flapan, the left-wing political activist and editor of *New Outlook* who inaugurated the assault on alleged 'Zionist myths', made no bones about his political motivations in rewriting Israeli history, presenting his book as an attempt to 'undermine the propaganda structures that have so long obstructed the growth of the peace forces in my country'.[2] However, soon after, a group of Israeli academics and journalists gave this approach a scholarly imprimatur, calling it the 'new history'.[3] Its foremost spokesmen include Avi Shlaim of Oxford University, Benny

Morris of Ben-Gurion University in Beersheba and Ilan Pappé of Haifa University. Other prominent adherents include Tom Segev of the *Haaretz* newspaper, Benjamin Beit Hallahmi of Haifa University, and researchers Uri Milstein and Yosi Amitai.

Above all, the 'new history' signifies a set of beliefs: that Zionism was at best an aggressive and expansionist national movement and at worst an offshoot of European imperialism;[4] and that it was responsible for the Palestinian tragedy, the continuing Arab–Israeli conflict, and even the Middle East's violent history.

In an attempt to prove that the Jewish State was born in sin, the 'new historians' concentrate on the war of 1947–49 (in Israeli parlance, the War of Independence). Deriding alternative interpretations as 'old' or 'mobilized', they dismiss the notion of a hostile Arab World's seeking to destroy the Jewish State at birth as nothing but a Zionist myth. They insist that when the Jewish Agency accepted the UN Resolution of November 1947 (partitioning Mandatory Palestine into Arab and Jewish states), it was less than sincere.

It is obviously a major service to all concerned to take a hard look at the past and, without political intent, to debunk old myths. Is that what the 'new historians' have done? I shall argue that, quite the contrary, they fashion their research to suit contemporary political agendas; worse, they systematically distort the archival evidence to invent an Israeli history in an image of their own making. These are strong words; the following pages shall establish their accuracy.

A number of scholars have already done outstanding work showing the faults of the 'new history'. Itamar Rabinovich (of Tel Aviv University) has debunked the claim by Shlaim and Pappé that Israel's recalcitrance explains the failure to make peace at the end of the 1947–49 War.[5] Avraham Sela (of the Hebrew University) has discredited Shlaim's allegation that Israel and Transjordan agreed in advance to limit their war operations so as to avoid an all-out confrontation between their forces.[6] Shabtai Teveth (David Ben-Gurion's foremost biographer) has challenged Morris's account of the birth of the Palestinian refugee problem.[7] Robert Satloff (of the Washington Institute for Near East Policy) has shown, on the basis of his own research in the Jordanian national archives in Amman, the existence of hundreds of relevant government files readily available to foreign scholars,[8] thereby demolishing the claim of the 'new historians' that 'the archives of the Arab Governments are closed to researchers, and that historians interested in writing about the Israeli–Arab conflict perforce must rely mainly on Israeli and Western archives'[9] – and with it, the justification for their almost exclusive reliance on Israeli and Western sources.

This essay addresses an altogether different question. The previous critics have looked at issues of politics or sources; we shall concentrate on the accuracy of documentation of these self-styled champions of truth and morality. By looking at three central theses of the 'new historians', this research reveals a completely different picture from the one that 'new historians' themselves have painted. However, first, let us examine whether the alleged newness of this self-styled group is justified.

New Facts?

The 'new historians' claim to provide factual revelations about the origins of the Arab–Israeli conflict. According to Shlaim, 'the new historiography is written with access to the official Israeli and Western documents, whereas the earlier writers had no access, or only partial access, to the official documents'.[10]

The earlier writers may not have had access to an abundance of newly declassified documents, which became available in the 1980s, but recent 'old historians', such as Rabinovich and Sela, have made no less use of them than their 'new' counterparts, and they came up with very different conclusions. Which leads to the self-evident realization that it is not the availability of new documents that distinguishes the 'new historians' from their opponents but the interpretation they give to this source material.

Further, much of the fresh information claimed by the 'new historians' turns out to be old indeed. Consider Shlaim's major thesis concerning the secret contacts between the Zionist movement and King Abdallah of Transjordan. He claims that 'it is striking to observe how great is the contrast between accounts of this period written without access to the official documents and an account such as this one, based on documentary evidence'.[11] Quite the contrary, it is striking to see how little our understanding has changed following the release of state documents. Shlaim himself concedes that the information:

> ...that there was traffic between these two parties has been widely known for some time and the two meetings between Golda Meir [Acting Head of the Jewish Agency's Political Department] and King Abdallah in November 1947, and May 1948 have even been featured in popular films.[12]

Indeed, not only was the general gist of the Abdallah–Meir conversations common knowledge by 1960,[13] but most of the early writers had access to then-classified official documents. Dan Kurzman's 1970 account of that meeting is a near verbatim narration of the report prepared by the Jewish Agency's Political Department adviser on Arab affairs, Ezra Danin.[14] Shlaim also relies on Danin's report, adding nothing new to Kurzman's revelations.

Similarly, Shlaim places great stress on a February 1948 meeting between the Prime Minister of Transjordan, Tawfiq Abul-Huda, and the foreign secretary of Great Britain, Ernest Bevin, claiming that the latter at that time blessed an alleged Hashemite–Jewish agreement to divide Palestine. However, this meeting was already known in 1957, when Sir John Bagot Glubb, the former commander of the Arab Legion, wrote his memoirs,[15] and most early works on the Arab–Israeli conflict used this information.[16]

Morris's foremost self-laudatory 'revelation' concerns the expulsion of Arabs from certain places by Israeli forces, at times through the use of violence. This was made known decades earlier in such works as: Jon and David Kimche's *Both Sides of the Hill*; Rony Gabbay's *A Political Study of the Arab–Israeli Conflict*; and Nadav Safran's *From War to War*.[17]

Eager to debunk the perception of the 1947–49 War as a heroic struggle of the few against the many, the 'new historians' have pointed to an approximate numerical parity on the battlefield.[18] Yet this too was well known: schoolchildren could find it in historical atlases, university students in academic books.[19] Ben-Gurion's autobiographical account of Israel's history, published nearly two decades before the 'new historians' made their debut on the public stage, contains illuminating data on the Arab–Israeli military balance; his edited *War Diaries*, published by the Ministry of Defence Press in 1982, give a detailed breakdown of the Israeli order of battle: no attempt at a cover-up here.[20]

New Interpretations?

As for new interpretations, some are indeed new, but only because they are flat wrong. Ilan Pappé has gone so far as to argue that the outcome of the 1947–49 War had been predetermined in the political and diplomatic corridors of power 'long before even one shot had been fired'.[21] To which, one can only say that the State of Israel paid a high price indeed to effect this predetermined outcome: the war's 6,000 fatalities represented one per cent of Israel's total Jewish population, a proportionately higher human toll than that suffered by Great Britain in the Second World War.[22] Further, Israel's battlefield losses during the war were about the same as those of the Palestinians; and, given that its population was roughly half the latter's size, Israel lost proportionately twice the percentage of the Palestinians.[23]

Other interpretations ring truer, but only because they are old and familiar. Shlaim concedes that his charge of Jordanian–Israeli collusion is not a new one but was made decades before him.[24] In fact, this conspiracy theory has been quite pervasive. In Arab historiography of an anti-Hashemite caste, 'the collusion myth became the crux of an historical indictment against the King for betraying the Arab national cause in Palestine'.[25] On the Israeli side, both left- and right-wingers have levelled this same criticism at the government's conduct of the 1947–49 War. Shlaim has hardly broken new ground.

Shlaim's main claim to novelty lies in his alleged challenging of 'the conventional view of the Arab–Israeli conflict as a simple bipolar affair in which a monolithic and implacably hostile Arab world is pitted against the Jews'.[26] However, this 'conventional view' does not exist. Even such passionately pro-Israel feature films on the 1947–49 War as *Exodus* and *Cast a Giant Shadow* do not portray 'a monolithic and implacably hostile Arab world pitted against the Jews', but show divided Arab communities in which some leaders would rather not fight the Jews and others would co-operate with the Jews against their Arab 'brothers'. Also what applies to popular movies applies all the more to scholarly writings. Not one of the studies by the 'old historians' subscribes to the stereotypical approach attached to them by Shlaim. Here is what the semi-official history of the 1947–49 War, prepared by the History Branch of the Israeli Defence Forces (IDF) and published in 1959, had to say about the issue:

> The 'Palestine War' gave the Arabs in general, and the Arab League in particular, the first opportunity to demonstrate, both externally and internally, that the Arabs were a cohesive political and military force. However, such factors as interpersonal squabbles, competition among leaders and commanders, conflicting interests among the various Arab League members, etc., prevented the co-ordination and the orchestrated employment of all military forces.[27]

The same applies to Morris. His claim that 'what happened in Palestine/Israel over 1947–49 was so complex and varied...that a single-cause explanation of the exodus from most sites is untenable'[28] echoes not only Aharon Cohen's and Rony Gabbay's conclusions of 30

years earlier[29] but also the standard explanation of the Palestinian exodus by such 'official Zionist' writers as Joseph Schechtman: 'This mass
flight of the Palestinian Arabs is a phenomenon for which no single
explanation suffices. Behind it lies a complex of apparently contradictory factors.'[30]

Even the claim to novelty is not new! Aharon Klieman, the quintessential 'old historian', wrote in his study of Hashemite–Zionist
relations, published just two years before Shlaim's book, that:

> it has been a commonplace to present the Palestine or the Arab-
> Israeli conflict in all its historical stages as a simple bilateral con-
> flict...It is a mistake to present the Arab side to the equation as a
> monolithic bloc. The 'Arab camp' has always been divided and at
> war with itself.[31]

At times, the 'new historians' themselves realize that they are recycling
old ideas. For example, Shlaim acknowledged that their arguments were
foreshadowed by such writers as Israel Baer, Gabriel Cohen and Meir
Pail.[32] In all, the 'new historians' have neither ventured into territory
unknown to earlier generations of scholars, nor made major factual discoveries, nor provided truly original interpretations, let alone developed
novel historical methodologies or approaches. They have relied on precisely the same research methods and source-material as those whose work
they disdain – the only difference between these two groups being the
interpretation given to their findings. The 'new historians' make three
main claims about the Zionist movement in the late 1940s: it secretly
intended to expel the Palestinians; it conspired with King Abdallah to dispossess the Palestinians of their patrimony; and it won British support for
this joint effort. Let us now turn to the accuracy of those interpretations.

Pushing out the Arabs

Morris writes that 'from the mid-1930s most of the Yishuv's leaders,
including Ben-Gurion, wanted to establish a Jewish state without an
Arab minority, or with as small an Arab minority as possible, and supported a "transfer solution" to this minority problem'.[33] He argues that
the transfer idea 'had a basis in mainstream Jewish thinking, if not actual
planning, from the late 1930s and 1940s'.[34] However, Morris, the 'new
historian' who has made the greatest effort to prove this thesis, devotes
a mere five pages to this subject. He fails to prove his claim.

First, the lion's share of his 'evidence' comes from a mere three
meetings of the Jewish Agency Executive (JAE) during 7–12 June 1938.

Five days in the life of a national movement can scarcely provide proof of long-standing trends or ideologies, especially since these meetings were called to respond to specific *ad-hoc* issues. Moreover, Morris has painted a totally false picture of the actual proceedings of these meetings. Contrary to his claim that the meetings 'debated at length various aspects of the transfer idea',[35] the issue was discussed only in the last meeting, and even then as but one element in the overall balance of risks and opportunities attending Britain's suggested partition rather than as a concrete policy option. The other two meetings did not discuss the subject at all.[36]

Second, Morris ignores the fact that the idea of transfer was forced onto the Zionist agenda by the British (in the recommendations of the 1937 Peel Royal Commission on Palestine) rather than self-generated.[37] He downplays the Commission's recommendation of transfer, creates the false impression that the Zionists thrust the idea on a reluctant British Mandatory Power (rather than vice versa), and misleadingly suggests that Zionist interest in transfer long outlived the Peel Commission.[38]

Third, and most important, Morris systematically falsifies evidence, to the point that there is scarcely a single document he relies on that he does not twist and mislead, either by a creative rewriting of the original text, by taking words out of context, or by truncating texts and thereby distorting their meaning. For example, Morris finds an alleged Zionist interest in the idea of transfer lasting up to the outbreak of the 1948 War. Yes, Morris concedes, Ben-Gurion in a July 1947 testimony: 'went out of his way to reject the 1945 British Labour Party platform "International Post-war Settlement" which supported the encouragement of the movement of the Palestine Arabs to the neighbouring countries to make room for Jews'.[39] But he insinuates that Ben-Gurion was insincere: in his heart of hearts, he subscribed to the transfer idea at the beginning of the 1947–49 War. Becoming a mind-reader, Morris discerns a transfer in a Ben-Gurion speech in December 1947:

> There was no explicit mention of the collective transfer idea...
> However, there was perhaps a hint of the idea in Ben-Gurion's speech to Mapai's supporters four days after the UN Partition resolution, just as Arab-Jewish hostilities were getting under way. Ben-Gurion starkly outlined the emergent Jewish State's main problem – its prospective population of 520,000 Jews and 350,000 Arabs. Including Jerusalem, the State would have a population of about one million, 40 per cent of which would be non-Jews. 'This fact must be viewed in all its clarity and sharpness. With such a

> [population] composition, there cannot even be complete certainty
> that the government will be held by a Jewish majority…There can
> be no stable and strong Jewish state so long as it has a Jewish major-
> ity of only 60 per cent.' The Yishuv's situation and fate, he went
> on, compelled the adoption of 'a new approach…[new] habits of
> mind' to 'suit our new future. We must think like a state.'[40]

Morris creates the impression here that Ben-Gurion believed that only
transfer would resolve the problem of a substantial Arab minority in the
Jewish State.

Is this mind-reading of Ben-Gurion correct? Was there really a hint
of the transfer idea in his speech? Here is the text from which Morris
draws his citation:

> In the territory allotted to the Jewish State there are now above
> 520,000 Jews (apart from the Jerusalem Jews who will also be citi-
> zens of the State) and about 350,000 non-Jews, almost all of whom
> are Arabs. Including the Jerusalem Jews, the State would have at
> birth a population of about one million, nearly 40 per cent of which
> would be non-Jews. This [population] composition does not con-
> stitute a solid basis for a Jewish state; and this fact must be viewed
> in all its clarity and sharpness. In such composition there cannot
> even be complete certainty that the government will be held by a
> Jewish majority…There can be no stable and strong Jewish state so
> long as she has a Jewish majority of only 60 per cent, and so long
> as this majority consists of only 600,000 Jews…
>
> We have been confronted with a new destiny – we are about to
> become masters of our own fate. This requires a new approach to
> all our questions of life. We must re-examine all our habits of mind,
> all our systems of operation to see to what extent they suit our new
> future. We must think in terms of a state, in terms of independ-
> ence, in terms of full responsibility for ourselves – and for others.[41]

The original text suggests that Morris has distorted the evidence in
three ways.

First, Morris omits Ben-Gurion's statement that there can be no stable and strong Jewish state so long as the Jewish majority 'consists of
only 600,000 Jews'. He distorts Ben-Gurion's intention by narrowing
the picture to a preoccupation with the 60:40 per cent ratio, when its real
scope was a concern for the absolute size of the Jewish population.

Second, Morris creates the impression that Ben-Gurion's call for a
'new approach…[new] habits of mind' applied to the Arab minority

problem, implicitly referring to transfer. In fact it applied to the challenges attending the transition from a community under colonial domination to national self-determination.

Third, he omits Ben-Gurion's statement on the need to take 'full responsibility for ourselves – and for others'. Who are these others but the non-Jewish minority of the Jewish State?

Worse, Morris chooses to rely on a secondary source (an edited version of Ben-Gurion's diary) rather than consult the primary document; and for good reason, for an examination of the original, with text Morris's secondary source had omitted, would easily dispel the cloud of innuendo with which Morris surrounded Ben-Gurion's speech:

> There can be no stable and strong Jewish state so long as it has a Jewish majority of only 60 per cent, and so long as this majority consists of only 600,000 Jews.
>
> From here stems the first and principal conclusion. The creation of the State is not the formal implementation process discussed by the UN General Assembly...To ensure not only the establishment of the Jewish State but its existence and destiny as well – we must bring a million-and-a-half Jews to the country and root them there. It is only when there will be at least two million Jews in the country – that the State will be truly established.[42]

This speech contains not a hint of the transfer idea. Ben-Gurion's long-term solution to the 60:40 per cent ratio between the Jewish majority and non-Jewish minority is clear and unequivocal: mass Jewish immigration.

As for the position of the Arabs in the Jewish State, Ben-Gurion could not be clearer:

> We must think in terms of a state, in terms of independence, in terms of full responsibility for ourselves – and for others. In our state there will be non-Jews as well – and all of them will be equal citizens; equal in everything without any exception; that is: the State will be their state as well.[43]

Ben-Gurion envisaged Jewish–Arab relations in the prospective Jewish State to be based not on the transfer of the Arab population but as a true partnership among equal citizens; not 'fortress Israel', a besieged European island in an ocean of Arab hostility, but a Jewish–Arab alliance.

These passages make it clear that Benny Morris has truncated, twisted and distorted Ben-Gurion's vision of Jewish–Arab relations and the Zionist position on the question of transfer. All this is especially strange given Morris's contention that the historian 'must remain hon-our-bound to gather and present his facts accurately'.[44]

Collusion Across the Jordan

Shlaim traces Israel's and Transjordan's alleged collusion to a secret meeting on 17 November 1947, in which King Abdallah and Golda Meir supposedly agreed to frustrate the impending UN Resolution on Palestine and instead divide the country between themselves. He writes that:

> In 1947 an explicit agreement was reached between the Hashemites and the Zionists on the carving up of Palestine following the termination of the British mandate…it was consciously and delib-erately intended to frustrate the will of the international commu-nity, as expressed through the United Nations General Assembly, in favour of creating an independent Arab state in part of Palestine.[45]

Is there any evidence for this alleged conspiracy? No, none at all. First, a careful examination of the two documents used to substantiate the claim of collusion – reports by Ezra Danin and Eliyahu Sasson, two Zionist officials – proves that Meir implacably opposed any agreement that would violate the UN Partition Resolution passed 12 days later. In no way did she consent to a Transjordanian annexation of Arab areas of Palestine. Rather, Meir made it eminently clear that:
• Any Zionist–Hashemite arrangement would have to be compatible with the UN Resolution. In Danin's words: 'We explained that our matter was being discussed at the UN, that we hoped that it would be decided there to establish two states, one Jewish and one Arab, and that we wished to speak now about an agreement with him [that is, Abdallah] based on these resolutions.'[46] In Sasson's words: 'Replied we [are] prepared [to] give every assistance within [the] frame [of the] UN Charter.'[47]
• The sole purpose of Transjordan's intervention in post-Mandatory Palestine would be, in Meir's words, 'to maintain law and order and to preserve peace until the UN could establish a government in that area',[48] namely, a short-lived law-enforcement operation aimed at facil-itating the establishment of a legitimate Palestinian government. Indeed, even Abdallah did not expect the meeting to produce any concrete agreement. In Danin's words: 'At the end he reiterated that

concrete matters could be discussed only after the UN had passed its resolution, and said that we must meet again immediately afterwards.'[49]

Second, Meir's account of her conversation with Abdallah – conveniently omitted in this context by Shlaim (though he cites it elsewhere in his study) – further confirms that Mandatory Palestine was not divided on 17 November 1947:

> For our part we told him then that we could not promise to help his incursion into the country [that is, Mandatory Palestine], since we would be obliged to observe the UN Resolution which, as we already reckoned at the time, would provide for the establishment of two states in Palestine. Hence, we could not – so we said – give active support to the violation of this resolution.[50]

Third, Shlaim's account is predicated on the idea of a single diplomatic encounter profoundly affecting the course of history. He naively subscribes to the notion that a critical decision about the making of war and peace or the division of foreign lands is made in the course of a single conversation, without consultations or extended bargaining. This account reflects a complete lack of understanding about the nature of foreign policy-making in general and of the Zionist decision-making process in particular.

Fourth, as mere Acting Head of the Jewish Agency's Political Department, Meir was in no position to commit her movement to a binding deal with Abdallah, especially since that deal would run counter to the Jewish Agency's simultaneous efforts to win a UN resolution on partition. All she could do was try to convince Abdallah not to violently oppose the impending UN Partition Resolution and to give him the gist of Zionist thinking.

Fifth, Meir's conversation with Abdallah was never discussed by the Jewish Agency Executive, the Yishuv's effective government. The Yishuv's military operations during the 1947–49 War show not a trace of the alleged deal in either their planning or their execution. Quite the contrary, the Zionist leadership remained deeply suspicious of Abdallah's expansionist ambitions up to May 1948.

Lastly, while the Jewish Agency unquestionably preferred Abdallah to his Palestinian rival, the former Jerusalem Mufti, Hajj Amin al-Husseini, this preference did not lead the agency to preclude the possibility of a Palestinian state. As late as 8 December 1948 (or more than a year after Abdallah and Meir had allegedly divided Palestine), Ben-Gurion stated his preference for an independent Palestinian state to Transjordan's annexing the Arab parts of Mandatory Palestine. 'An

Arab State in Western Palestine is less dangerous than a state that is tied to Transjordan, and tomorrow – probably to Iraq,' he told his advisers. 'Why should we vainly antagonize the Russians? Why should we do this [that is, agree to Transjordan's annexation of Western Palestine] against the [wishes of the] rest of the Arab States?'[51]

In short, not only did the Zionist movement not collude with King Abdallah to divide Mandatory Palestine between themselves, but it was reconciled to the advent of a Palestinian state. Abdallah was the one violently opposed to such an eventuality and who caused it to fail by seizing the bulk of the territory the United Nations had allocated to the Palestinians.

Collusion with Great Britain

Shlaim writes that 'Britain knew and approved of this secret Hashemite–Zionist agreement to divide up Palestine between themselves, not along the lines of the UN partition plan.'[52] This alleged British blessing was given in the above-noted conversation between Bevin and Abul-Huda, in which the foreign secretary gave the Transjordanian Prime Minister:

> The green light to send the Arab Legion into Palestine immediately following the departure of the British forces. But Bevin also warned [Trans]jordan not to invade the area allocated by the UN to the Jews. An attack on Jewish state territory, he said, would compel Britain to withdraw her subsidy and officers from the Arab Legion.[53]

This thesis is fundamentally flawed. True, the British were resigned to Transjordan's military foray into post-Mandatory Palestine, but this was not out of a wish to protect Jewish interests. Rather, it was directed against those interests: Israel was intended to be the victim of the Transjordanian intervention – not its beneficiary.

• Contrary to Shlaim's claim, the British Government did not know of a Hashemite–Zionist agreement to divide up Palestine, both because this agreement did not exist and because Abdallah kept London in the dark about his contacts with the Jewish Agency. The influential British ambassador to Amman, Sir Alec Kirkbride, was not aware of the secret Meir–Abdallah meeting until well after the event.[54] How then could the British bless a Hashemite–Zionist deal?

• Glubb's memoirs alone indicate that Bevin gave Abul-Huda a green light to invade while warning him, 'do not go and invade the areas allotted to the Jews'.[55] In contrast, declassified British documents unequivocally show that Bevin neither encouraged Abul-Huda to invade the Arab parts of Palestine as 'the obvious thing to do', as claimed by Glubb, nor warned him off invading the Jewish areas. Bevin said only that he 'would study the statements which his Excellency had made'.[56] Shlaim's choosing of an old and partisan account over a newly released official document suggests a desperate attempt to prove the existence of such a warning.

• The British archives are bursting with evidence that the foreign secretary and his advisers cared not at all whether or not Abdallah transgressed Jewish territory; they only wanted to be sure he did not implicate Britain in an embarrassing international situation. Shortly after the Bevin–Abul-Huda meeting, Bernard Burrows, head of the Eastern Department, wrote (with Bevin's approval) that:

> It is tempting to think that Transjordan might transgress the boundaries of the United Nations Jewish State to the extent of establishing a corridor across the Southern Negeb [that is, Negev] joining the existing Transjordan territory to the Mediterranean and Gaza…[thereby] cutting the Jewish State, and therefore Communist influence, off from the Red Sea.[57]

More importantly, on 7 May 1948, a week before the all-Arab attack on Israel, Burrows suggested the Foreign Office intimate to King Abdallah that 'we could in practice presumably not object to Arab Legion occupation of the Nejeb [that is, Negev]'.[58] In other words, not only was the Foreign Office not opposed to Transjordan's occupation of the Jewish State's territory, but it encouraged Abdallah to go in and occupy some 80 per cent of it.

• Having grudgingly recognized their inability to prevent the partition of Palestine, British officialdom wished to see a far smaller and weaker Jewish state than that envisaged by the UN Partition Resolution and did its utmost to bring about such an eventuality. Limitations of space do not allow a presentation of the overwhelming documentary evidence of British efforts to cut Israel 'down to size' and stunt its population growth through the prevention of future Jewish immigration.[59] Suffice to say that British policy-makers sought to forestall an Israeli–Transjordanian peace agreement unless it detached the Negev from the Israeli State.

Conclusions

Recently declassified documents in Israeli and Western archives fail to confirm the picture of the origins of the Arab–Israeli conflict painted by the 'new historians'. The self-styled 'new historiography' is really a 'distoriography'. It is anything but new: much of what it presents is old; and much of the 'new' is distortion. The 'new historians' are neither new nor true historians but rather partisans seeking to give academic credibility to long-standing misconceptions and prejudice on the Arab–Israeli conflict. To borrow the words of the eminent British historian E.H. Carr: what the new historians are doing is to 'write propaganda or historical fiction, and merely use facts of the past to embroider a kind of writing which has nothing to do with history'.[60]

Returning to political issues of today: the Palestinian claim to national self-determination stands on its own and does not need buttressing by historical falsification. Quite the contrary, fabricating an Israeli history to cater to interests of the moment does great disservice not only to historical truth but also to the Palestinians that the 'new historians' seek to champion. Securing the future means coming to terms with one's past, however painful that might be, not denying it.

NOTES

1. Reprinted by permission from *Middle East Quarterly* (June 1996); all rights reserved.
2. Simha Flapan, *The Birth of Israel: Myths and Reality* (New York, 1987), p. 4; *see also* pp. 10 and 233.
3. The 'new historians' make much of their relatively young age: 'Most of them, born around 1948, have matured in a more open, doubting, and self-critical Israel than the pre-1967, pre-1973, and pre-Lebanon-War Israel of the old historians'. Of course, biological age indicates little about outlook. The opponents of the 'new historians' also matured 'in a more open, doubting, and self-critical Israel', many of them belonging to the same age-group and having lived in the same milieu as the 'new historians'. Moreover, some 'new historians' are older than the 'old' historians, especially Flapan, who was born in 1911 and is thus precisely a member of that generation that 'had lived through 1948 as highly committed adult participants in the epic, glorious rebirth of the Jewish Commonwealth', and that was consequently derided by the 'new historians' as being 'unable to separate their lives from the events they later recounted, unable to distance themselves from and regard impartially the facts and processes through which they had lived'. Benny Morris, *1948 and After: Israel and the Palestinians* (Oxford, 1994), p. 7.
4. Avi Shlaim writes:
   > At the time of the Basle Congress, Palestine was under the control of the Ottoman Turks. It was inhabited by nearly half a million Arabs and some 50,000 Jews...But, in keeping with the spirit of the age of European imperialism, the Jews did not allow

these local realities to stand in the way of their own national aspirations.
Avi Shlaim, *Collusion Across the Jordan: King Abdullah, the Zionist Movement, and the Partition of Palestine* (Oxford, 1988), pp. 2–3.

Ilan Pappé has been far more outspoken in articulating Zionism as a brand of Western colonialism that 'gained control over a land that is not theirs at the end of the nineteenth century'. *See*, for example, 'Damning the Historical Forgery', *Kol Ha-ir*, 6 October 1995, p. 61.

5. Itamar Rabinovich, *The Road Not Taken: Early Arab–Israeli Negotiations 1947–1949* (New York, 1991).

6. Avraham Sela, 'Transjordan, Israel and the 1948 War: Myth, Historiography, and Reality', *Middle Eastern Studies* (1992), pp. 623–89.

7. Benny Morris, *The Birth of the Palestinian Refugee Problem* (Cambridge, 1987), p. 286; and Shabtai Teveth, 'The Palestine Arab Refugee Problem and its Origins', *Middle Eastern Studies* (1990), pp. 214–49.

8. Robert Satloff's review of Morris's *Israel's Border Wars*, in *Middle Eastern Studies* (1995), p. 954.

9. Benny Morris, 'A Second Look at the "Missed Peace", or Smoothing Out History: A Review Essay', *Journal of Palestine Studies* (1994), p. 86.

10. Avi Shlaim, 'The Debate about 1948', *International Journal of Middle East Studies* (1995), p. 289. *See also* Morris, *1948 and After*, p. 7.

11. Shlaim, *Collusion*, p. viii.

12. Shlaim, 'The Debate about 1948', p. 296.

13. Jon Kimche and David Kimche, *Both Sides of the Hill* (London, 1960), p. 60; Marie Syrkin, *Golda Meir: Woman with a Cause* (London, 1964), pp. 195–202.

14. Dan Kurzman, *Genesis 1948: The First Arab–Israeli War* (New York, 1970), pp. 42–4.

15. Sir John Bagot Glubb, *A Soldier with the Arabs* (London, 1957), pp. 63–6.

16. For example, Kurzman, *Genesis 1948*, pp. 116–17; Zeev Sharef, *Three Days* (London, 1962), p. 77; and Kimche and Kimche, *Both Sides of the Hill*, p. 39. As we shall see shortly, the newly released official British documents do shed fresh light on the Bevin–Abul-Huda meeting but completely opposite from that claimed by Shlaim.

17. Kimche and Kimche, *Both Sides of the Hill*, pp. 227–8; Rony Gabbay, *A Political Study of the Arab–Israeli Conflict: The Arab Refugee Problem (A Case Study)* (Geneva, 1959), pp. 108–11; and Nadav Safran, *From War to War: The Arab-Israeli Confrontation, 1948–1967* (Indianapolis, 1969), pp. 34–5.

18. Morris, *1948 and After*, pp. 13–16; Shlaim, 'The Debate about 1948', pp. 294–5.

19. *See*, for example, Moshe Lissak, Yehuda Wallach, and Eviatar Nur (eds), *Atlas Karta Le-toldot Medinat Israel: Shanim Rishonot, Tashah-Tashak* (Jerusalem, 1978); Safran, *From War to War*, p. 30

20. David Ben-Gurion, *Medinat Israel Ha-mehudeshet*, Vol. 1 (Tel Aviv, 1969), pp. 70–1, 98, 102, 106, 115; David Ben-Gurion, *Israel: A Personal History* (London, 1972), pp. 61, 90; and G. Rivlin and E. Oren (eds), *Yoman Ha-milhama, Tashah-Tashat* (Tel Aviv, 1982), 3 Vols [particularly Vol. 3], pp. 1013–19.

21. Ilan Pappé, *The Making of the Arab-Israeli Conflict, 1947–1951*, London, 1992, p. 271.

22. *See*, for example, Martin Gilbert, *The Second World War* (London, 1990), p. 746; and *National Register of the United Kingdom and the Isle of Man: Statistics of Population on 29 September 1939* (London, 1939).

23. 'Casualties in Palestine since the United Nations Decision, Period 30 November, 1947 to 3 April, 1948', CO 733/483/5, p. 19.

24. Shlaim, 'The Debate about 1948', p. 296. On the Jordanian side, Colonel Abdallah

at-Tall, who served as a messenger between King Abdallah and the Zionists during the armistice talks at the end of the 1947–49 War, then defected to Egypt and wrote about his experiences in *Karithat Filastin: Mudhakkirat Abdallah at-Tall, Qa'id Ma'rakat al-Quds* (Cairo, 1959). On the Israeli side, Lieutenant-Colonel Israel Baer, an adviser to Ben-Gurion later convicted of spying for the Soviet Union, told about the negotiations in *Bithon Israel: Etmol, Ha-yom, Mahar* (Tel Aviv, 1966).

25. Sela, 'Transjordan, Israel and the 1948 War', pp. 623–4. *See also* his article 'Arab Historiography of the 1948 War: The Quest for Legitimacy' in Laurence J. Silberstein (ed), *New Perspectives on Israeli History* (New York, 1991), pp. 124–54.

26. Shlaim, 'The Debate about 1948', p. 297.

27. IDF's History Branch, *A History of the War of Independence* (Tel Aviv, 1975), p. 71.

28. Morris, *The Birth*, p. 294.

29. Gabbay, *A Political Study of the Arab–Israeli Conflict*, pp. 54, 85–98; and Aharon Cohen, *Israel and the Arab World* (London, 1970), pp. 458–66.

30. Joseph B. Schechtman, *The Arab Refugee Problem* (New York, 1952), p. 4.

31. Aharon Klieman, *Du Kium Le-lo Shalom* (Tel Aviv, 1986), pp. 15–16.

32. Shlaim, 'The Debate about 1948', p. 289. And, years earlier, Arnold Toynbee, Alfred Lillienthal, Noam Chomsky and Edward Said all used these same arguments.

33. Morris, *1948 and After*, p. 17. 'Yishuv' refers to the Jewish community in Palestine before the establishment of Israel.

34. Morris, *The Birth*, p. 24.

35. *Ibid.*, pp. 25–6.

36. Protocol of the Jewish Agency Executive meetings of 7, 9 and 12 June 1938, Central Zionist Archives (CZA), Jerusalem.

37. The Peel report suggested the partition of Mandatory Palestine into two states, Arab and Jewish: To reduce frictions between the two communities, the commission also suggested a land and population exchange, similar to that effected between Turkey and Greece after the First World War. See 'Palestine Royal Commission, *Report.* Presented by the Secretary of State for the Colonies to Parliament by Command of His Majesty, July 1937', Cmd. 5479, London, 1937, pp. 291–5. There being far more Arabs in the Jewish state-to-be than the other way round (225,000 versus 1,250), Ben-Gurion and some other Zionist proponents of partition viewed this exchange (or transfer, as it came to be known) as a partial compensation for the confinement of the prospective Jewish State to a tiny fraction of the Land of Israel. Yet they quickly dismissed this idea, as shown by the fact that not one of the 30-odd submissions the JAE made to the Palestine Partition Commission (the Woodhead Commission, 1938) suggested population exchange and transfer.

38. Morris, *The Birth*, pp. 27–8.

39. *Ibid.*, p. 28.

40. *Ibid.*

41. Ben-Gurion, *Yoman Ha-milhama*, Vol. 1, p. 22.

42. David Ben-Gurion, *Ba-ma'araha* Vol. 4, Pt 2 (Tel Aviv, 1959), pp. 258–9.

43. *Ibid.*, p. 260.

44. Morris, *1948 and After*, p. 47.

45. Shlaim, *Collusion Across the Jordan*, p. 1; Ari Shlaim, *The Politics of Partition* (Oxford, 1990), p. viii (this is an abridged and slightly revised edition of *Collusion*). Other 'new historians' have taken up this thesis. Thus, Pappé:

> The common ground for the agreement was a mutual objection to the creation of a Palestinian state…The Jewish Agency in particular abhorred such a possibility,

asserting that the creation of a Palestinian state would perpetuate the ideological conflict in Palestine.
(*The Making of the Arab–Israeli Conflict*, p. 118).

46. Ezra Danin, 'Siha Im Abdallah, 17 November 1947', CZA, S25/4004.
47. Sasson to Shertok, 20 November 1947, CZA, S25/1699.
48. Danin, 'Siha Im Abdallah'.
49. *Ibid.*
50. Golda Meir's verbal report to the Provisional State Council on 12 May 1948, Israel State Archives, *Provisional State Council: Protocols, 18 April–13 May 1948* (Jerusalem, 1978), p. 40.
51. Ben-Gurion, *Yoman Ha-milhama*, Vol. 3, 18 December 1948, p. 885.
52. Shlaim, 'The Debate', p. 297.
53. *Ibid.*, p. 293.
54. *See*, for example, Kirkbride's telegram to Bevin dated 17 November 1947, displaying total ignorance of the Abdullah–Meir meeting, which was held that very day (FO 816/89). For further evidence of British ignorance of the alleged Hashemite–Jewish deal, see a personal and secret letter from H. Beeley, Eastern Department, Foreign Office, to T.E. Bromley, 20 January 1948, FO 371/68403/E1877; Michael Wright, 'Brief for Conversation with Transjordan Prime Minister on Palestine', 6 February 1948, FO 371/6837/E1980G.
55. Glubb, *A Soldier with the Arabs*, p. 66.
56. Mr Bevin to Sir Alec Kirkbride (Amman), 'Conversation with the Transjordan Prime Minister', 9 February 1948, FO 371/68366/E1916/G.
57. Memorandum by Bernard Burrows, 9 February 1948, FO 371/68368/E296.
58. Bernard Burrows, 'Palestine After May 14', 7 May 1948, FO 371/688/54/E6778.
59. For a discussion of this issue, see Efraim Karsh, *Fabricating Israeli History: 'The New Historians'* (London, 1997/2000), Chapters 4 and 5.
60. E.H. Carr, *What is History?* (Harmondsworth, 1984), p. 29.

11

Revisionists, Arabists and Pure Charlatans[1]

I

Until the summer of 2001, Joseph J. Ellis was one of America's most celebrated academics. A Ford Foundation Professor of History at Mount Holyoke College – one of the country's top women's colleges – his book, *Passionate Sage: The Character and Legacy of John Adams* was published in 1993 to critical acclaim. Four years later Ellis rose to national prominence with a best-selling biography of Thomas Jefferson, which won the National Book Award; and then went on to win the 2001 Pulitzer Prize for History with yet another bestseller –*Founding Brothers: the Revolutionary Generation*. In a promotional campaign for *Founding Bothers* in the summer of 2001, a long line of fans waited in the hallowed halls of the National Archives for Ellis to sign copies. It is hardly surprising, therefore, that the American academic world, indeed the public at large, was deeply shaken when, on 18 June 2001, the *Boston Globe* revealed that Ellis had fabricated a past in which he claimed to have been a platoon leader with the 101st Airborne Division in Vietnam; to have been in the village of My Lai just before the notorious massacre; to have served on General William C. Westmoreland's staff; and, once back in the United States, to have become an anti-war protester and a civil-rights activist. The truth, as the *Globe* found out, was that Ellis had never set foot in Vietnam during the war. Having received a reserve commission in 1965 upon graduating from college, he was allowed to defer active service for four years while working on his doctorate.

Reeling in disbelief, Mount Holyoke College ordered an investigation into the matter, and on 17 August issued an official statement rebuking Ellis for violating 'the ethics of our profession and the integrity we expect of all members of our community' and announcing his suspension for one year without pay, as well as his consensual abdication from his endowed chair 'until such time as the Trustees may wish to reinstate it'.

This move was favourably received within the profession. Anita Jones, Executive Director of the American Historical Association, described the Ellis case as 'a disturbing issue'. 'Professors have an obligation in the classroom to be forthright and truthful about their own personal experiences,' she said. Similar sentiments were voiced by Robert Keiser, of the American Association of University Professors, while the Pulitzer Prize winning historian David J. Garrow argued that any professor who told these kinds of lies should be banned from a classroom. 'He lied in *class*,' he said. 'If he were telling lies in a local bar, who cares?'[2]

Though none of Ellis's critics have directly charged him with extending his fabrication into his history books – with his colleagues and his publisher, the highly respectable firm of Knopf, specifically denying any such a possibility – the seeds of doubt have been sown. As a local newspaper put it: 'How can you trust a historian who makes up history?'[3]

How indeed? Yet there is at least one field in which history is being made up with impunity as a matter of course, albeit under the flashy title of 'revisionism': modern Middle Eastern studies. Had Ellis been a scholar of, say, the Arab–Israeli conflict, he would probably have got away with inventing not only his personal past but his research findings as well. Let me explain the grounds for this belief.

II

In the late 1990s I took issue with a group of Israeli academics and journalists who called themselves the 'new historians', and who claimed to be offering a revisionist history of the origins of the Arab–Israeli conflict in general and the 1948 War in particular.

To start with, I showed that there was nothing revisionist about their work. Far from unearthing new facts or offering fresh interpretations that would transform the general understanding of events, the 'new historians' were effectively reiterating the standard Arab narrative of the conflict, in an attempt to give it academic respectability. Moreover, while this group insists on tracing its origins, indeed its *raison d'être*, to the opening of the Israeli State Archives in the late 1980s, an examination of their works easily reveals a highly eclectic and superficial use of these archives. Thus, for example, while claiming to have overturned the 'myth of the few [Jews] against the many [Arabs]' during the 1948 War, Avi Shlaim, at Oxford University, had not even attempted to tap the archives of the Israeli Defence Forces (IDF) and its pre-state precursor, the Hagana; both of which contain millions of declassified documents relating to the issue. Similarly, in his book on *The Birth of the Palestinian Refugee Problem, 1947–1949*, Benny Morris, at Ben-Gurion University in Beersheba, presents the Hagana and the IDF as the main instigators of the Palestinian exodus, again without reference to archival material held by these two military organizations.

Apparently in response to my repeated criticisms, Morris has recently conceded that 'when writing *The Birth of the Palestinian Refugee Problem, 1947–1949* in the mid-1980s, I had no access to the materials in the IDFA [IDF Archive] or Hagana Archive and precious little to first-hand military materials deposited elsewhere'. 'None the less', he hastened to reassure his readers, 'the new materials I have seen over the past few years tend to confirm and reinforce the major lines of description and analysis, and the conclusions, in *The Birth*.'[4] In other words, the foremost 'new historian' admits both to having written the single most influential 'revisionist' work without the use of the most important archives, and to having a preconceived view of what his archival findings would be.

Far more disturbing than this feigned revisionism is the liberty that the 'new historians' take with their evidence, in an attempt to invent an Arab–Israeli history in an image of their own devising. This ranges from the more 'innocent' act of reading into documents what is not there, to tendentious truncation of source material in a way that distorts its original meaning, to 'creative rewriting' of original texts by putting words into people's mouths.

Consider David Ben-Gurion's comment (in an October 1937 letter to his son):

> We do not wish and do not need to expel Arabs and take their place. All our aspiration is built on the assumption – proven throughout all our activity – that there is enough room for ourselves and the Arabs in Palestine.

In his Hebrew-language writings, Morris has cited Ben-Gurion correctly.[5] However, in the English version of *The Birth*, Morris himself misrepresents Ben-Gurion as saying the opposite: 'We must expel Arabs and take their place.'[6] Could it be because he knew his audience would not be able to check for itself the wording of the original Hebrew document?

Alternatively, take Morris's citation of Prime Minister Ben-Gurion at the Israeli Cabinet meeting of 16 June 1948:

> But war is war. We did not start the war. They made the war, Jaffa went to war against us. So did Haifa. *And I do not want those who fled to return*. I do not want them again to make war.[7]

The key sentence here is Ben-Gurion's assertion that 'I do not want those who fled to return'. The trouble is, nothing of this sort is found in the actual text of the meeting protocol, which reads as follows:

> But war is war. We did not start the war. They made the war. Jaffa waged war on us, Haifa waged war on us, Beit-Shean waged war on us. And I do not want them again to make war.[8]

Yet again, in the Hebrew version of his article Morris refrained from attributing the fabricated sentence to Ben-Gurion.[9] Could it be because Israeli readers can check for themselves the wording of the original text?

Similarly, Morris has Ben-Gurion telling a Jewish Agency Executive meeting (on 7 June 1938) that:

> 'The starting point for a solution of the Arab problem in the Jewish State' was the conclusion of an agreement with the Arab States that would pave the way for a transfer of the Arabs out of the Jewish State to the Arab countries.[10]

Again, there is no mention in the original protocol of any such transfer agreement. It is entirely of Morris's own making. The original text reads as follows:

> The starting point for a solution of the question of the Arabs in the Jewish State is, in his [that is, Ben-Gurion's] view, the need to prepare the ground for an Arab–Jewish agreement.[11]

III

Any self-respecting academic discipline would not tolerate such distortions of the research process. However, such is the politicization of modern Middle Eastern studies, especially in relation to the Arab–Israeli conflict, that partisan rewriting of history in line with contemporary political agendas has not only become the norm, its practitioners are even applauded as courageous 'revisionists' presenting their discoveries at a considerable professional, if not personal, risk to themselves. 'The historian who reveals undesirable truths, who challenges or explodes myths', complained Professor Ze'ev Sternhell of the Hebrew University of Jerusalem, 'is perceived [in Israel] as a troublemaker, an enemy of the people.'[12] Dr Ilan Pappé (of Haifa University) has gone a step further by calling for 'some kind of international protection' for Israel-based researchers of the *nakba* (as Palestinians call the 1948 War).[13]

Nothing can be further from the truth. Not only have the 'new historians' *not* faced the slightest risk to their careers – the humanities and social sciences faculties in most Israeli (and Western) universities are dominated by like-minded academics – but their writings have brought them instantaneous 'celebrity' status that would have otherwise been unattainable. For what could possibly provide better 'proof' of the validity of the Arab narrative than 'inside evidence' by Israeli scholars on the basis of (allegedly) declassified Israeli documents? Indeed, Palestinian and Arab establishments have quickly embraced the 'new historians'. Prominent Palestinian politicians, such as Hanan Ashrawi and Abu Mazen, refer regularly to their 'findings' in support of Palestinian territorial and political claims from Israel. The partisan *Journal of Palestine Studies* (*JPS*) has not only thrown its doors open to this group but has turned them into its favourite contributors. Since the late 1980s it has featured at least seven articles by both Shlaim and Morris, in addition to a string of review essays: far more than any Palestinian or Arab scholar, with the sole exception of Edward Said.

The *JPS* has also used the 'new historians' as its foremost demolition team, particularly against works by Israeli historians deemed most damaging to the Palestinian narrative. In 1994, for example, Morris wrote a lengthy and venomous review of *The Road Not Taken*, an account of early Arab–Israeli peace talks by Professor Itamar Rabinovich of Tel Aviv University. Yet this review pales in comparison to his fifteen-page assault on the first edition of my book *Fabricating Israeli History: The 'New Historians'* – the longest review-essay ever published by the *JPS*.[14]

Last but not least, the *JPS* has turned the 'new historians' into regular commentators on contemporary Israeli–Palestinian affairs, where their adherence to the truth has been no stricter than in their 'historical' studies. Thus, for example, having traced the origins of Yitzhak Rabin's assassination to a mixture of the 'national–religious tradition of ideological and actual lawlessness' and 'the older tradition of "Revisionist" terrorism', Morris argues that:

> During the late 1960s and the 1970s, Gush Emunim continuously broke the law in its campaign to set up Jewish settlements in the West Bank. The Labour-led governments of the day, under Prime Ministers Levi Eshkol, Golda Meir, and Yitzhak Rabin, continually bent to their will.[15]

However, Gush Emunim was established in March 1974, in the twilight of the Yom Kippur War, and as such could not have 'continuously broke[n] the law' during the late 1960s. Nor could Prime Ministers Meir and Eshkol have 'continually bent to their will': if only because the former had resigned her post before the start of the Gush's activities while the latter had died five years before the establishment of Gush Emunim. But why be bothered by facts?

The new historians' partisanship has also served as an entry ticket to the influential Arabist club (comprising scholars of the Middle East and veterans of institutions dealing with the region, such as foreign ministries, oil companies, economic/financial organizations, etc.), and its attendant access to academic journals, respected publishing houses and the mass media. Shlaim, for instance, was the primary academic consultant to a six-part BBC television series about the Arab–Israeli conflict, produced on the occasion of Israel's fiftieth anniversary, which cast the Jewish State in the role of the regional villain. Morris was the moving spirit behind a televised documentary on the Palestinians by an Israeli expatriate. 'We perform at weddings and bar mitzvas', the leading 'new historian' Tom Segev joked about this group's popularity.[16] Indeed, admiring reports on the 'new historians' feature regularly in the Western press.

This state of affairs is not difficult to understand. Half-a-century after Israel's creation and its victory over the concerted Arab attempt to destroy it at birth, these heroic events seem to have been all but forgotten. Not only is there widespread ignorance in the West regarding the origins of the Arab–Israeli conflict and the reasons for its persistence, but Middle Eastern studies have increasingly fallen under the sway of the Arabists and/or scholars of Arab descent, as a glance at the membership list of the American Middle East Studies Association (MESA) and its European counterparts will easily reveal. Moreover, for quite some time the Arab oil-producing countries have been penetrating the foremost Western universities and academic publishing houses by subsidizing publications and extending generous grants for the establishment of endowed chairs and research centres, over which they exercise a lasting control. Finally, since democracy is an extremely rare commodity in the Middle East, and since students of the region's contemporary affairs are anxious to maintain free access to its countries, they exercise a strict self-censorship, avoiding anything that smacks of criticism of local societies and regimes, however brutal and repressive they might be.

Consider, for example, a doctoral student who wanted to research contemporary Syrian state-sponsored terrorism. It did not take him long to realize that the topic would make him a *persona non grata* in Syria (and Lebanon) and would isolate him among fellow Arabists, and he changed his research focus and its time frame. Or consider an international conference on Iraq, held at the Royal Institute of International Affairs (or Chatham House as it is commonly known after the building in which it resides), shortly before the Iraqi invasion of Kuwait in August 1990. All participants, British, Europeans and Americans, went out of their way to heap praise on Saddam Hussein's regime and to rub shoulders with the senior Iraqi officials in attendance (notably Nizar Hamdoon, then Iraq's Deputy Foreign Minister). A respected American Arabist even applauded the desert concentration camps, in which the Iraqi authorities had herded dozens of thousands of Kurds exiled from their homes during and after the Iran–Iraq War, as decent hamlets. When the handful of Iraqi expatriates, who had somehow managed to obtain invitations to the conference, tried to voice criticism of the repressive nature of the Iraqi regime, they were peremptorily silenced by the moderators, with some of them being unceremoniously ushered out of the discussion hall.

This trend has not been confined to academia. In today's global village, where events in one part of the world are instantaneously transmitted around the globe, reaching the public and the policy-makers at the same moment, Arabists have gradually become key shapers of public opinion in their field of specialty. It is they who interpret the Middle East to the general public whenever there is a fresh conflagration in this volatile area; and it is they who regularly give the benefit of their opinion to government and congress. The Arabist presence has been particularly conspicuous on television, where the proliferation of around-the-clock news channels has generated a cosy symbiosis between broadcasters and pundits: the former are in constant need for commentary while the latter are eager to ply their merchandise, come what may. A good case in point is the recent whitewashing by Western broadcasters and pundits of the extent of Palestinian rejoicing over the World Trade Center atrocity, and their acquiescence in the Palestinian Authority's violent suppression of the freedom of information by preventing the distribution of photographs and videos of these celebrations.

In this disturbing atmosphere, where propaganda is often substituted for scholarship, Israel has increasingly been cast in the role of the regional villain and implicated in every Middle Eastern crisis over several decades, regardless of any actual connection. Also, whoever dares to challenge this comfortable consensus is subjected to massive retaliation, or rather a defamation campaign, aimed at 'shooting the messenger' before he or she has been given the opportunity to speak.

IV

Such has been the reaction of the 'new historians' and their sympathizers to my book, *Fabricating Israeli History: The 'New Historians'*: a sustained campaign of personal smear and innuendo aimed at discrediting my professional credentials. Boasting he had never read the book, Morris dismissed it as 'idiotic slander indicative of the man himself, who is probably seeking to promote his own personal interests' (what particular interests could be promoted by going against the grain Morris did not say);[17] while Pappé derided me as a 'court historian'. 'Perhaps in the patriotic Israeli colony in London there still exist the fighting spirit and the readiness to fight for Zionism to the last drop of ink,' he wrote,[18] as if there is something fundamentally wrong when expatriate Israelis rebut historical fabrications (though, of course, not when they fabricate in the first place).

Omer Bartov, an Israeli history professor at Brown University, expressed similar sentiments. In a review of *Fabricating Israeli History* in London's *Times Literary Supplement*, Bartov made no attempt to rebut any of my factual assertions, which in itself is hardly surprising given that his field of research is modern German history. Instead he made a number of wholly irrelevant comments regarding my (alleged) personal background, aimed at discrediting my academic integrity. In an attempt to portray me as part of the Israeli defence establishment – the current version of the much-maligned 'Orientalist' – Bartov claimed that I began my 'specialization in Middle Eastern affairs as an officer in Israeli Army Intelligence'. In fact, I acquired my first academic degree in Arabic and modern Middle Eastern history prior to joining the army, and during my military service dealt with superpower involvement in the Middle East rather than with Arab affairs. But then, what is the relevance of my educational background to the validity of my assertions? What counts is their factual basis. Similarly, Bartov finds a fundamental incongruity between my criticism of the 'revisionist' writings and my long-standing support for Palestinian self-determination,[19] as if one's contemporary political views should necessarily influence one's historical propriety.

Indeed, a vivid illustration of the political agenda underlying the 'new historiography' has been afforded by Benny Morris's apparent about-face following the outbreak of Palestinian violence in the autumn of 2000. So long as the Oslo peace process appeared to be edging towards a two-state solution – Israel and a Palestinian state in the West Bank and Gaza – Morris had no compunction about charging Israel with the 'original sin' of dispossessing the Palestinians and perpetuating the conflict with the Arab World. Yet, when in the summer of 2000 the Palestinian leader, Yasser Arafat, rebuffed Prime Minister Ehud Barak's generous territorial concessions and, rejecting Israel's very right to exist, unleashed a tidal wave of violence, Morris changed tack. Departing from the line he and his fellow 'new historians' had been toeing for more than a decade, he blamed the persistence of the Arab–Israeli conflict on the Palestinians' intransigence and their rejection of all compromise solutions since the 1930s.[20] However, would a true historian discard his own archival research on a specific historical period, without the discovery of new documentary evidence, merely on account of political developments taking place some half-a-century after the original events? Hardly. For all of Yasser Arafat's shortcomings, including his failure to accept Morris's definition of a 'fair' solution to the Israeli–Palestinian dispute, this does not change one iota in the historical record of the 1948 War and its aftermath.

Even when criticism of *Fabricating Israeli History* has ostensibly moved from the personal to the professional sphere, it has never genuinely attempted to grapple with the book's central thesis, let alone refute its factual assertions. Instead, the critics have misrepresented its substance altogether. Consider, for example, the assertion by Joel Beinin of Stanford University, one-time President of the Middle East Studies Association, that, 'by returning the debate to the arena of intellectual history, Karsh...avoids engaging [Benny] Morris's archival discoveries'.[21] In fact, my book has nothing to do with 'intellectual history', its exclusive concern being to engage the 'new historians'' archival 'discoveries'. Indeed, after both *The Economist* and the *Times Literary Supplement* cited a number of Morris's factual falsifications exposed by my book,[22] Morris begrudgingly conceded the validity of my claim, while simultaneously seeking to disguise their real nature. 'Karsh has a point', he wrote to the *Times Literary Supplement*. 'My treatment of transfer thinking before 1948 was, indeed, superficial.' He also acknowledged my refutation of his misinterpretation of an important speech made by David Ben-Gurion on 3 December 1947: '[Karsh] is probably right in rejecting the "transfer interpretation" I suggested in *The Birth* to a sentence in that speech'.[23] Elsewhere he admitted that: 'Karsh appears to be correct in charging that I "stretched" the evidence to make my point.'[24] However, the issue is not the misinterpretation of a specific sentence in Ben-Gurion's speech, or even the 'stretching of evidence': it is the deliberate and complex attempt to misrepresent the contents of the speech so as to portray a false picture of the moral and political worldview of Israel's founding father.

Shlaim resorts to even cruder means to discredit my rebuttal of his conspiracy theory of an Anglo–Transjordanian–Zionist collusion to disinherit the Palestinians. Rather than engage my archival discoveries, he dismissed my criticism as based on a single 'unimportant and insignificant document', written by 'a middle-level career civil servant' and deemed 'not suitable for circulation outside the Foreign Office'.[25] This is an incredible charge indeed, given that two full chapters in *Fabricating Israeli History*, containing hundreds of documents from official British archives, are dedicated to the rebuttal of the conspiracy charge.

But the story does not end here, for Shlaim chose to misrepresent the nature of the above document and its significance. First, this was not an obscure document by a middle-level career civil servant but rather a summary of a crucial consultation, held by Foreign Secretary Ernest Bevin with his key advisers immediately after his meeting with the Transjordanian Prime Minister, Tawfiq Abul-Huda. The consultation addressed the critical issue of Transjordan's possible incursion into Palestine after the termination of the British Mandate, raised by Abul-Huda during the meeting, and its implications. Second, contrary to Shlaim's claim, the memorandum was circulated well beyond the bounds of the Foreign Office, as clearly evidenced by the comment on the foot of the page: 'This was briefly discussed with the S.of S. [that is Bevin] who did not object to the substance of the above minute being confidentially discussed with the State Depat [*sic*]. I attach a draft tel.'[26]

In short, Shlaim has totally misrepresented the above memorandum, turning black into white. Again, this is not a matter of academic sophistry but rather a deliberate distortion of archival evidence so as to defend an important but false aspect of his thesis. I challenged Shlaim to publish the sources of his (mis)representation of the document.[27] He never did.

The only sympathizer of the 'new historians' willing to acknowledge the nature of my criticism and its far-reaching implications has been Professor William Quandt of the University of Virginia. 'Karsh is not talking about differences of interpretation, of nuanced readings of texts', he wrote in a review of *Fabricating Israeli History*, 'he is making a different and more damaging accusation – namely, that these academics are deliberately misleading readers. That is, they know what the record says and choose to distort it.' 'Along with plagiarism', he continued, 'fabrication is the worst accusation one academic can make against another.'

Do I succeed in making my case? Here, Quandt is reluctant to break rank: 'I do not come away convinced, although in some cases he does raise points that seem to warrant examination of the originals.'[28] But then, why not press this point to its logical conclusion and conduct an 'examination of the originals' prior to writing the review, so as to inform the readers of your findings? Don't they deserve an analysis that gets to the bottom of things, rather than an open-ended question?

V

That Quandt alone, among mainstream Middle Eastern scholars, has been prepared to admit what *Fabricating Israeli History* is all about is a sad testament to the prejudice and dogmatism which has plagued this field of studies over the past few decades. There is no real freedom of expression, no revisionism in the true sense of the word: only founding myths and preconceived dogmas to which scholars must conform, such as the presentation of Israel as 'the bad guy', to use Edward Said's words, and the Arabs as hapless victims of Zionist and Israeli aggression.[29] 'Revisionism', in this Orwellian environment, means simply the rewriting of history in line with these dogmas. If this requires the substitution of fiction for fact, so be it.

Needless to say, it has been taken for granted that the Arab narrative of the conflict needs no revisionist history. 'It is important to stress that for all their flaws, the versions of history produced by th[e] traditional Arab historiography are fundamentally different from the Israeli myths of origin,' Rashid Khalidi of the University of Chicago has recently argued:

> This is true notably because it is not a myth that a determined enemy bent on taking control of their homeland subjected the Palestinians to overwhelming force. It is not a myth, moreover, that as a result of this process the Palestinian people were victims, regardless of what they might have done differently in this situation of formidable difficulty, and of the sins of omission or commission of their leaders. In this case, as in so much else in the conflict, there can be no facile equivalence between the two sides, however much some may long for the appearance of Palestinian 'new historians' to shatter the 'myths' on the Arab side.[30]

This blind nationalist belief in one's absolute justice may have some merit at the level of political polemics. As a historical statement it has none at all. During the past decade Israeli and Western archives have declassified millions of records, including invaluable contemporary Arab and Palestinian documents, relating to the 1948 War and the creation of the Palestinian refugee problem. These make it possible to establish that, contrary to Khalidi's assertion, the Palestinian tragedy was by no means a foregone conclusion: it could have been averted altogether had the Palestinians and the Arab States accepted the UN Partition Resolution of 29 November 1947 and opted for peaceful coexistence with their Jewish neighbours rather than attempt to ethnically cleanse this community. This mass of documentation also proves beyond any reasonable doubt that, far from being an act of expulsion, the mass Arab flight was a direct result of the fragmentation and lack of cohesiveness of Palestinian society, which led to its collapse under the weight of the war it had initiated and whose enormity it had failed to predict. But then, why tap this indispensable mine of information if the historical narrative has already been decided?

VI

Another founding myth of modern Middle Eastern history views Western imperialism as the foremost source of regional instability. According to this conventional wisdom, the European Powers – Britain, France, Russia, and Italy – having long coveted the declining Ottoman Empire, exploited its entry into the First World War in order to carve it into artificial entities, in accordance with their imperial interests, and in complete disregard of the yearning of the indigenous peoples for political unity. In order to do so, they duped the naive and well-intentioned Arab nationalist movement into a revolt against its Ottoman suzerain, only to cheat it of the fruits of its efforts. The European powers broke the historical unity of this predominantly Arab area, thus sowing the seeds of the endemic malaise plaguing the Middle East to this day.

As with the Arab–Israeli conflict there has been no real revisionism applied to this dogma. The only scholar to have attempted to do so was the eminent British historian, Elie Kedourie (1926–92), and he paid dearly for his moral and scholarly integrity. His refusal to revise his dissertation so as to bring it into line with the misconceptions of his examiner, H.A.R. Gibb (later Sir Hamilton Gibb), the Laudian Professor of Arabic at Oxford University and the leading Orientalist of the day, cost Kedourie his ultimate objective: his doctorate. When Kedourie later led the assault on the blame-the-West thesis,[31] the dogmatic denizens of Middle Eastern studies shunned him.

A similar treatment was meted out to me and my wife upon the publication of our co-authored, *Empires of the Sand: The Struggle for*

Mastery in the Middle East, 1789–1923 (Harvard University Press, 1999) – a comprehensive reinterpretation of the origins of the modern Middle East. Denying primacy to Western imperialism and attributing equal responsibility to regional powers, it refuted the orthodox belief in a long-standing European design on the Middle East culminating in the destruction of the Ottoman Empire, as well as the notion that the European powers broke the Middle East's political unity by carving artificial states out of the defunct entity. No less important, *Empires of the Sand* laid to rest the popular myth of 'Perfidious Albion', proving that it was Britain's Arab war allies who duped the largest empire on earth into backing the 'Great Arab Revolt', rather than the other way round.

It is hardly surprising, therefore, that the book has incurred the ire of the Arabist establishment. Scathing indictments have been made, on the basis of hearsay, without writers taking the trouble to read the book. A leading Orientalist has even urged fellow academics to place negative reviews on the website of a leading internet bookstore so as 'to warn' potential readers of our book.

Following a lengthy pre-publication review of *Empires of the Sand* in the *Chronicle of Higher Education*, Ken Cuno of the University of Illinois quickly alerted fellow members of the Middle East Social and Cultural History Association (MESCHA), an informal network of scholars and graduate students, of the new threat to their cherished dogmas and conceptual frameworks.

> I have just submitted a comment to a 'colloquy' site created by the *Chronicle of Higher Education* with regard to a pre-reviewed book by Efraim and Inari Karsh entitled *Empires of the Sand* (Harvard, due out in December)

he wrote without the benefit of reading a single sentence of our book.

> Never mind the Karshes' book. What I am more concerned about is the *Chronicle* author's [that is, reviewer's] evident conviction that what is new and cutting-edge in our field is old-fashioned political history cum polemic. Consider the damage that will do. Maybe if they hear from enough of us that something else is going on they might take notice. Maybe even in the form of another article entitled something like 'Middle East Historians Protest Out of Date Image of their Field'.

Cuno's letter elicited a string of enthusiastic responses from his colleagues. Though none of them had read the book, and some had not even read the *Chronicle* review, these staunch Arabists unquestioningly rallied to the call to discredit a scholarly work, the actual substance of which they were totally ignorant. 'I think Ken's idea is good, and the most efficient way to do it is to have him or someone write a letter, and e-mail it to us for signatures,' wrote Nikki Keddie of the University of California, Los Angeles. 'The letter should be consensual enough in its views so most of us will sign.' After reading the *Chronicle* review her alarm seemed to have intensified and she suggested a more comprehensive struggle against the book:

> I no longer think a group letter important; better to stress having people like Carl Smith who both know the documents and can make general points give specific answers; and best of all doing so after reading the book. But others of course can contribute answers that are useful.

Joel Beinin concurred. 'I agree with the general thrust of Ken Cuno's comments and warning about the Karshes' new book,' he wrote.

> I was not planning on writing anything about this book before having a chance to read it (is that too old-fashioned now?) but I have reviewed a previous opus of Ephraim Karsh on the Israeli 'new historians' which may give those interested an idea of what kind of person/scholar he is.

Beinin's reluctance to review a book without reading it first is to be commended; far less so his readiness to warn readers away from a scholarly work he has never read, or to dismiss it out of hand merely on the basis of an author's perceived personality. However, this is precisely how this group has sought to confront the presumed 'threat' of our book: not a scholarly debate on facts and theses but a character assassination couched in high pseudo-academic rhetoric. 'This is not the first time that Efraim Karsh has written a highly self-important rebuttal of revisionist history,' wrote Yezid Sayigh of Cambridge University. 'He is simply not what he makes himself out to be, a trained historian (nor political/social scientist).'

Leave aside the fact that both my training (undergraduate degree in modern Middle Eastern history and Arabic language and literature, and a doctorate in political science and international relations) and my research output refute Sayigh's assertion. His misleading misrepresentation of my scholarly background is wholly irrelevant. *Fabricating Israeli History* has nothing to do with *Empires of the Sand*, which is a wholly different work in terms of scope, time frame and historical methodology. But Sayigh is not the person to be bothered by such

niceties. Having told his colleagues how 'Morris and Shlaim *et al.*
"swept the floor" with Karsh on methodological and documentary
grounds' (although so far it is Morris, rather than myself, who has
admitted mistakes and backtracked on his earlier claims), Sayigh urges
the writing of:

> ...robust responses [that] make sure that any self-respecting
> scholar will be too embarrassed to even try to incorporate the
> Karsh books in his/her teaching or research because they can't
> pretend they didn't know how flimsy their foundations are.

Mary Ann Fay from the American University of Sharjah seems to
share his view. 'Why this book?', she protested.

> It is appalling to think that the wider academic community believes
> that all we do is 'old' history but what is even worse is the notion
> that our work still has to be judged for legitimacy (or illegitimacy)
> on where we stand in relation to Palestine.

Had Fay taken the trouble to read the book, she would have easily
discovered that it has nothing to do with the Palestine Question. Only
one of its 21 chapters (12 pages out of 400) deals with the origins of the
Balfour Declaration, and even this, from a predominantly Great Power
perspective. There is a discussion of Palestine in a couple of other chapters, but then again, not from the perspective of an Arab–Jewish conflict
but rather as an illustration of the perennial tension between imperialism and nationalism. *Empires of the Sand* simply ends before this conflict
began to transcend its embryonic phase, and its scope is far wider than
this localized feud.

Since we have seen the nature of Shlaim's and Morris's responses to
Fabricating Israeli History, it takes no great imagination to guess the
essence of the 'robust responses' envisaged by Sayigh. Indeed, when
such robust responses were published, they made no greater an effort
than Sayigh to grapple with the book's thesis or to rebut its factual
assertions. Consider, for example, the criticism by Richard Bulliet of
Columbia University of our claim that 'the price of Ottoman imperialism was often paid for by its national minorities'. Referring to our
description of a large-scale massacre of Armenians in Baku in
September 1918, Bulliet argues that since Baku lies:

> ...some 500 miles beyond the Ottoman frontier[,] to the degree
> Armenians in Baku were a national minority, surely they were a
> national minority in the Russian, rather than in the Ottoman,

Empire. But to have said so would not so well have served the Karshes' interest.[32]

This is wrong not just by a mile, but by 500 miles. The Armenians of Baku were not massacred by the Russians, as implied by Bulliet, but rather by Ottoman forces that had occupied the city, together with vast Russian territories. Bulliet seems blissfully unaware of the history of the war in the Middle East: Russian forces in Transcaucasia went into rapid disintegration following the revolutionary upheavals of 1917, and Ottoman forces reached Baku the following year. To the degree Armenians in Baku were a national minority in the autumn of 1918, they were a national minority in the (temporarily) expanded Ottoman, rather than Russian Empire. They were slaughtered precisely because of this fact. Bulliet's error is an appalling example of ignorance in a professional historian.

However, the story does not end here. In noting the Baku massacre as the sole basis for our assertion that 'the price of Ottoman imperialism was often paid for by its national minorities', Bulliet withholds from his readers the existence of an entire chapter dedicated to the Ottoman repression of Armenian nationalism in the late nineteenth and early twentieth centuries.

As the largest and most vibrant nationally aware minority in Turkey-in-Asia, the Armenians were seen by their Ottoman imperial master as the foremost internal threat to that part of the empire. Hence the brutal campaign of repression of 1895–96, in which some 100,000–200,000 people perished, and thousands more fled to Europe and America; hence the massacre of thousands of Armenians in 1909; and, hence the genocidal policies against the Armenians during the First World War. All this is documented at considerable length and detail in our book.

Indeed, what credential did Bulliet possess, that a leading journal in the field should ask him to review our book? He is a medievalist who has done no research or writing on the subject. But in his spare time, he propagates the view of the Middle East and its nations as hapless victims of Western imperialism. In Middle Eastern Studies, this in itself is a sufficient credential to pronounce on anything. In his review, Bulliet rushes to absolve the Ottomans of responsibility for crimes they committed to keep their own empire intact. The evidence be damned – for it would not so well have served Bulliet's interest.

VII

This conventional view – absolving Middle Easterners and blaming the West – is academically unsound and morally reprehensible. It is academically unsound because the facts tell an altogether different story of modern Middle Eastern history, one that has consistently been suppressed because of its incongruity with the politically-correct dogmas of the Arabist establishment. And it is morally reprehensible, because denying the responsibility of individuals and societies for their actions is patronizing in the worst tradition of the 'white man's burden' approach, which has dismissed regional players as half-witted creatures, too dim to be accountable for their own fate. As Lawrence of Arabia, perhaps the most influential early exponent of this approach, described the Arabs:

> They were a limited, narrow-minded people, whose inert intellect lay fallow in incurious resignation. Their imaginations were vivid, but not creative... They did not understand our metaphysical difficulties, our introspective questioning. They knew only truth and untruth, belief and unbelief, without our hesitating retinue of finer shades.[33]

Little wonder therefore that *Empires of the Sand* was more favourably received by Middle Eastern intellectuals, fed up with being talked down to, and open to real revisionism of their region's history after suffering decades of condescension from their paternalistic champions in the West.

NOTES

1. A short version of this article was published in *Middle East Quarterly* (2002).
2. *Chronicle of Higher Education*, 13 July 2001; Christopher Chow, 'The Greatest Dishonor', *Accuracy in Academia* (www.academia.org/news/greatest_dishonor.html), 2 July 2001.
3. Dennis Loy Johnson, 'The History Lesson of Joseph Ellis', *Mobylives*, 20 June 2001.
4. Benny Morris, 'Revisiting the Palestinian Exodus of 1948', in Eugene L. Rogan and Avi Shlaim (eds), *The War for Palestine: Rewriting the History of 1948* (Cambridge, 2001), p. 37.
5. *See*, for example, Benny Morris, *Leidata Shel Be'ayat Ha-plitim Ha-palestinim 1947–1949* (Tel Aviv, 1991), p. 45.
6. Benny Morris, *The Birth of the Palestinian Refugee Problem, 1947–1949* (Cambridge, 1987), p. 25.
7. Morris, 'Falsifying the Record: A Fresh Look at Zionist Documentation of 1948', *Journal of Palestine Studies* (1995), p. 58 (emphasis added).
8. Israel State Archives (ISA), Protocol of the Provisional Government Meeting of 16 June

1948, pp. 35–6.
9. Morris, 'A New Look on Central Zionist Documents', *Alpayim*, 16 (1996), p. 99.
10. Morris, *The Birth*, p. 24.
11. Central Zionist Archives (CZA), Protocol of the meeting of the Jewish Agency Executive of 7 June 1938, pp. 11–12. For further fabrications by Morris and his fellow 'new historians' see Efraim Karsh, *Fabricating Israeli History: The 'New Historians'* (London, 2000) [2nd, exp. edn]; Efraim Karsh, 'Morris and the Reign of Error', *Middle East Quarterly*, (1999), pp. 15–28.
12. *Rive: Review of Mediterranean Politics and Culture* (1996), p. 48.
13. Ilan Pappé, 'The Tantura Case in Israel: the Katz Research and Trial', *Journal of Palestine Studies* (2001).
14. Benny Morris, 'A Second Look at the "Missed Peace", or Smoothing Out History: A Review Essay', *Journal of Palestine Studies* (1994), pp. 78–88; Benny Morris, 'Refabricating 1948: Review Essay', *Journal of Palestine Studies* (1998).
15. Benny Morris, 'After Rabin', *Journal of Palestine Studies* (1996), pp. 84, 86.
16. Michael Kennedy, 'Rewriting History', *Inquirer Magazine* 1 February 1998, p. 12.
17. For my interview and Morris's response *see*, 'The Charge: Historical Fabrication', *Ha-aretz Weekly Magazine*, pp. 16–18.
18. Ilan Pappé, letter to *Ha-aretz Weekly Magazine*, 9 May 1997.
19. Omer Bartov, 'Of Past Wrongs – and their Redressing', *Times Literary Supplement*, 31 October 1997, p. 14.
20. *See*, for example, his interview in *Yediot Aharonot: Seven Day Supplement*, 23 November 2001.
21. Yoel Beinin, review of *Fabricating Israeli History*, in *Middle East Journal* (1998), p. 448.
22. 'The Unchosen People', *Economist*, 19 July 1997, p. 92; *Times Literary Supplement*, 14 November, 1997, p. 19.
23. Benny Morris, *Times Literary Supplement*, 28 November 1997, p. 17. The term 'transfer' refers to the alleged Zionist design to remove the Palestinians from their patrimony.
24. Morris, 'Refabricating 1948', p. 83.
25. Avi Shlaim, 'A Totalitarian Concept of History', *Middle East Quarterly* (1996), p. 55; Shlaim's response to my interview with *Ha-aretz Weekly Magazine*, 2 May 1997, p. 18.
26. Memorandum by B.A.B. Burrows, 9 February 1948, FO 371/68368/E2696.
27. Efraim Karsh, 'Historical Fictions', *Middle East Quarterly* (1996), p. 60.
28. William Quandt, review of *Fabricating Israeli History*, in *MESA Bulletin*, 32 (1998), p. 118.
29. *Sunday Times*, 20 June 1993.
30. Rashid Khalidi, 'The Palestinians and 1948: The Underlying Causes of Failure', in Shlaim and Rogan (eds), *The War for Palestine*, pp. 16 17.
31. *See*, for example, Elie Kedourie, *England and the Middle East: The Destruction of the Ottoman Empire, 1914–1921* (London/Boulder, CO, 1987) [first published in 1956]; Elie Kedouri, *In the Anglo-Arab Labyrinth: The McMahon–Husayn Correspondence and Its Interpretations, 1914–1939* (Cambridge, 1976); [reprinted by Frank Cass, 2000].
32. Bulliet's review of *Empires of the Sand*, in *Middle East Journal* (2000), pp. 667–8.
33. T.E. Lawrence, *Seven Pillars of Wisdom: A Triumph* (Garden City, NY, 1935), p. 38.

Index

Abbas, Mahmoud 156
Abdallah Ibn Hussein 132; imperial ambitions
2–4, 7, 108–9, 121–4, 163; and the Zionist
movement 105, 107–24, 170–4, 178–80;
opens Transjordan's borders to Palestinian
refugees 161
Abdul Hamid 16, 21–3, 25–8, 195
Abul Huda, Tawfiq 172, 180–1
Acre 143
Afghanistan 31, 94
Albania 54
Aleppo 6, 57, 62–3, 100
Alexandria 20, 23–5, 56, 100
Algeria 53, 86
Ali, Muhammad 7, 15, 53
Amman 146
Antonius, George 58
Aqaba 56
Arab anti-Semitism 97–106
Arab Bureau 6, 57
Arab Co-operation Council (ACC) 90
Arab Higher Committee (AHC) 130–1, 133–4;
forcing Haifa Arabs to leave 145–8; forc-
ing Tiberias Arabs to leave 160
Arab–Israeli conflict xi, 71, 72, 74–7, 87–94
Arab League 8, 84, 89, 115, 116, 117, 118, 123,
148, 158; urges Arab states to open their
borders to Palestinian refugees 161–2
Arab Liberation Army (ALA) 162
Arab nationalism (see pan-Arabism)
Arafat, Suha 104
Arafat, Yasser 9, 90, 92, 94, 104–5, 147, 166,
167
Armenians 6, 64, 66, 157, 200–1
Asad, Bashar 104
Asad, Hafiz 4, 9, 12, 74, 77, 89, 91, 103, 104,
166
Ashrawi, Hanan 127–8, 148, 156
Asia Minor 2, 26
Asquith, Herbert 44
Assyrians 6, 64
Austria-Hungary 21, 30–4, 44, 53
Azzam, Abd al-Rahman 8, 117, 118, 148, 158,
161

Aziz, Tariq 84, 86
Azuri, Najib 2

Baghdad 7, 11, 59, 63, 65, 88, 98
Baker, James 91
Balfour Declaration 102
Balkan Wars (1912–13) 30, 31, 32, 35
Balkans 32, 33, 41, 53
Barak, Ehud 94, 155
Basra 7, 63
Ba'th 11, 88
Begin, Menachem 74, 88, 89
Beirut 6, 47, 57, 63–4, 100
Beisan 160
Ben-Gurion, David; and Palestinian state 108,
120–1; and peace 120–1; and equality of
Israel's Arabs 157; and the 'transfer' solu-
tion 178, 188–9, 194; and Transjordan's
intervention in Palestine 115–17
Bethman-Hollwegg, Theobald von 33–5
Bevin, Ernest 172, 180–2, 195
Black Sea 45–6, 47, 48
Brezhnev, Leonid 76
Brzezinski, Zbigniew 81
Britain 2, 3, 6, 84, 115, 116, 118, 120, 121;
and the Ottoman Empire 30–2, 35–7,
40–51; occupies Egypt (1882) 15–29;
turns down Ottoman offer to take over
Egypt 21–2; destroys the Ottoman
Empire 52–68, 197–202; and the 'Great
Arab Revolt' 54–64; and First World War
promises 57–64, 197–202; and the
Palestine Mandate 107–8, 129, 133,
135–41, 143–4, 162–3, 172–5, 180–1, 195
Bulgaria 31, 40, 41, 54, 157
Bunche, Ralph 120
Burrows, Bernard 181
Bush, George 83, 85, 87
Bush, George W. 94

Cairo 6, 16, 17, 19, 44, 56, 57, 59, 60, 61, 101,
130
Camp David Accords (1978) 93–4
Camp David summit (2000) 155

Carter, Jimmy 74, 80
Chechens 6, 93
China 71
Churchill, Winston 43, 44, 103; requisitions
    Ottoman ships 35–7; on creation of the
    new Middle East 65; establishes
    Transjordan 121–2
Christopher, Warren 88
Clinton, Bill 87, 94
Clinton, Hillary 104
Cold War xi, 66, 71–94
Constantinople 6, 23–4, 25, 26, 45, 57 (*see also*
    Istanbul)
Creech Jones, Arthur 163
Crimean War (1854–55) 53
Crusaders 8, 158
Cuellar, Javier Perez de 86
Cunningham, Alan 115, 144, 159–60, 163
Cyprus 31

Damascus 3, 7, 9, 62–3, 100, 146
Danin, Ezra 107–11, 124, 178–80
Declaration of Principles (1993) 9, 92
Deir Yasin 139, 152 fn 44
Disraeli, Benjamin 17, 27
Djavid Pasha 36, 42, 45
Djemal Pasha 32, 36, 39, 41
Dufferin, Lord 21–2, 26–7, 28

Eastern Question 52–4
Eban, Abba 117–18
Egypt 6, 7, 8, 12, 31, 32, 35, 42, 44, 47, 53, 55,
    56, 57, 59, 66, 78, 83, 89, 90, 94, 101, 116,
    132, 134, 163, 166; union with Syria 3;
    occupied by Britain (1882) 15–29; and the
    Soviet Union 74–6, 78; official anti-
    Semitism 103–4, 106
Eilath, Eliyahu 116
Eitan, Rafael 89
Ellis, Joseph 186–7
Enver Pasha 32, 33, 35–7, 39, 40–1, 42, 43, 45,
    46–7
Eshkol, Levi 190–1

Fahd, King 85
Faisal Ibn Hussein 7, 9, 12, 59, 62–3; King of
    Iraq 3, 122; dismissive of non-Hijazi
    Arabs 6; imperial ambitions 2–4
Faisal, King 101
Falkenhayn, Erich von 39
Ferdinand, Frantz 32
Ferry, Jules 17
Fertile Crescent 2
Finland 71, 157
First World War 1, 2, 7, 10, 30–56, 197–202
France 3, 7, 17–25, 53, 55, 81, 86, 101; and
    the Ottoman Empire 30–2, 36, 40–51;
    and First World War agreements 59–64
Freycinet, Charles de 20, 24–5

Gaddafi, Muammar 89, 101
Galilee 135, 163
Galili, Israel 158
Gambetta, Leon 17–18, 21
Gaza Strip 8, 90, 94, 104, 155, 162–3
Gemayel, Bashir 89
Geneva conference (1973) 76
Germany 21; and the Ottoman Empire 30–40,
    54
Ghoury, Emile 162
Gibb, Hamilton 197
Giers, Mikhail Nikolaevich 40–1, 42, 45, 48
Gladstone, William Ewart 17–19, 20–1, 22, 24,
    25, 27
Glaspie, April 83
Glubb Pasha 172, 180–1
Golan Heights 77
Gorbachev, Mikhail 71, 77, 90, 91
Granville, Lord 17–18, 22, 28
Great Arab Revolt 2, 7, 54–7
Greater Syria 1, 2, 3, 4, 9, 109
Greece 6, 33, 36, 42, 54, 66, 157
Grey, Edward 40, 42, 44, 45–8, 60
Gromyko, Andrei 76
Gulf conflict (1990–91) 71, 82–7
Gulf states 11, 56, 89, 92
Gush Emunim 190–1

Hagana 129, 132–3, 137–40, 148; tries to con-
    vince Haifa Arabs to stay 141–5; acknow-
    ledges Arab equality in Israel 158
Haifa 127–48, 160, 161, 188
Hajj Ibrahim, Rashid 102, 130–1, 133–4
Hama 62–3
Hashemites 1–4, 6, 12, 54–64
Hebron 163
Hijaz 6, 55, 57, 59, 63, 64
Hitti, Philip 9, 163
Hizbullah 11
Hogarth, David 6, 57
Homs 62–3, 100
Horovitz, David 117–18
Husri, Abu Khaldun Sati 7, 52
Hussein Ibn Ali: imperial ambitions 2, 5, 6, 7;
    launches the 'Great Arab Revolt' 54–7,
    67–8; corresponds with McMahon 58–64
Hussein Ibn Talal 68, 105
Hussein, Saddam 1, 4, 8, 11, 68, 82–7, 89, 91–2
Husseini, Hajj Amin 108, 110, 117, 120, 130–2,
    158, 161
Husseini, Faisal 167
Husseini, Jamal 141, 162

Ibn Saud, Abd alAziz 32, 56, 61
Idrisi, Muhammad 56, 61
India 31, 35, 44, 63, 66, 157
Indian Ocean 2
Intifada 90
Iran 8, 31, 66, 74, 94, 158, 192; and the

United States 78–82; and the Soviet Union 79–80; Islamic republic 9–11, 68, 82, 88, 89
Iran–Iraq War 11, 71, 82, 88, 192
Iraq 2, 3, 6, 7, 9, 11, 12, 90, 94, 98, 119, 121, 134, 162 (*see also* Mesopotamia); invades Kuwait 74, 82–7
Ireland 18
Ismail Pasha 15, 21
Israel 4, 8, 9, 11, 74–6, 84, 163; and the Gulf conflict 91–2; and peace process 87–94; and Arab anti-Semitism 97–105
Istanbul 21–3, 26, 31, 40, 41, 44, 48
Italy 21, 53

Jaffa 56, 63, 102, 159, 160, 188
Jagow, Gottlieb von 33–5
Jerusalem 63–4, 87, 98, 100, 108, 119, 139, 155, 161, 176
Jewish Agency 107–8, 111–17, 174–5, 178–80
Jews 6, 10, 12, 64, 92, 97–105, 123, 135, 136, 139, 156
Jibril, Ahmad 9
Johnson, Lyndon 79
Jordan 3, 4, 8, 9, 90, 105, 163, 165 (*see also* Transjordan)

Kawakibi, Abd al-Rahman 2
Kedourie, Elie 65–6, 99, 197
Khalidi, Hussein 160
Khatib, Muhammad Nimr 103, 132, 162
Khomeini, Ayatollah Ruhollah 1, 9–11, 68
Kirkbride, Alec 120, 180
Kissinger, Henry 78
Kitchener, Horatio Herbert 44
Klibi, Chadly 84
Kurds 6, 12, 64, 92, 157, 192
Kuwait 7, 12, 56, 59, 61, 82–7

Lawrence of Arabia 4, 6, 57, 64, 202
League of Nations 102
Lebanon 3, 4, 9, 66, 74, 89, 116, 132, 161, 165, 191
Lebanon War (1982–85) 89
Levy, Shabtai 131, 134, 140
Lewis, Bernard 52, 99
Libya 4, 53, 89
Lloyd George, David 44
London Convention (1841) 37
Lydda 160–1

Macedonia 31
Madrid Conference (1991) 87, 91
Malet, Edward 17, 19
Mallet, Louis 40, 41, 42, 43–4, 45–8
Mansur, Anis 98, 100
McMahon, Arthur Henry 55, 58–64
Mecca 55
Mediterranean 2, 35–7, 45, 167

Meir, Golda 107–15, 116, 117, 118, 123, 124, 143, 146, 172–3, 178–80, 190–1
Mesopotamia 56–7, 59, 62, 66, 122 (*see also* Iraq)
Mitterand, Francois 86
Moltke, Helmut von 35
Mubarak, Husni 83
Muhammad, Prophet 7, 10, 99, 100, 102, 105

Nasser, Gamal Abdel 1, 3, 4, 8, 12, 75, 101, 166
Nazareth 143
Negev 181
'New historians' 128, 169–97; abusive towards their critics 193–202
Nicolson, Arthur 27
Nixon, Richard 76, 78, 79

October War (1973) 74, 75, 76, 78, 190
Organisation of Petroleum Exporting Countries (OPEC) 83–4
Oslo process 87–8, 104, 155, 193
Ottoman Empire xi, 4, 121, 197–202; and the Egyptian crisis (1882) 15–29; and the First World War 30–51; misleads the Entente Powers 40–9; destruction of 1, 2, 5, 6, 10; creation of the modern Middle East 52–68; position of Jews 98–100; mistreatment of Armenians 200–1
Oz, Amos 156, 165

Pahlavi, Muhammad Reza 78–82
Pakistan 157
Palestine 3, 9, 56, 103, 107–24; and First World War promises 62–4; Palestine Liberation Organization (PLO) 9, 74, 75, 77, 89–92, 94, 165; Palestine question 8–9; Palestine War (1948) xii, 3, 8, 127–48, 157–63, 169–82; Palestinian anti-Semitism 102–5; Palestinian state 107, 117–21; Palestinian dispersal 127–48, 157–63, 172, 174–8, 196–7; 'right of return' 155–67, 169
Palestinians xii, 1, 8, 12, 94, 102–3, 127–48, 169–82, 193; blame Arab states for their 1848 'catastrophe' 162–3
Pan-Arabism 1–3, 5, 8, 10, 11, 12, 57
Paris Peace Conference (1919) 2
Peel Commission 122, 175
Persia (*see* Iran)
Persian Gulf 2
Picot, George 59

Quwaitly, Shukri 139–40

Rabin, Yitzhak 92, 190
Rifai, Samir 122
Romania 33, 44, 54; Russia 21, 59, 68, 81, 200–1 (*see also* Soviet Union); and the Ottoman Empire 30–51, 53, 54

Rwanda 71, 93

Sadat, Anwar 74–6, 78, 87, 101, 105
Said, Edward xi, 52, 87
Said, Nuri 3, 7, 9
Sakakini, Khalil 102–3
Salomon, Yaacov 140, 146
Samaria 163
Sanders, Otto Liman von 34, 41
Sarajevo 32
Sasson, Eliyahu 107–11, 113, 115, 116, 117, 118, 124
Saudi Arabia 3, 11, 84, 91, 109, 121
Sayyadi, Abu al-Huda 26–7
Sazonov, Sergei 41–2, 44, 48
Serbia 33, 34, 44, 54
Seymour, Beauchamp 23–5
Shamir, Yitzhak 90
Sharabi, Hisham 5, 159
Sharett, Moshe 114, 116; and Palestinian state 108, 117–20
Sharif of Mecca (*see* Hussein Ibn Ali)
Sharon, Ariel 89
Shi'ites 11
Shiloah, Reuben 116
Shitrit, Bechor Shalom 119
Sidqi, Ismail 117
Six Day War (1967) 3, 74
Somalia 93
Souchon, Wilhelm 37–9, 45
Soviet Union 71–8, 79, 92–4, 121 (*see also* Russia)
Spain 8, 158
Stockwell, Hugh 135–6, 138–41
Sudan 57
Suez Canal 22, 23–4, 28
Sykes, Mark 6, 59
Sykes-Picot Agreement 57–64
Syria 2, 3, 7, 9, 12, 56, 57, 59, 63, 64, 89, 103, 104, 116, 132, 134, 165, 191; intervention in Lebanon 4, 74; and Israel 75–7; and the Soviet Union 75–7; and 1948 War 39–40, 162, 163

Taba summit (2001) 155

Tal al-Kabir 27
Talaat Pahsa 32, 33, 36, 39, 40, 46–7
Tawfiq Pasha 15, 16, 19–20, 21, 25, 26
Thrace 31, 41
Tiberias 160
Tirpitz, Alfred von 24–35
Transcaucasia 11,
Transjordan 9, 12, 103, 107, 109, 110, 115–21, 132, 134, 170, 172, 178–82 (*see also* Jordan)
Troutbeck, John 162–3
Tunisia 17, 53
Turkey 6 (*see also* Ottoman Empire)
Turki, Fawaz 128–9, 148
Turkey (*see* Ottoman Empire)

Umayyads 4, 7
United Nations 11, 74, 86, 98; partition resolution xii, 107, 109, 114, 118–19, 127, 129, 157, 170; relief and aid agency (UNRWA) 165–6; resolution 194 164–5; resolution 242 75, 88, 155; special commission for Palestine (UNSCOP) 117–18
United States xii, 1, 68, 72–3, 76; and Iran 78–82; and the invasion of Kuwait 82–7; and Palestinian–Israeli negotiations 87–94
Urabi, Ahmad 16–17, 18, 19–21, 22, 23, 25, 26, 27

Vance, Cyrus 81

Wahhabiya 66
Weizmann, Chaim 101
Wangenheim, Hans von 33–5, 37–9
West Bank 3, 8, 90, 94, 155, 163
Western imperialism xi, xii, 1, 2, 11, 15, 52–4
Wilhelm, Kaiser 34–5, 36
Wilson, Woodrow 59
Woodhead, Commission 122

Yemen 3, 6, 44, 90
Yugoslavia 66, 93

Zionist movement xii, 8, 107–24; and Abdallah 178–80; and Partition resolution 107–11, 118–19; anti-Zionism 97–105